Wayne Westphal Barrow

Guyana's Elections 2020

Guyana's Elections 2020

The 153-Days Saga

Wayne Westphal Barrow

ISBN: 979-8-7584-7694-9

Cover design by: Usama Zaheen

Printed in the United States of America

ACKNOWLEDGEMENTS

I thank Heavenly Father for planting the seed of inspiration in my mind about this subject area about which I am very passionate and for providing a rounded education which facilitated this project.

It takes not one person but a team of persons to grow an idea into reality, something that can be seen, touched, and even tasted. My friends, sisters and children have been a great source of motivation and that is why this book have been completed. Thank you for giving of your time to read and make comments on the book. Your commitment and dedication are most laudable.

To my Eternal Companion, Zailoon, who walked with me every step of the journey and has always been my cheerleader, your friendship, kindness and love has made this life worth living. Thank you for your editing skills and recommendations. Had I listened to you the book would have read smoother and would have been shorter.

CONTENTS

Wayne Westphal Barrow

PREFACE

"The best laid schemes o' mice an' men often go awry." Robert Burns

Coming to Guyana! That's what I call my sojourn to Guyana, a very different place. Having planned to reside in Guyana for a 2 year-period, I have been here for over 30 years awaiting change, socially, politically, and emotionally.

I arrived in Guyana from Barbados on March 15, 1989, 3 years before its first democratically sanctioned elections and exactly 31 years to the date of its 7th elections all of which were fraught with drama and intrigue. Every election period is one of quiet desperation and muted anxieties. To say that the election atmosphere in 1992 was normal would be to stretch the truth. Barbados, my perfect isle of calmness and organization and great governance, is a paradise in comparison to this active waterfalls' country of political mischief and electoral manipulation. To the majority of Guyanese whom I had befriended, this was considered *'acceptable around this time.'* Bewildered, I never voiced my political feelings except in the company of foreign nationals who could speak freely of Manifestoes, Economic and Social plans and party preferences.

The latter part of the 20th century in Guyana was a time when racial tensions were high, and the Guyana dollar was being devalued at an alarming rate. Citizens made a bee line to the embassies of the ABCE[1] countries seeking political asylum before *'leaving on a jet plane'*; never to be heard from again. A poster, of which I had grown fond, was posted on one of the walls of the office of a European NGO and read, *"Will the last person leaving the country, please turn off the lights!"* Within that statement is encapsulated the zeitgeist for the period between 1989-2000. Times were tough.

From my youth, I had heard of the plight of the Guyanese which never seemed to end. Political mechanizations dominated every aspect of the life of the Guyanese. It is all pervasive and taints the aesthetics of the country.

When my son, Shayne, was 5 years old, he had been up to mischief for which he was scolded. When I attempted to ascertain the reason for the breach of the rules, his response was, *"I don't know why I did it?"* I pressed him again and again reminding him that there were house rules and a value system of which he was aware and to which he must subscribe. The consequences of his actions and challenges were due to insufficient life skills, knowledge and a strong desire to experiment and take risks. He was

[1] America, Britain, Canada and Europe

childish and ignorant of so many things. That, I understood, and that could be remedied over the next couple of years. Of course, constant discipline and greater knowledge allowed for a bit of brain-rewiring and critical thinking.

However, in Guyana, any of the political parties in power, can be likened to the scorpion in the Persian fable of The Scorpion and the Turtle. The scorpion's behavior is mind bogglingly self-sabotaging. He and the turtle had come to an agreement prior to crossing the river. In the middle of the river, the scorpion who is riding on the back of the turtle strikes venomously. Both are at risk of drowning. The turtle, resigned to his fate, asked, "*Why did you do it?*" The scorpion's response was, "*It's just my nature!*" The leaders from the two main political parties and correspondingly, their parties' sycophants appear to have been stuck in a holding pattern for generations. It's the younger generation that must ensure that the current and future politicians raise their game. The voters can do this by embracing smaller, more competent, professional groupings of new, untainted political parties.

This book covers the actual sentiments of casual observers, the average Guyanese voters, and the members of the international communities during Elections 2020. Additionally, it details the apparent post-elections electoral manipulations for a period of 153 days when the world stood in awe of the drama that unfolded. It was political theatre at its most dramatic. Each chapter may be read as a self-contained narrative some of the contents of which the reader may find repetitive. It serves it purpose.

I would hope that generations of Guyanese may reflect on the contents of this book and smile knowing that this was all part of a warped sense of their history that has long been forgotten. I can only pray that generations from now, no one will ever refer to these dark days except in jest or as the Pavlovian effect to peruse Martin Carter's body of Resistance Poem, ***This Is The Dark Time My Love***. It is written in a lighthearted manner and should not detract from the intensity of the emotions which flowed during this period nor the pain that was caused to families on both sides of the racial divide.

All too often, in Guyana, the will of the political leaders overshadow that of the will of the majority of the people by a series of political and judicial gerrymandering. Guyana is a counterfeit democracy which was catering to the approval of the international community while neglecting its citizens and gambling with their public health given Covid-19 and the safety of the communities.

Independence must mean the collective desire and ability to govern oneself in a manner that is pleasing to the majority who are industrious and law-abiding. A people must always stand united against tyranny and bad governance, especially during challenging times. Let us not forget Syria and Afghanistan and our neighbor, Venezuela!

CHAPTER 1: PRE-ELECTIONS ACTIVITIES

"Governments must urgently address the corrupting role of big money in political party financing and the undue influence it exerts on our political systems". Delia Ferreira Rubio, Chair, Transparency International

What is striking about 2020 is that it started off as a syzygy between the dreaded Covid-19 pandemic, the bicentennial celebration of the restoration of the gospel of Jesus Christ, the discovery and production of oil and gas and Guyana's long-drawn-out Elections. From an astrological standpoint, syzygy is when the sun, moon and earth are aligned. It results in a solar or lunar eclipse. In any event, the human response has always been a combination of awe, anxiety, and transformational thinking.

No one, not the bookies, seers nor revelators could have predicted the devastating impact of the Covid-19 coronavirus[1] which paralleled the 1918 Spanish flu pandemic in response. Millions of lives have been lost, economies broken, and lifestyles altered. Lives have been changed forever as has the earth's overall environment.

Guyana witnessed the celebration of the Bicentennial 200th Anniversary of the Restoration of the Gospel[2] as declared by the Church of Jesus Christ of Latter-day Saints and the 30th Anniversary of the dedication of the land of Guyana for the preaching of the gospel by Apostle M. Russell Ballard. It could not have been more meaningful at this time. In 2020, all religious meetings came to a sudden halt as preaching of the gospel was not considered an essential service by world governments. All places of worship remained closed for beyond five months. All citizens of Guyana were invited by their leaders to pray unceasingly, to fast as a means of ending the scourge of the coronavirus and to quell the tensions (racial and physical) between the supporters of the major political parties. At no time in the history of Guyana have the citizens prayed more earnestly save it be for the 2005 deluge which threatened the lives of those on coastal locations.

When the land of Guyana was dedicated for the preaching of the gospel by Apostle Russell M. Ballard 30 years ago, much success was foreseen. It was predicted that economic circumstances would improve and that the national leaders would have the vision of things to bring about employment and a comfortable lifestyle to the people of Guyana. As the years have unfolded, the predictions have manifested themselves, bit by bit and in no small way either. The onus is on the citizens of Guyana to demand good governance.

The Guyana Elections 2020[3] was held on March 2, 2020, and was fraught with much concern after being declared free and fair by over a dozen Elections Observers and the multiple party representatives. Elections results were declared after a record-breaking 153 days from Elections Day; 89 days after the Recount *(agreed to by all political parties)* started and after multiple judicial interventions by the political sycophants of various political parties.

To fully understand the confluence of the four factors mentioned above as it relates to 2020, one must consider that since 2015, America's biggest energy company, Exxon Mobil, led a consortium which had found multi-billion-dollar recoverable resources (8 billion barrels of oil) in the deep waters 200 km off the coast of Guyana. Over 16 discoveries have been made in an area covering 26,800 square kilometers[4]. The Consortium is made up of ExxonMobil's affiliate Esso Exploration and Production Guyana Limited which is the operator and holds 45 percent interest in the Stabroek Block. Hess Guyana Exploration Limited, holds 30 percent interest and CNOOC Petroleum Guyana Limited, a wholly owned subsidiary of China National Offshore Oil Corporation (CNOOC) Limited, holds 25 percent interest.

Based on the high quality of oil and the high level of production, these findings will bring in tens of billions of US dollars of revenue into Guyana, a developing country. Revenues from oil and gas sales could catapult Guyana among the richest countries in the world and by extension, transform the living conditions of approximately three-quarters of a million citizens.

December 20, 2019 was a red-letter day in the history of Guyana. First oil is normally projected 8 years after discovery but 5 years later, after the discovery of oil in Guyana, production was ahead of schedule. Three months later, $ 54.9M[5] was deposited in the United States of America Federal Reserve Bank by Shell Western Supply and Trading Limited on behalf of the Bank of Guyana. Guyana is the nation to which wealthy and powerful investors, hungry for huge returns on investments, will be descending like hawks to capitalize on the many opportunities that will present themselves. According to Christopher Sheldon, World Bank Practice Manager, Energy and Extractives Global Practice, "*Resource wealth can lift people out of poverty and boost human capital. But a robust policy framework with strong regulations and institutions is an essential prerequisite. Through this technical assistance the World Bank will contribute to strengthening Guyana's institutions and enhancing its legal and regulatory framework, maximizing the benefits of its natural resources.*"

In the World Bank's semi-annual report[6] which was published in April 2020, on Latin America and the Caribbean, Guyana's gross domestic product (GDP) was projected to grow by 8.7 per cent and 2.6 per cent in 2021 and 2022, respectively. The World Bank also predicted that within the Latin American and Caribbean region, the economy would contract by 4.6% but Guyana would enjoy a growth of 51.7% despite the negative economic impacts brought on by the Covid-19 pandemic. The International Monetary Fund (IMF)'s predictions have been as generous as the World Bank's granted that the oil reserves were conservatively estimated at $100 billion. Guyana happens to be one of the top 5 fastest growing economies in the world as was reported by NSADAQ back in June 2019[7].

Whoever controls the oil and gas holds the key to political longevity in a country that is divided along racial lines since the time when the founding leaders of the PPP-C and the PNC-R, the late Dr. Cheddie Jagan and the late Mr. Forbes Burnham, respectively split and went their separate ways, ideologically. The two major political parties have been playing dangerous politics games since the intervention of the CIA in the domestic affairs of the nation during the early 1960s. Hence, Elections 2020 was bound to have some sparks which led to a conflagration, almost.

Guyana's tribal politics, liken to that of Kenya, places the two major political parties and the goals of their leaders above that of the needs of the populace and the desire to bring the nation out of poverty. Enrichment and power drive these hollow men whose interests are of a personal nature and who serve themselves ahead of their people. They are encouraged by their supporters who embrace yardfowlism. Yardfowlism is a term that is used predominately in Barbados and refers to the nature and character of political sycophants. A yard fowl is a chicken which runs around the yard foraging for food. It tends to focus all its attention on the person who feeds it. It will follow mindlessly, the hands that feed it even when the food has disappeared.

The myopic views of the leaders of the two major political parties have been the leading cause of the standoffs between them both at all elections and the violence which follows. Every government of the two major parties, in turn, suck all the juice and nutrients out of the fruits of the labor of the Guyanese economy and leave the non-germinating seed for the party which takes over. It is a Ground Hog Day phenomenon which is now seared into the psyche of both major players with the hot iron of complacency and avarice. Consequently, the Elections 2020 is a situation of when the elephants fight, it is the grass that suffers, an African proverb which aptly sums it up. Both parties are wont to destroy Guyana's reputation and economy by risking economic sanctions and the psychological trauma of its citizens, an indifference that is unpalatable, but which plays out in Guyana ad nauseum.

The political chicanery of the last 153 days tested the fabric of the various agreements and Charters signed by the Government of the Cooperative Republic of Guyana. From the Region, the Charter of Civil Society[8] for the Caribbean Community adopted in 1997, from the Americas, the Inter-American Democratic Charter of the OAS[9] adopted in September 2001 and internationally, the United Nation's International Covenant on Civil and Political Rights adopted in December 1966.

At Article VI, Political Rights, Item 1 of the Charter of Civil Society states: *"The States shall ensure the existence of a fair and open democratic system through the holding of free elections at reasonable intervals, by secret ballot, underpinned by an electoral system in which all can have confidence and which will ensure the free expression of the will of the people in the choice of their representatives."*

Given the vitriolic attacks on the smaller members states of CARICOM by academically sound Ministers of the Government of Guyana and spokespersons of the APNU+AFC party, Mr. Joseph Harmon, Mr. Raphael Trotman and even the President of the Cooperative Republic of Guyana, His Excellency Brigadier Granger; it is presumed that devoid of humility and without historical perspective, they were fighting for their political lives and their attacks were their last throes of survival. These bedraggled leaders with their short memories seem to have forgotten that Guyanese fled to the Caribbean islands to get away from the dictatorship of the past and the dire economic strains foisted upon them.

Chairman of the Alliance For Change (AFC), Mr. Raphael Trotman, declared that the smaller member states could not understand Guyana's current political situation and would not be in a position to guide nor assist Guyana as it was a *"Guyana problem[10]."* The criticism from Government supporters came at a time when the leaders of CARICOM countries expressed grave concern at the *"transparent effort to alter the results of an election."* According to Prime Minister of St Vincent and the Grenadines, Dr. Ralph Gonsalves then Chairman of the Caribbean Community (CARICOM), *"I am satisfied that CARICOM will not stand by idly and watch the recount which was properly done for the results to be set aside."*

What Dr. Edwin Carrington, former Secretary General of the Caribbean Community (CARICOM), stated in his introduction to the Charter was that *"The commitment which our Member States have solemnly undertaken with this Charter is a tangible demonstration of the Region's belief in the democratic process."* In its preamble, the representatives of the governments are determined to *"uphold the right of people to make political choices."*

Clearly, any representative of any Member State declaring that the Caribbean Community should butt out is either acting in a manner devoid of the understanding of the Agreements to which their government has assented or are demonstrating gross ignorance or have reach a level of despotism that must be checked. Less we forget, it was CARICOM which brokered an agreement between the two major political (PPP-C and the PNC-R) parties in the aftermath of the December 1997 elections impasse.

The Organization of American States is the world's oldest regional organization and the principal multilateral organization for the Western Hemisphere. Guyana, one of the 35 member states since 1991, subscribes to the ideal and objectives of the Inter-American Democratic Charter, Declarations and Resolutions of the OAS and its relevant Treaties and Agreements[11].

The Coalition leaders, in particular, the Minister of Foreign Affairs, Dr. Karen R. V. Cummings, should be familiar with the Inter-American Democratic Charter of the OAS adopted in September 2001. Reference is made to Articles 21 and 25.

Article 21*: When the special session of the General Assembly determines that there has been an unconstitutional interruption of the democratic order of a member state, and that diplomatic initiatives have failed, the special session shall take the decision to suspend said member state from the exercise of its right to participate in the OAS by an affirmative vote of two thirds of the member states in accordance with the Charter of the OAS. The suspension shall take effect immediately.*

Article 25*: The electoral observation missions shall advise the Permanent Council, through the General Secretariat, if the necessary conditions for free and fair elections do not exist.*

Chief of the Electoral Observation Mission of the Organization of American States (OAS) at the March 2020 Elections, former Prime Minister of Jamaica, Mr. Bruce Golding, said, *"You know it takes an extraordinarily courageous mind to present fictitious numbers when such a sturdy paper trail exists. And this is being illustrated now as the recount proceeds."* In a statement from the OAS on April 15, 2020; the people of Guyana were reminded that the OAS' Mission *"remains engaged to assist the people of Guyana in ensuring that their will prevails and that Guyana's position as an internationally respected democracy is restored and preserved."*

Mr. Joseph Harmon, Campaign Manager for the APNU+AFC, again spoke of external interference in Guyana's affairs when he addressed the OAS Observer Mission in Guyana by stating, *"Mr. Golding's statement, coming from a former CARICOM Head of Government, smacks of gross disrespect for a sovereign state and for the ongoing process which has been supported by CARICOM. The APNU+AFC Coalition calls on all Guyanese to disregard these distant voices and pay attention to the unfolding situation at the Arthur Chung Conference Centre where the recount is unmasking the PPP fraud at the March 2, 2020, elections."*

Ignorance compounded with arrogance continued to be a blindfold to those who were intent on getting their way even when the Rule of Law came into play.

Another Agreement which was trampled at the expediency of projecting a false narrative was the UN-adopted International Covenant on Civil and Political Rights (ICCPR) which was acceded to in February 1977. The reason that there is a focus on these areas of regional and international support is to acknowledge that Guyanese need to remember that in this world of globalization, they need each other and the tactics of the 1960s will not work in the era and age of digital convergence.

The United Nations has affirmed that political rights are human rights. And citizens have a right to participate in political affairs as outlined in the ICCPR. According to the United Nation's Article 25:

"Every citizen shall have the right and the opportunity, without any of the distinctions mentioned in Article 2 and without unreasonable restrictions:

(b) To vote and to be elected at genuine periodic elections which shall be by universal and equal suffrage and shall be held by secret ballot, guaranteeing the free expression of the will of the electors;"

The UNDP has been supportive of Guyana's election process since 1991 by providing technical assistance and a large amount of funds. It was instrumental is strengthening the Guyana Electoral Commission (GECOM) to handle the 1992 and 1997 general elections and the 1994 Local Government elections by modernizing the registration and electoral processes and playing a major role in facilitating the electoral observation process for them.

The Economist Intelligence Unit's Democracy Index[12] in 2019 rated Guyana at number 72 of 167 countries assigning Guyana as a *"flawed democracy"* with a score of 6.15 (on a scale of 0-10) down 0.52 from 2018. The USA is positioned at number 25, while Trinidad and Tobago is at number 44, with its neighbor, Suriname, at 49 falling into the same *"flawed democracy"* status as Guyana.

The Democracy Index is based on five categories: electoral process and pluralism; civil liberties; the functioning of government; political participation; and political culture. Each country is classified as one of four types: 1. full democracy, 2. flawed democracy, 3. hybrid regime, 4. authoritarian regime. According to the report, almost half of (48.4%) the world's population live in a full democracy, flawed democracy or hybrid regime. 22 countries are considered full democracies. Norway tops the index with a score of 9.87 with North Korea at 167 at the bottom of the ladder with a score of 1.08.

Guyana has a multi-party parliamentary democracy and is governed by the Legislature, the Executive and the Judiciary. The Constitution and the Representation of the People Act make provisions for the election of members of the National Assembly (unicameral legislature) under a system of Proportional Representation and elections are constitutionally due every five years as per article 69 (4) of the Constitution. It is usually fixed to be held, specifically on a Monday.

Under Article 51 of the Constitution of Guyana, the Parliament of Guyana[13]consists of the President and the National Assembly and is responsible for making and amending the laws of Guyana including the Constitution. The National Assembly has sixty-five elected members of which twenty-five are elected from the ten geographical constituencies and forty are awarded at the national level on the basis of block votes secured, using the LR-Hare Formula as prescribed by the Elections Laws (Amendment) Act 15 of 2000 (Sections 11 and 12). No less than one-third of the seats of the national top-up list is reserved for women as provided for in the Elections Laws (Amendment) Act No. 15 of 2000. In addition, the National Assembly includes a maximum of four non-voting ministers and two non-elected non-voting parliamentary secretaries appointed by the President.

The Judiciary branch consists of the Supreme Court of Judicature: The High Court and the Court of Appeal, with right of final appeal to the Caribbean Court of Justice (CCJ). The courts determine and interpret the law and are required to be independent and impartial and subject only to the Constitution of Guyana and the law.

The Judiciary through the High Court is responsible for determining challenges to elections and electoral disputes which are submitted to it for adjudication by way of an elections petition as outlined in Article 64 of the Constitution of Guyana. The Chancellor of the Judiciary is the chief representative of the judicial authority of Guyana. Never in the history of Guyana has the Judiciary been put to the test as frequently and as robustly as during the period March 2020 – July 2020 inclusive. It would be prudent to add that candidates, parties, electors, and voters may submit cases to the judiciary in order to settle elections disputes.

During the Elections 2020, members of the APNU+AFC led the charge to the courts even as far as the Caribbean Court of Justice on multiple occasions. Every case was lost by them but there was a heightened awareness that the voice of the people can and will be heard and that the process of change is inevitable in Guyana as it relates to the electoral process and politics.

There are two significant events which have shaped the course of Guyana's Elections 2020 but which have its genesis in the unilateral selection of a Chairperson for the Guyana Elections Commission

(GECOM) and the No Confidence motion against the APNU+AFC led government. There are no conspiracy theories being laid before you. However, as Robert Burns declared over two hundred years ago, *"the best laid plans of mice and men, often go awry!"*

GECOM[14] is headed by a chairman and six commissioners. As outlined in in the Constitution Amendment Act No. 2 of 2000, the Chairman shall be a person who holds, has held or is qualified to hold the office of Judge of the High Court or the Court of Appeal or any other fit and proper person who is appointed from a list of six persons, who are not unacceptable to the President, submitted by the Leader of the Opposition after he has meaningfully consulted with the non-governmental political parties represented in the National Assembly.

If the Leader of the Opposition does not submit such a list of persons then the President shall appoint a person who holds, has held or is qualified to hold the office of Judge of the High Court or the Court of Appeal. The President appoints the Chairman of the Guyana Elections Commission from this list of names as prescribed in section 3 in the Constitution Amendment Act No. 2 of 2000.

The first niggling issue that will be addressed is the length of time that it took to agree upon a Chairman for GECOM after three lists were presented to His Excellency President David A. Granger on three separate occasions, the last being August 25, 2017. President Granger did not make known his reasons for rejecting the third list of nominees only indicating for the third time that it was unacceptable. Subsequently, he appointed Retired High Court Judge, Justice James Patterson, 84 years old, on October 19, 2017, who later demitted office on June 24, 2019, because of the Caribbean Court of Justice (CCJ)'s ruling and much pressure from the Opposition.

There is a general belief that the unilateral appointment of Justice Patterson was one of the many steps in the erosion of democracy in Guyana. Inept council from the Attorney General may have served to balance the scales of justice against this presumption. The fact that the CCJ had to council both the President and the Leader of the Opposition to communicate in good faith and have a confab prior to the submission of another List would suggest that the leaders of both the major parties operate in isolation of each other and merely tolerate each other. Such behavior is beyond childishness and is driven by narcissism and selfishness. Given the electoral shenanigans of Elections 2020, one hesitates to guess whether this was one of the many steps in a masterplan that was foiled or rather began to unfurl along the way.

On October 4, 2018, Mr. Anil Nandlall took the matter of the rejection of the three lists and the appointment of Justice Patterson to Guyana's Court of Appeal. Having previously received an unfavorable ruling from

Chief Justice (Ag.) Roxane George-Wiltshire of the High Court that his client's challenge was misconceived, he took the matter to the Court of Appeal which reaffirmed the decision of the High Court.

It was former President Jimmy Carter of the Carter Centre who advanced a solution to a possible impasse in a proposal known as the Carter Formula back in 1990 which was incorporated into the 1999 Act that led to amendment of the Constitution. Act (2) of 2002. *"The Court noted therefore that the evolution of Article 161 (2) had been characterized by a significant shift from exclusivity and unilateralism on the part of the President to inclusion and consensuality involving the Opposition Leader,"* said Justice Saunders of the CCJ[15].

The Caribbean Court of Justice, Guyana's highest court of appeal, ruled on June 18, 2019, that the process of selection of Justice James Patterson was flawed and that his unilateral appointment as Chair of GECOM was in breach of the Constitution. Furthermore, Justice Maureen Rajnauth-Lee reasoned that by giving reasons for the rejection of the nominees List, President Granger would be engendering greater public trust and confidence in the Elections Commission as is the premise of the Carter Formula.

On July 26, 2019, Justice Claudette Singh was sworn in as the GECOM Chair given that both the Leader of the Opposition and President Granger found common ground. She oversaw one of the most trying of elections in Guyana's history where she managed a Secretariat tainted with corrupted officials.

The second niggling issue was more a thorn in the flesh for the APNU+AFC government which lost a No-Confidence[16] motion when one of its MPs, Mr. Charrandas Persaud of the Alliance for Change (AFC), voted with the opposition on December 23, 2018. This action took great courage from Mr. Persaud whose grievances were many and were even shared by citizens of Guyana interested in the development of the country. This single act was a shock that rippled through the National Assembly on the shout of *"Yes"* by Mr. Persaud. His vote was a vote of conscience, care for the people of Guyana, courage and patriotism. That single act of defiance toppled the APNU+AFC-led government.

Elections, due in March 2019, did not occur until March 2, 2020, one year later due to political maneuverings by the incumbent, President David. A Granger. The citizens of Guyana, since 2015, were relying on President Granger who failed to reach out effectively to the PPP-C and bring social cohesion and electoral reform to the country in a manner pleasing to most Guyanese. The country deeply needed it. He did not treat the anti-corruption fight as a priority which was welcomed by supporters and non-supporters, alike.

Mr. Persaud brought to the forefront, the concerns constantly voiced by an involved and vigilant people whose voices were muffled and not reflected in the various projects and decisions being made by the Coalition Government. There was very little input from the coalition partner, the AFC. His action highlighted the inner workings of the ruling party and the fracture between the PNC and its coalition partners. Among Mr. Persaud's concerns were the Coalition's bold move to increase the salaries of the MP by 50%, the closure of sugar estates leaving thousands of workers out of jobs and the unprofessional and incompetent negotiations with Exxon Mobil in the absence of a regulatory and environment framework in preparation for first oil.

The No-Confidence vote was a stress test for the racial unity of the divided Afro-Guyanese and the Indo-Guyanese and of the democratic institutions. It cemented in the psyche of the citizens, the scant indifference of the President for the laws of the land. Guyana has now become, because of the shenanigans of the current administration, the most litigious society in CARICOM relative to the elections process. Mr. Persaud's vote triggered a litany of legal skirmishes in the courts of Guyana.

On June 18, 2019, the CCJ[17] declared that the motion of no confidence in the Government was validly passed and that according to the Constitution of Guyana, the Cabinet inclusive of the President was required to resign if the Government was defeated by the **majority vote** of all the elected members of the National Assembly on a vote of confidence. Another provision of the Constitution as guided by Article 106 requires elections to be held within **three months** of the defeat of the Government on a motion of confidence, unless two-thirds of the National Assembly determined a longer period before the holding of elections.

The Speaker of the Assembly declared that the motion had been validly passed. However, the Government of Guyana neither resigned nor announced impending elections. In determining the majority, the CCJ believed the **'half plus one' rule** was not applicable as was submitted by lawyers defending the Government. The Court stated that the majority was clearly at least 33 votes after the Guyana's Court of Appeal bent over backwards to prove that it was 34, an overture by the APNU+AFC coalition.

One cannot help but judge the Government's actions over these legal tirades which would lead ultimately to their political demise. Justice Winston Anderson of the CCJ who heard the appeals on the majority rule (34 vs 33) describes the Government's approach as *"wholly untenable and without merit."* Justice Wit reminded the people of Guyana that the provisions of the Articles 106(6) and (7) is intended to *"bring Guyana back from an authoritarian presidential regime to a more democratic one."*

It is a pernicious act of an autocratic leader to abuse the judicial system to its end, in particular, one, that can be easily manipulated due to the level of corruption in the judiciary and the Guyana Police Force. Attorney Ms.

Kim Kyte-Thomas, who represented the Chairman of GECOM, Justice Claudette Singh, summed up the approach of the APNU+AFC government as *"frivolous, vexatious and amounts to an abuse of the courts process."*

Exactly four weeks after the Gazetted declaration of a winner in the Guyana Elections 2020, the APNU+AFC Coalition party filed its election petition on August 31, 2020, at the High Court to set aside the March 2, 2020, election and put the PPP-C Government out of office by ordering fresh elections. The petition was officially lodged with the Supreme Court Registry by the former President of the Cooperative Republic of Guyana, Brigadier David A. Granger, the Opposition Leader, Mr. Joseph Harmon, the AFC chairman, Mr. Khemraj Ramjattan among other senior APNU+AFC leaders who were in attendance. The applicants, Ms. Claudette Thorne and Mr. Heston Raymond Bostwick[18], as citizens of Guyana, requested that the court determines chiefly whether the *"elections have been lawfully conducted or whether the results have been, or may have been affected by any unlawful act or omission and in consequence thereof, whether the seats in the National Assembly have been lawfully allocated."* The Petition was thrown out on April 26, 2021, by Chief Justice (ag) Roxane George-Wiltshire.

A second petition was filed on September 17, 2020, on behalf of the APNU+AFC Coalition to increase the odds of the petitions' success by applicants with loyalties to the Coalition. The petitioners, Ms. Monica Thomas and Ms. Bernnan Joette Nurse, were employed as Assistants of the Opposition leader, Mr. Joseph Harmon. The petition accused GECOM of failing to execute several of its constitutional and statutory duties, including failing to complete house-to-house registration and verifying the Official List of Electors (OLE). Other issues covered include ghost voting, voter impersonation and anomalies of which the Coalition complained during the Recount process which would have invalidated the integrity of the election process. This Petition also fell by the wayside.

The Eleventh Parliament of Guyana was dissolved on December 30, 2019, and approximately nineteen months after the passage of the no-confidence motion against the APNU+AFC Coalition government, the Twelfth Parliament opened at 10:00 hrs. at the Arthur Chung Conference Centre (ACCC), Liliendaal, Greater Georgetown on September 1, 2020. There was no pomp and ceremony for the Opening of the Parliament by the Head of State. Members of Parliament were sworn in, along with a Speaker, Mr. Manzoor Nadir and a Deputy Speaker, Mr. Lennox Shuman.

The Clerk of the National Assembly, Mr. Sherlock Isaacs, had asked that Members of Parliament who held dual citizenship to provide evidence that they have relinquished such, in conformity with Article 155 (1) (a) of the constitution of Guyana. This approach would prevent challenges like that which existed at the time of the no-confidence motion. On the advice of the Ministry of Health and the Guyana Defence Force, the Parliamentarians sat six feet apart following the Covid-19 Guidelines and would only return to the Parliament Chamber, Public Buildings, Brickdam, Georgetown on the advice of the Minister of Health.

CHAPTER 2: ELECTORAL MANIPULATION
- INVISIBLE RIGGING -

"There is no act of treachery or meanness of which a political party is not capable; for in politics there is no honor." Benjamin Disraeli

The electoral drama within Guyana needs to be presented within the context of the wider international community. With regards to political integrity and the rule of law, it would be disingenuous to ostracize the country pretending that it stands in isolation of the world.

The absence of political integrity, over generations, has led to the subtle undermining of democracy in Guyana. The absence of this ethical standard has led to vote tampering, cheque book voting, ballot box stuffing and a host of behavioral patterns that are border line illegal. According to Nic Cheeseman and Brian Klaas[19] in How to rig an Election, there are 6 subcategories of electoral manipulations and three of these, form a part of Guyana's electoral history on a consistent basis.

The Global Corruption Barometer is an analysis published by Transparency International and is the largest survey in the world tracking public opinion on corruption. 40% of the Guyanese population believe that corruption increased in 2019 and close to 27% paid a bribe during 2018[20]. The most bribed institution was the police force at a bribery rate of 40%. 20% of Guyanese rated the judges and magistrates as corrupt, 27% the local government officials, 36% the Members of Parliament, and a whopping 42% regarded the Guyana Police Force as corrupt. Incredibly, 67% of the people of Guyana believe that the government is doing a good job at fighting corruption and 82% of them believe that ordinary people can make a difference at fighting corruption, and this was demonstrated during the Elections 2020 through the pervasive use of social media.

Guyana's Corruption Perceptions Index[21] score of 40 is not one to be proud of, particularly as it ranks 85 out of 180 countries. The Corruption Perceptions Index ranks 180 countries and territories by their perceived levels of public sector corruption, according to experts and business owners. Corruption in Guyana has reached endemic proportions due to multiple factors ranging from extreme poverty and open racism to, more so, a high level of nepotism. During 2019-2020, the people of Guyana sparked a movement where they had been demanding that the political players be more honest and provide Guyanese with opportunities needed for personal and national growth.

Elections 2020, more than any other election in the history of Guyana, saw the flow of large amounts of monies into electoral campaigns anticipating the taste and feel of the Oil and Gas spin offs. The wealthy in Guyana continues to get richer while the poor continues to struggle thereby creating an environment ripe for crime and thus feeding the drug trade and human trafficking interests. Guyana, still remains in 2019, a hub for the trafficking of drugs according to Mr. Michael Atherley, Director of National Anti-Narcotics Agency (NA-NA).[22]

A comparative analysis of the delays of election results in some of the ABCE countries and some of their record-breaking events, Guyana's elections process in placed in perspective. The United Kingdom[23] has an estimated population of 65 million (83 times that of Guyana) on a land area of 242,500 square kilometers. If we think that 153 days to await results caused anxiety in Guyana and the Caribbean Region, then we can only imagine what the British were thinking when their elections results were delayed by 22 days. Once more, the delays were man-made. It was the aftermath of the Second World War which ended on May 8, 1945. U.K. Elections 1945 happened on July 5, 1945[24], and with so many servicemen posted overseas, it was not until July 26, 1945, that the overseas votes were brought to Britain which saw the British replacing Prime Minister Winston Churchill's Conservative party with that of the new Prime Minister Clement Attlee of the Labour party. Apparently, from the date of elections until the date when results were announced, no mention was made of them on the radio broadcasts. This behavioral pattern is highly unlikely in Guyana given the prevalence of the internet.

The United States of America[25], one of the ABCE countries, is approximately 9.8 million square kilometers and made up of 50 states. It is the fourth largest country by land area with a 2019 estimated population of 328 million. Its longest election results delay was 5 days. Guyana is 215,000 square kilometers which is 45 times smaller than the USA by land area but with the USA having 400 times the population size.

Apparently, when Mr. Abraham Lincoln won the elections over incumbent Mr. John Buchanan on November 6, 1860, with the exception of the postmaster, all the federal officers in South Carolina resigned the next day[26]. The results of the voting were telegraphed throughout most of the country within 24 hours of the close of the polls. On November 7, 1860, Pony Express riders carried word of Mr. Abraham Lincoln's election as President from Fort Kearney, Nebraska to Placerville, California in a record 5 days. This was considered one of the most significant accomplishments by the Pony Express. The Pony Express[27] was a mail service delivering messages, newspapers, and mail using relays of horse-mounted riders that operated from April 3, 1860, to October 24, 1861, between Missouri and California in the United States of America. Again, the delay of the results was created by people.

The second time that the results of a presidential election, the 54th quadrennial presidential elections, in the USA were delayed was when it was held on November 7, 2000. Republican George W. Bush lost the popular vote to Democrat Al Gore by more than a half million votes but beat Gore in the Electoral College by a count of 271-267[28]. This was the closest elections since 1876. As a result, the Bush campaign filed an appeal with the U.S. Supreme Court, asking it to delay the Recount until it could hear the case. On December 9, 2000, the Court issued a stay on the Recount. George W. Bush had the distinction of being the governor of Texas and was the eldest son of George H. W. Bush, the 41st president of the USA.

Twenty years ago, the Presidential Elections 2000 reminded the Americans that their democracy was imperfect and was just as corrupted as that of the developing countries. A series of ensuing legal battles led the Supreme Court, in a highly controversial (5-4) decision, to declare George W. Bush the winner of Florida and the winner of the presidential elections to become the 43rd president of the USA on January 20, 2001. The deciding ballots from the State of Florida were disputed and as such the elections remained unresolved for five weeks. Mr. Al Gore did not pursue further legal action for the sake of the nation. On December 13, 2000, Vice President, Mr. Al Gore, conceded defeat offering words of unity, *"And tonight, for the sake of our unity as a people and the strength of our democracy, I offer my concession."*[29]

Guyanese were concerned that their beloved country's elections process would lend itself to a record being created for the longest delay in the conclusion of elections and to the declaration of a winner. 153 days is a long time given the paltry population of three quarters of a million for an area of approximately one quarter of a million square kilometers, for anyone to patiently await the outcome of a free and fair elections. Trinidad and Tobago, with a population of 1.3million inhabitants, held their elections on August 10, 2020, and the winner, Dr. Keith Rowley of the PNM, was declared the winner within 24 hours.

The government of war-torn Iraq held parliamentary elections on March 7, 2010. It was the second parliamentary election since Mr. Saddam Hussein was deposed in 2003. However, a government was not formed until December 21, 2010, after a total of 289 days. On October 1, 2010, a new government was formed with Prime Minister Nouri Al-Maliki leading a coalition. Iraq broke the record for the longest period for a country without a government during war time and that is why it is in the Guinness Book of World Records[30].

The Guinness Book of World Records[31] recorded Belgium as the country which registered the longest time to form a government after elections, during peacetime. On June 13, 2010, elections for the Federal Parliament were held and this was during the midst of the 2007-2011 Belgian political instability. After 541 days, on December 5, 2011, Belgium's King Albert II appointed a new cabinet and a new prime minister, Mr. Elio di Rupo, whose new government took office on the following day and included a coalition of the Liberal, Socialist and Christian Democratic parties from both Flanders and Wallonia. What the above-mentioned countries have in common with Guyana is a level of political and social instability and lack of progress on electoral reformation.

Wikipedia defines *"Electoral fraud, sometimes referred to as election fraud, election manipulation or vote rigging, is illegal interference with the process of an election, either by increasing the vote share of the favored candidate, depressing the vote share of the rival candidates, or both[32]."* The manipulation is an undemocratic effort to curtail the rights of the citizens of any country.

The strategies and implementation of those strategies were so sinister in their divisiveness and lack of ingenuity, that it would have taken minds mired in evil but lacking in impulse control and tactical know how to construct the narrative.

The first sub-category of election manipulation which emerged from the Elections 2020 process was the intimidation of the international Elections Observers. On March 5, 2020, the Minister of Foreign Affairs, Ms. Karen Cummings, summoned the observers to a meeting at GECOM's Region Four office at High & Hadfield Street, Georgetown. This event was a risky attempt at elections manipulations which backfired leaving the international community and the people of Guyana stunned. The British High Commissioner, Mr. Greg Quinn, responded that the international observers were following a code of conduct and that the Minister's suggestion that the observers were peddling misinformation was inaccurate.

The Government of Guyana issued a Statement upon the reaction of the members of the Observer Missions indicating that it regretted any misunderstanding the comments of the Foreign Affairs Minister may have caused when she threatened to strip the International Observers of their accreditations and after the head of the Commonwealth Observer Mission, former Barbados Prime Minister Owen Arthur responded angrily, *"I speak on behalf of the Commonwealth, the largest concentration of people in the world and I am not going to have, not me, the Commonwealth, disrespected by a threat to take away the accreditation of the Commonwealth."* Many of the international observers felt intimidated and were concerned that the electoral process was being eroded. Minister Cummings premise was to caution the diplomats and observers about issuing premature statements about the Elections 2020 but it was done in a very heavy-handed manner.

On March 20, the Carter Center signaled their desire to return to Guyana to participate in the National Recount alongside the CARICOM Observer team. It did not happen. The Coalition government ensured that it did not.

On January 2, 2020, within the afternoon period when supporters of the PPP-C were rallying in Sophia, they met with concerted, heavy resistance by activists from the APNU+AFC party which blocked the streets and threw missiles to impede their progress in a predominantly APNU+AFC stronghold. PPP-C paraphernalia was removed as is the practice by the supporters of both major parties. A practice that is undemocratic and unconstitutional. Former Attorney General and PPP-C member, Mr. Anil Nandlal reported the incident[33] to the Police Commissioner, Mr. Leslie James. During this silly season, war lines are drawn, and the divisions are re-entrenched. Both major parties are adept at these strategies to divide and rule.

Throughout the month of July 2020, supporters of the APNU+AFC coalition gave vent to their dissatisfaction with the rulings of the various courts dealing with the resolution of elections challenges. They protested in the streets, free of protective masks against Covid-19 and in breach of the safety regulations against the orders of the National Covid-19 Task Force though supporters of the Opposition PPP-C were quickly warned against congregating.

One particular gathering that is worth mentioning was the gathering of APNU+AFC supporters on July 11, 2020, in front of State House after the CCJ's ruling in the presence of President David A. Granger. One of the supporters bellowed, *"Tell we what we want to hear, not what you want to tell we!"* It was presumed that this was a request of the President to authorize the unleashing of violence on the populace and to make the situation in Guyana, untenable. All these illegal protesters marched through the streets to the blowing of horns and the music of the song, *"Let the Blow Blow Blow!"*

Another method of electoral manipulation was the use of the Guyana Police Force to disrupt the tabulation of Region Four's votes. A decision was made, other than by the legal authority of the GECOM's Returning Officer Mr. Clairmont Mingo to remove the local and international observers along with accredited individuals from the GECOM command center. According to the Representation of the People Act, Section 84 (1), it is the Returning Officer who has the authority to have persons present during the period of tabulating and verifying of votes.

One of the victims of the indiscriminate use of excessive force by the Guyana Police Force was Assistant Police Commissioner, Mr. Edgar Thomas, who was relieved of his Commanding Officer position in Region Four A, after refusing to execute an order that was unlawful. Men of integrity fall by the wayside when their professional responsibilities do not conform to the dictatorial commands of those in authority bent on manipulation of the elections process. This style was reminiscent of the Burnham era of electoral rigging.

On March 18, 2020, the Georgetown Chamber of Commerce and Industry (GCCI)[34] accused the Guyana Police Force (GPF) of adopting an aggressive posture against political parties and accredited observers. The GCCI, a local accredited observer, observed that *"Members of the GCCI's electoral observer team were present on the evening of March 16th, 2020, at the compound of the Arthur Chung International Conference Centre (ACICC) when a group of accredited observers and party agents who had convened a peaceful gathering outside of the building were confronted by riot police and forced to leave the premises. The GCCI can confirm that the observers and party representatives who attempted to question and gain clarity on the orders were subsequently threatened with incarceration."* Once more, the GPF's professionalism and impartiality were brought into question and clearly demonstrated that both major political parties have used the GPF to their political advantage.

A month later, the International Center for Democracy (ICD)[35] penned a letter to the Commissioner of Police, Mr. Leslie James, attempting to ascertain the reason for not arresting the REO for Region Four, Mr. Clairmont Mingo, the Chief Elections Officer (CEO) and also the Deputy CEO for fraudulently tampering with the Statements of Poll (SoPs) for Region Four in favor of the APNU+AFC and for making a fraudulent declaration.

The climate of fear in Guyana is created first in the minds of the electorate by the indifferent leaders and supporters of the two major political parties. Elections periods in Guyana have historically been periods of insensitive speech, repeated pronouncements of racial epithets and information that is so far from the truth that they form parts of anecdotes.

Hate speech and misinformation is part of the electoral manipulation strategy of the two major political parties. What the pandemic of 2020 had revealed to the world was that the citizens of the world tolerated the lies, half-truths and fear mongering of their political leaders. The constant threat of violence can be unnerving to the recipients of such threats which have contributed to the progressively lower rates of turnout for voting in some areas of Guyana. Repression does lead to the reduction in the votes of the

Opposition parties in many countries and it is no less so in Guyana. So pervasive is this strategy that the Ethnic Relations Commission (ERC) on February 13, 2020, invited the eleven contesting political parties to sign on to the Code of Conduct for elections by urging all parties to *"to work towards eliminating such public displays through a more responsible approach in an effort to ensure that the remaining period of the campaign is free of ethnic division, discrimination, hate speech, incitement and provocation.*[36]"

Elaborate threads of fake news were planted with unmatched frequency on every popular social media platform known to the Guyanese but in a manner so crude as to warrant scrutiny. So many interpretations of the Laws of Guyana were peddled in a systematic manner via mainstream media that the supporters of the two major parties settled within their Information Bubble less reasoning and commonsense disentangled the lies from the facts. Things got so heated during the Elections 2020 that commentators on Social Media blogs were called in and reprimanded by the ERC and warned about fear mongering and the spouting of racial terms. The Cyber Crime Act of 2016 was tested to its max as persons who posted threats and incurred the wrath of other races were invited to take a trip to the Police Headquarters.

One of the most popular Facebook commentators during the Elections 2020 was the Guyanese Critic, Mr. Mikail Rodrigues. Based on his free and liberal form of speaking, he incurred the wrath of supporters of the APNU+AFC coalition. One of the Ministers of Government, along with an entourage of supporters, protested in front of the commentator's house causing much disruption to his life. On August 11, 2020, his house was riddled with bullets[37]. The perpetrators of this act had not been found at the time of publication of this book but the matter was being investigated by the GPF. Facebook's live streaming of the event evoked intense, raw emotions of hate, racism, and man's inhumanity to man.

Misinformation came in the form of WhatsApp videos and audio recordings and an all-out bombardment on the Facebook platform. These newer and more effective ways of inflaming the ethno-political polarization can only lead to situations liken to that of Kenya, Zimbabwe and Cambodia, powder keg moments away from being lit. What is unfortunate is that the largely educated populace is encapsulated in a political bubble of tribalism.

A bloated Official List of Electors (OLE) may be a source of voter manipulation given that ghost voting had occurred in Guyana, in the past. The two major parties had ample time to sanitize the voters list. However, whatever the motives may be, it has been a source of contentions for several elections starting in 1992. The PPP-C had the greatest amount of time to correct the OLE but did not, knowing that an unsanitized OLE is an obstacle to a free and fair elections process. They supported House-to-

House Voter registration but opposed the process when the coalition government demanded it be conducted before general and regional elections were held.

GECOM confirmed that the OLE contained 661,028 eligible voters, an invitation for illegitimate voting. Dr. Tara Singh[38] posited that given a population of 746,955[39] in 2012 according to the 2012 Population & Housing Census Final Results of the Bureau of Statistics, there are approximately 479,545 eligible voters above the age of 18 years. It is this same OLE which the CEO, Mr. Lowenfield, used in dropping over 115,000 voters from the list because of voter impersonation and other challenges. The integrity of any OLE provides confidence and trust in the democratic process of free and fair elections.

Once more, the APNU+AFC coalition government turned to the courts (High Court and Court of Appeal) regarding the House-to-House Registration (H2H) in what former Attorney General, Mr. Anil Nandlall, referred to as a tactic to delay the setting of an early elections date.

Justice Claudette Singh, Chairman of GECOM, made a unilateral decision to end the H2H registration on August 31, 2019, and to merge the data garnered by the H2H exercise with the National Register of Registrants Database as per the ruling of the Chief Justice Roxane George-Wiltshire. Secondly, the Commission published the Preliminary List of Electors (PLE) and this was followed by a Claims and Objections (C&O)[40] exercise which started on October 1, 2019, and was completed on November 18, 2019.

It is important to record instances where a flawed democracy and a full democracy tend to merge. In the United States, on November 11, 2016, a federal judge issued a restraining order to stop North Carolina state and county election boards from mass purging voters from its electoral rolls[41]. The electoral boards began illegally removing voters from the roll after an instance of a single letter from a voter's home address was returned to sender. North Carolina National Association for the Advancement of Colored People brought the court challenge. In Guyana, it was the opposition parties and political activists who fought the encroachment on democratic rights.

On reflection, back in 1997, the PPP-C government voted to make possession of a valid ID card[42] a requirement to vote which was contrary to the Constitution. The High Court received an Elections Petition by Ester Perreira, a PNC supporter. After two years of hearings, the High Court judge, Justice Claudette Singh, the current chairman of GECOM, ruled that the ID card requirement was unlawful and declared Guyana's 1997 general elections null and void because of fraud. The court found that about 30,000 persons, some one-tenth of Guyana's eligible voters, were disenfranchised by the illegal requirement and that there was evidence of missing ballot boxes from opposition strongholds.

On November 29, 2019, the PPP-C launched their elections campaign with the promise of enacting campaign finance legislation to curb elections corruption. The premise behind the proposal was to ensure that all monies received from companies within the petroleum sector were disclosed. Dr. Bharat Jagdeo[43], leader of the Opposition, PPP-C party proclaimed that, *"We have to ensure that foreign money doesn't play a role in influencing national policy, particularly in these sectors that are so crucial to the wellbeing of Guyanese because you can possibly sell policies that can harm the whole country."*

During Elections 2020, the business sector was focused on the outcome of the elections results. Companies and supporters of the Opposition PPP-C were known to have doled out monies to the APNU+AFC coalition supporters in exchange for votes. The supporters were required to take a snapshot of the ballot paper with a valid X next to their party symbol. Given the outcome of the Elections 2020, this may have been a successful strategy given the vote distribution in Coalition strongholds.

In the final report of the European Union Elections Mission, one of the 26 recommendations included the introduction of strong campaign financial legislation. The Citizenship Initiative (TCI)[44], in October 2019, made public its campaign finance information following its commitment to transparency. It was the only political party to do so. Of the $ 2.5M raised by TCI from approximate 30 donors, $ 2.0M of the donations was spent by January 31, 2020. This was a start in the right direction and should have encouraged the larger parties to follow suit and should be demanded by the electorate.

In the absence of campaign financial legislation, nothing prevented the political parties in Guyana from splurging in a bid to acquire maximum votes. There was no level playing field when it came to spending monies to lure the electorate, in particular, by the incumbent. Electoral campaigns were the ideal opportunities to misuse government funds and it was done by the APNU+AFC government when it acquired in May 2019, 10,000 Buju Banton tickets at a total cost of $ 50M[45]. The funds were taken from the Lotto Fund. Entertainment for the supporters would seem to declare the intentions of the party that spends a great deal of money, that is, our promises are sound and we intend to please you. Cheque book politics was alive and striving in Guyana, more so, during Elections 2020 and with so much at stake.

It is eerily coincidental that the Working People's Alliance (WPA) commemorated the 40th Anniversary of the assassination of Dr. Walter Rodney who met his death on June 13, 1980, by a bomb hidden in a walkie-talkie. The Anniversary occurred at a time in Guyana's history when its citizens were trying to prevent undemocratic means and atrocities in the aftermaths of the transparent rigging of the Elections 2020.

According to the National Security Archive, George Washington University, the U.S. Embassy in Guyana in 1980 had strong evidence to believe that the death of internationally known historian and activist Walter Rodney was caused by the Forbes Burnham PNC government and that Gregory Smith was the Government's agent responsible. Supporting documentation was also found in the form of the February 13, 2016, Commission of Inquiry[46] *"appointed to enquire and report on the circumstances surrounding the death in an explosion of the late Dr. Walter Rodney."* One of the key findings was that there was a conspiracy involving the Guyana Defense Force (GDF), the Guyana Police Force (GPF) and others to kill Dr. Rodney and that former President Forbes Burnham had to be aware of it.

Dr. Rodney was the leading figure in the resistance movement against the authoritarian and repressive Government of President Forbes Burnham of the People's National Congress (PNC). His active protests against human rights violation and the rigging of elections led to his early demise.

President Forbes Burnham of the People's National Congress (PNC) rigged three consecutive General Elections and the July 10, 1978, Referendum. Consequent upon his actions the 1980 Constitution provided him with unmatched powers thereby paving the way for the continuous rule of Guyana, a dictatorship, in essence. Of course, since 1964 the U.S.A. preferred Mr. Forbes Burnham's PNC government over the more openly Marxist-oriented ideology of Dr. Cheddi Jagan, leader of the main opposition People's Progressive Party (PPP). The U.S.A's Cold War policy during that period tolerated human rights abuses at the expediency of a partnership against the Soviet Union's rising hegemony in Latin America and the Caribbean.

Elections 2020 was no different to the elections of the 1960s-1990s. The ubiquitous social media platforms provided the spotlight on the violent tactics of the incumbent's supporters. A number of WhatsApps videos that were circulating highlighted the tactics of intimidation of the APNU+AFC party supporters through predominantly Indo-Guyanese areas, mainly along the East Coast Demerara which brought back the fears and anxieties of the 1960s under the late President Forbes Burnham.

Rigging by the PNC-dominated APNU+AFC coalition has evolved in a frightening way, no longer subtle, it is blatant, self-defeating and goes against the campaign theme of Honesty and Integrity as portrayed by the incumbent. The ballot stuffing strategy as carried out during the Elections 2020 in Guyana duplicated in so many ways, the Kenyan Elections 2017. Kenya's elections were the blueprint for the APNU+AFC coalition government. This strategy is normally a last resort which could not pass a forensic audit and was very high risk. However, what was absent was the political instability that followed with over one thousand deaths for which the people of Guyana are all grateful chiefly due to the leverage of the

ABCE countries, the local private sector groups and the personal sanctions against those who were implicated in the rigging.

Questions have also been raised around the independence of GECOM and allegations of internal manipulation by staffers within the Commission. On June 16, 2020, the three-member CARICOM Scrutinizing Team rendered their Report on Elections Recount 2020 citing that the political nature of the Commission prevents it from being an impartial body and from being independent. *"Indeed from its beginning, given the essential political distrust and ethnic polarization in the country, GECOM was never conceptualized as an institution which exemplified autonomy from partisan political influences."* Clearly, there is a need for electoral reform. However, we have heard these recommendations since 1992. Since the two major political parties' approach will remain the same every election period, it is unlikely that any changes will occur unless a Joker Effect presents itself.

The next chapter will relate the details of the Elections 2020 Ballot Stuffing in a way that only a sociopathic mind could devise.

CHAPTER 3: GUYANA ELECTIONS COMMISSION
- ELECTIONS PROCESS -

"If you look at their voting habits and their eating habits, you realize people are stupid." RuPaul

Within a democracy, flawed or counterfeit, elections are a given. Institutions are set in place to ensure that the voting process flows smoothly with the minimum of disruptions and mechanisms are structured to prevent electoral manipulation. It was the year 2020 and Elections 2020 was set for March 2, 2020. What could possibly go wrong?

Elections 2020 was destined to be the Election of all Elections given the discovery of oil and gas and the hope of great wealth for the politicians and their sycophants. From as far back as the controversial, unilateral selection of the Chairman of the Guyana Elections Commission (GECOM) to the protracted outcome of the No-Confidence Motion and the abuse of the judicial system, the citizens of Guyana knew that a tsunami of anxiety coupled with the restrictions of the Covid-19 pandemic were bound to happen. With all its twists and turns, Elections 2020 reached its climax in March 2020, then it fizzled in July 2020.

With 42 days remaining in 2018, on November 19, 2018, the Honorable Minister of Finance, Mr. Winston Jordan, announced that $ 5.4 billion dollars[47] was allocated in the 2019 Budget for GECOM to conduct the elections scheduled for 2020. If quality elections are required, then a quality electoral commission is a must. GECOM is responsible for the unenviable task of administering all national, regional and local government elections within Guyana's legislative framework. It sets the policy for voter registration and maintenance of the voters' list. Under Section 17 of the Election Laws Amendment Act 2000, there shall be a Permanent Secretariat to GECOM to *"ensure institutional memory and capacity and the Commission shall be responsible for the efficient functioning of the Secretariat."*

According to GECOM, *"The Secretariat also performs the tasks of the National Registration Centre under the National Registration Act, Chapter 19:08 and the CEO acts as the National Commissioner for Registration. The National Registration Centre has responsibility for the registration of electors and maintenance of the registers whereas the Secretariat has responsibility for administering elections. GECOM is constitutionally obliged to act with impartiality and fairness in the execution of its duties (162 (1) [b], Constitution (Amendment) Act)."* GECO[48], as an Electoral Management body, is required to be insulated from executive interference in the performance of its functions.

The first female Chairman, Justice Claudette Singh, was appointed from a list of six candidates who either held or were qualified to hold the office of Judge of the High Court or the Court of Appeal or any other fit and proper person *"who are not unacceptable to the President, submitted by the Leader of the Opposition after he has meaningfully consulted with the non-governmental political parties represented in the National Assembly."*

The Constitution (Amendment) Act No. 2 of 2000[49] provided for the appointment of six members of the Commission, three each from the government and the Opposition parties, respectively. During Elections 2020, the government commissioners were Mr. Vincent Alexander, Mr. Charles Corbin and Mr. Desmond Trotman. On the other hand, the representatives from the Opposition were Ms. Bibi Safora Shadick, Mr. Robeson Benn and Mr. Sase Gunraj. These commissioners are as non-objective as they come and are essentially filtering units for their respective party's views.

The main functions and responsibilities of the Election Officials and staff are stipulated by the Representation of the People Act Cap. 1:03 and the relevant subsidiary legislation. GECOM's Secretariat is led by the Chief Elections Officer (CEO), Mr. Keith Lowenfield, who was responsible for the appointment and removal of electoral officials such as the ten Returning Officers (RO) corresponding to the ten Electoral Districts, the Deputy Returning Officers (DRO) and the polling staff for elections day. The ROs are responsible for the supervision of the Polling Stations, ascertaining the total votes cast in favor of each List of Candidates in the supervised District, publicly declaring and publishing the votes recorded for each List of Candidates and promptly and accurately submitting the Statements of Poll (SOP) to the CEO. Mr. Lowenfield's contract was renewed in December 2019 even though the Commissioners of the Opposition PPP-C objected.

Infrastructurally, GECOM provided 2,339 polling stations for the Elections 2020 as opposed to 2,299 in 2015[50]. Given the sensitivity and perceived neutrality of polling stations located at private residences, there were only 92 such stations compared to the 166 house-based polling stations during the 2015 elections. To alleviate the challenge of voting as a consequence of the reduced number of house-based polling stations, 49 polling stations[51] were located in tents to accommodate over 10,000 voters throughout the length and breadth of Guyana. On February 7, 2020, one of the largest cargo planes ever to touch down at the Cheddie Jagan International Airport and to utilize the newly constructed Apron designed for Code D and E sized aircrafts landed in Guyana. The cargo plane, the Atlas Air (747-400), brought GECOM's ballot papers and blank Statements of Poll which were delivered to GECOM headquarters in Kingston, Georgetown securely.

A year prior to the Elections Day, on March 20, 2019[52], Opposition Leader, Dr. Bharrat Jagdeo of the PPP-C party, accused the APNU+AFC coalition Government of conspiring with the GECOM to rig the General and Regional Elections and to delay them beyond the constitutionally mandatory deadline. Dr. Jagdeo surmised that the government is too insistent on updating the OLE through H2H registration. Elections were constitutionally due within three months of the passage of the no-confidence motion against the Government. GECOM's Chairman, retired Justice James Patterson wrote President David A. Granger, informing him that General and Regional Elections could not be held before late November 2019, even though GECOM was constitutionally mandated to hold elections by March 21, 2019.

In July 2019, the leadership of the Opposition, the PPP-C, discouraged their supporters from supporting the House-to-House (H2H)[53] activity of GECOM which would violate the consequential orders of the Caribbean Court of Justice's (CCJ) rulings of June 18, 2019, and July 12, 2019.

The Claims and Objections (C&O) process ran for a period of 49 days from October 1st to November 18th, 2019, rather than the 35 days that was initially agreed upon at its September 24 statutory meeting. Objections to the inclusion of dead persons or disqualified otherwise were submitted to Registration Officers for them to hear and determine objections and appeals on November 20, 2019. Thereafter, all complete objections and applications were submitted to the Commissioner of Registration for corrections by November 25, 2019. The three Opposition-nominated Commissioners did not support the vote for an extended C&O period. This was the longest C&O period in Guyana's history.

President Granger on September 25, 2019, having met with the Chairman of GECOM Justice Claudette Singh, issued two proclamations for the holding of General and Regional Elections[54] on Monday, March 2, 2020. The President's powers are vested in him by Article 61 of the Constitution of Guyana to appoint by proclamation March 2, 2020, as the day for the election of members of the National Assembly and members of the Regional Democratic Councils as held under Article 60 (2).

Consequent upon the proclamation by His Excellency, President David A. Granger, the Disciplined Services[55], namely the Guyana Defence Force (GDF), the Guyana Police Force (GPF) and the Guyana Prison Service (GPS); voted on February 21, 2020, at 68 polling stations throughout the 10 Regions of the country. There are approximately 10,226 ranks of which 8,369 (81.8%) voted. 80.6% of the ranks of the GPF or 5,400 officers from a total of 6,702 voted. 83.6% or 2,359 soldiers of the 3,036 army ranks exercised their franchise. 88.1% or 430 officers of the GPS of the 488 members voted.

Retired Director of Prisons, Mr. Byron W. Henry[56], plead with the powers that be not to disenfranchise the Disciplined Services through a letter to the Editor of the Guyana Chronicle newspaper on March 1, 2020. He was rejecting claims of disenfranchisement by the Campaign Manager of the APNU+AFC, Mr. Joseph Harmon, and the President of the Guyana Veterans, Lieutenant Colonel Gomes, during the recounting period in May 2020.

On the day prior to Elections Day, the People's Progressive Party/Civic (PPP-C) objected to the use of aircrafts owned by businessman, Mr. Brian Tiwari of BK Tiwari[57], who had been known to financially support the APNU+AFC. Mr. Tiwari's aircrafts had been used to transport ballot boxes and polling officials on Monday's Elections Day. They believed that the process tainted the integrity of the elections because of political alignment to the governing party.

On the same day, March 1, 2020, Mr. Roy Beepat, Chairman of Giftland[58] made a couple of recommendations to GECOM so basic and so relevant to the situation in Guyana that it warranted an analysis of the electoral commission itself and its negligence on informing the general, local voting populace. Mr. Beepat made three recommendations given the nature and anxiety associated with the elections process in Guyana. In the same vein, the Chief of Mission of the OAS, Bruce Mr. Golding, recommended that *"the elections commission consider implementing a system to give preliminary results and make information available on elections day or the morning after[59]."*

He recommended that the details of the verified Statements of Polls (SOPs) be communicated to GECOM's ICT Unit, the results of the various Polling Stations be posted frequently on GECOM's website for viewing by the local and international communities throughout the course of the tallying process and that Preliminary Results be displayed at the end of the process. These recommendations would ensure transparency of the process, reduce fake news and defuse the tensions, both racial and physical, during and post election's day.

What mattered most to the political leaders at this time was the control of the ranks of the Disciplined Services. The government in power always had greater control over them as history has informed us. The Guyana Police Force's (GPF) mandate during the elections process was to maintain the safety and security of ballots and polling stations. They provided escort services for the ballot boxes which were transported to the Arthur Chung Convention Centre, Liliendaal, East Coast Demerara for Recounting. So important to the integrity are these security services that the Private Sector Commission, led by its Chairman, Captain Gerry Gouveia, met with the GPF on February 5, 2020, to discuss security arrangements for the elections to provide another level of assurances of free and fair elections.

Close to 51% of the eligible voters or 460,352 persons exercised their franchise freely on March 2, 2020, in all the 10 administrative Regions of Guyana. The electoral process was well managed and at best, one of the most peaceful elections with comparatively minimal violence. Local and international electoral observers played a crucial role in the resolution of some matters and were influential where it mattered most by supporting the electoral process.

Polling day was a bright sunshine day throughout Guyana. Exposure to voting in the Elections 2020 was positive and polling staff was generally polite and informed. Monday 2, 2020 was declared a Public Holiday by Minister of Public Security, the Honourable Mr. Khemraj Ramjattan, a decision that was somewhat late in coming. Hundreds of election observers were deployed throughout all electoral districts and included those from the Commonwealth, the OAS, the Carter Center, CARICOM, the Private Sector Commission, the Georgetown Chamber of Commerce and Guyana Bar Association being the most prominent of the observers fielding the largest contingencies of monitors.

At the Pearl Nursery School, East Bank Demerara, His Excellency President David A. Granger and his wife, Her Excellency Madam Sandra Granger and daughter Afuwa voted. On the other hand, the Presidential candidate for the PPP-C, Dr. Mohamed Irfaan Ali and his wife, Arya, voted at the Leonora Technical and Vocational Institute, West Coast Demerara. Generally, the tabulation process and verification were conducted in a transparent manner in spite of minor hiccups in all the electoral districts with the exception of Region Four, the most populous district. Representatives from the two major political parties, APNU+AFC and PPP-C, were present at all polling stations. It was anticipated that the election results would have been declared after three days based on the history of the past six elections.

The day after elections, businesses remained closed, windows were protected with plywood and secured against elections violence. It is said that when the Chinese-owned restaurants and supermarkets are closed, the fear must be real. APNU+AFC supporters were ever present on the roadways and hovered around the GECOM Command Centre.

The Chief Elections Officer (CEO), Mr. Keith Lowenfield, promised preliminary results throughout the day which never materialized, and this was accepted as being consistent with his modus operandi. The absence of preliminary results being issued on an on-going basis and analysis thereof, as occurs in almost every democratic country, is a feature of Guyana's elections landscape. Though GECOM had been warned about the paucity of information fed to the electors, it ignored the call which resulted in heightened tensions, race baiting, prognostications of doom and a variety of other social ills which raise their ugly heads every five years.

Consistent in every election has been the call for peace, calm and unity by members of the Diplomatic Corp, the leaders of the two main political parties and civil society. All the major news media supported this venture and elaborated on the benefits of democracy and a united Guyana. However, in the background, the political leaders continued to make statements which were very provocative and inflammatory which was brought on by their political impulse control disorder and which significantly impaired their judgement.

The Opposition PPP-C[60] called upon the Commissioner of Police to take steps to protect and preserve the official records of the Ministries of Government and State property. The call was made against the backdrop of attempts hatched to remove and destroy public documents and moveable State assets. The geographical challenges, minimal roadways and the lack of effective means of transportation prevented the declaration of Results within 24-hours.

The RO of Region Four, Mr. Clairmont Mingo, suspended counting at 8:30pm because of tiredness to the annoyance and frustration of the representatives of the multiple parties present and the elections observers.

During the evening period, large bodies of predominantly APNU+AFC supporters moved slowly and deliberately along the East Coast Demerara corridor from Buxton's Linetop as part of a premature victory procession. They walked, bicycled and travelled in cars and mini-buses. Loud honking car horns accompanied the procession, and the distinct sound of the vuvuzelas permeated the evening leaving the tremors of fear in the hearts of the Indo-Guyanese. It was a frightful atmosphere which normally preceded disruptive actions during this period.

The electoral drama unfolded on March 4, 2020, at the tabulation of the Region Four's votes at the Ashmin's Building on High & Hadfield Streets, Georgetown. From around 8:00 am, members of the various local and international Observer groups, GECOM Commissioners, High Commissioners of the ABCE countries and high-ranking members of the political parties contesting the Elections 2020 arrived at the GECOM

Command Centre. The Centre was filled with anticipation. GECOM's officials did not appear to have planned for a day of work. It was on this date that GECOM's cloak of political neutrality was stripped away, and it donned the impenetrable cloak of the APNU+AFC.

At approximately 11:00 am, Mr. Clairmont Mingo, the controversial Region Four Returning Officer and author of mischief and intrigue, fell ill and was removed from the premises by an ambulance attached to the Georgetown Public Hospital Corporation. He returned to the Command Centre a few hours later. Mr. Mingo's actions started a domino effect of political maneuverings which later escalated to all out racial tension and makeshift divisions in Guyana's morbid political game. His replacement, Registration Officer, Ms. Carolyn Mikhaik Duncan, fell ill in what was deemed a contrived sick out to interrupt the electoral process for Region Four.

By midday, the Results of all nine regional districts, except for Region Four, were announced. The APNU+AFC Coalition representatives made requests for recounts in Regions Two, Three, Five and Six which were won by the PPP-C. These efforts were designed to delay the process as was confirmed during the next 151 days.

The tabulation stopped and started several times throughout a period of five hours. The GECOM official who took over from Mr. Mingo began the count at 1:00 pm using an unverified spreadsheet instead of tabulating the Statements of Poll (SOPs) as required by the legislative provisions of Section 84 of the Representation of the People Act Cap 1.03 Revised Edition of the Laws of Guyana. The process was stopped after it was discovered that the numbers on the spreadsheet and the ones on the approved SOPs were not compatible. Consequently, representatives of political parties and observers held an emergency meeting[61] of approximately one hour with GECOM officials and this resulted in the spreadsheet application being set aside for the time being. For the next four hours, hardly anything of significance occurred to advance the completion of the verification process. To anyone who has watched paint dry, the feeling was the same.

While all the drama was being played out at the Command Centre, around 2:30 pm, supporters of President David A. Granger gathered at the campaign headquarters of the APNU+AFC on Lamaha Street, Georgetown and in tents on the Lamaha Embankment in a festive mood of celebration. By eventide, President David A. Granger addressed his supporters informing them that a declaration could not have been made and he plead for calm and peace. Similar tactics were used by the PPP-C which reminded their supporters that GECOM would declare results upon completion of the verification process.

Again, with the rhythm of a defective heart, the tabulation process resumed at 6:00 pm, but was halted after the two Deputy ROs complained of feeling unwell. This Comedy of Electoral Errors of Shakespearean dramatic intensity unfolded from the pages of a sociopathic mind and his cohorts. Frustration was marked on the faces of those who anticipated a simple tabulation process that would not have exceeded twenty-four hours.

Whoever had conceived this Electoral Manipulation Masterplan was knowledgeable of the game plan of the riggers of the Kenya's 200[62] elections. Kenya suffers from similar tribal politics and in 2007 over 300,000 persons were displaced and over 1,000 were killed. Here in Guyana, the media houses which were accredited by GECOM were banned from entering the Command Centre. Without a satisfactory explanation, they were barred from the GECOM Command Centre. They were in the dark as to the happenings within the Centre though they were fed sporadic, second-hand information from time to time by observers and party representatives. On the other hand, the international media roamed the hallways of the GECOM's Media Centre, freely. Daily and surreptitiously, the elements of democracy within the country were stripped repeatedly as orchestrated by unknown powers. Ranks of the Guyana Police Force formed a human barricade, intermittently throughout the day to prevent the local press from gathering details of the unfolding of an elections heist right under their noses. There was a clear violation of freedom of the press and an attempt to manipulate and disrupt the news and information flow.

About two hours to midnight, prior to welcoming the day when all hell would break loose; diplomats, observers and party representatives, desperate for rational answers and suspicious of GECOM's intentions; encircled the CEO, Mr. Lowenfield. Questions were posed and suggestions made to the CEO as a means of resolving the tabulation and verification delays and to hasten the declaration of the Region Four results. The CEO did not trust the DROs that were available but referred to a specific DRO that would be suitable for him, personally to complete the process. Like a deer caught in the headlight, Mr. Lowenfield[63] was dumbfounded as he struggled for answers and looked for a way to escape the questions. Former Attorney General, Mr. Anil Nandlall, supported suggestions for a resolution of the impasse. A restrained Presidential candidate for the PPP-C, Dr. Irfaan Ali, outlined Mr. Lowenfield's responsibilities with an expectation of a positive response. It did not happen as the CEO charged out of the Command Centre.

Again, the presence of mobile devices saved the day. Social media was replete with videos of the exchange between Dr. Ali, Mr. Nandlall and Mr. Mustapha of the PPP-C and Pastor Delwin Wint of the People's Republic Party from approximately forty different vantage points. The people of Guyana were wont to judge. If anyone needed additional evidence that

GECOM's Secretariat was not playing by the Laws of Guyana and were indifferent to the electors whom they had a responsibility to protect, then there it was.

In the good old days, Dr. Steve Surujbally, former GECOM's Chairman, would have already addressed challenges and uncertainties in a Press Conference designed only for bold and sensible media personnel. His Press Conferences were informative and direct and represented the best of TV drama in Guyana during elections time.

From 1992 with Mr. Rudy Collins through to Dr. Steve Surujbally, the Chairmen of GECOM have always made an impression of strong leadership. They had been vocal and opinionated, in control and mostly, fair. Elections 2020 revealed a hushed body of GECOM officials who did not lead the charge to have a credible tabulation and verification process which conformed to the will of the people and the rule of law. Justice Claudette Singh was a silent accomplice to the happenings which unfolded at GECOM or perhaps, wore a different mantle of leadership.

During the course of the day, the President of the Georgetown Chamber of Commerce and Industry (GCCI), Mr. Nicholas Deygoo-Boyer, appealed to the business community for a return to normalcy. Businesses were careful not to open for the protection of their staff members and property given that election-based violence is a constant in every election in Guyana. Georgetown, the capital city, was a silent zone for over a week and that impacted the economy of the country, negatively. Students had not been attending schools and there was a minimum student flow on the campus of University of Guyana too. No sensible warm-blooded Guyanese living in the rural areas had any intention of making a journey to Georgetown for fear of elections related intimidation or violence.

If the activities of the previous day were anything to go by, March 5, 2020, was going to be a doozy. When the tabulation restarted around 1:25 am, GECOM's management of its resources was a case study of *How Not To Manage Human Resources*. Consequently, the effective implementation of the tabulation and verification process and compliance with the electoral laws was checked. Staff was still on a sick out in spite of the urgency of the electoral matters, but they worked in fifteen minutes aliquots before retiring due to fatigue. The impetuous nature of the staff's actions was tantamount to a carefully orchestrated Game of Procrastination that could only have come from the mind of a Lewis Carrol-type conspirator.

By 1:40 am, the Data Entry Clerk, Mr. Enrique Livan, became tired after fifteen minutes of tabulating votes cast for the lists of candidates for District 4. He headed for a room on the upper level of the Command Centre, returned and removed the USB Flash Drive[64] which contained the data from the SOPs. Mr. Livan collected the laptop on which he was entering data, made a request of the Observers and party representatives to leave the room and proceeded to leave. Great concern, more so, suspicion on the part of the party representatives led to the arrival of members of the Criminal Investigation Department of the GPF and the CEO, Mr. Keith Lowenfiel, to resolve the matter.

Mr. Livan was escorted from the Centre by the police ranks. Two hours later, variances between what was entered into the computer and the tally from the SOPs were recognized. The CEO, Mr. Lowenfield, to pacify party representatives, with the notable exception of those of the APNU+AFC, ensured the printing of all data entered to that point and issued same to the party representatives. All tabulations came to end as party representatives left to prepare themselves for another day of uncertainty beginning at 9:00 am. On August 27, 2020, the Data Entry Clerk, now an Information Technology Officer at GECOM[65], was arrested; he was represented by attorney Mr. Eusi Anderson.

Bright and early in the morning, and before the start of the tabulation and verification process, like hawks, the representatives of the major parties, the small parties and local and international observers descended upon the GECOM Command Center. Former Presidents, Mr. Donald Ramotar and Dr. Bharat Jagdeo were present and represented the PPP-C. Former Ministers of Government representing the APNU+AFC coalition like Ms. Volda Lawrence and Mr. Basil Williams along with Mr. James Bond did not mingle.

By 10:30 am when the process had not restarted, frustration set in. Political representatives became agitated and walked out of the building. Opposition-nominated GECOM Commissioner, Mr. Sase Gunraj, could not provide an explanation for the delay. At this juncture, members of the Guyana Fire Service (GFS) and ranks of the Guyana Police Force (GPF) arrived on the scene due to an alleged bomb threat. Two large, bomb-sniffing dogs and their handlers entered the building and emerged within the hour. Barricades were placed around the building.

Members of the diplomatic corps and the elections observers assembled at the entrance to the Command Centre despite the bomb threat. Nothing short of an earthquake would phase these perceived defenders of democracy. Even though armed ranks of the GPF requested an evacuation of the Centre, PPP-C-nominated commissioners, party representatives and other stakeholders resisted, presuming that this was another ploy to modify the tabulation results and tamper with the SOPs.

Notwithstanding all the intrigue that was happening among the GECOM officials within the tabulation center, the former Minister of Foreign Affairs, Dr. Karen Cummings, threatened to revoke the accreditation of members of the International Observer Missions who were invited by the Government of Guyana to monitor the General and Regional

Elections 2020. Dr. Cummings met with the international observers in a room within the Command Centre and informed the international observers that she was advised to inform them of this request of which she was not in full agreement.

Dr. Cummings' misstep was as undiplomatic and unattractive as that of Attila the Hun. The repercussions were immediate. The observers felt threatened and were visibly upset given the tumultuous nature of the day's events. Former Prime Minister of Barbados and Head of the Commonwealth Observer (COG) Group, Mr. Owen Arthur[66], said animatedly, "I speak on behalf of the Commonwealth, the largest organization of people in the world, and I am not going to have, not me, the Commonwealth disrespected by a threat to take away the accreditation." He went so far as to remove his accreditation badge and gestured towards the Minister in an effort to return it to her. Mr. Arthur, a no-nonsense man, did not mince his words and made the matter known to the Commonwealth Secretary General, the Rt Hon. Patricia Scotland QC. Dr. Cummings promptly left the room on receipt of a mobile phone call chaperoned by the Deputy DEO, Mr. Roxanne Myers.

Grave concern was expressed by the British High Commissioner to Guyana, Mr. Greg Quinn. Western diplomats such as the American Ambassador, Ms. Sarah-Ann Lynch, Canadian High Commissioner to Guyana, Ms. Lilian Chatterjee and the European Union Ambassador to Guyana, Mr. Fernando Ponz Cantó and other diplomats were exposed to a high level of diplomatic discomfort. High Commissioner Quinn's response to the Minister was, *"This is the GECOM building. Is it appropriate for you to be having this meeting with us in this building?"* At best, Dr. Cummings was acting as an emissary of the leaders of the APNU+AFC. At worse, she was a novice at it because of her ambivalence. The behavioral pattern displayed here in Guyana are like that of the political parties in Azerbaijan where observers are intimidated and even violently attacked. Dr. Cummings sounded the death knell of APNU+AFC's dominance in Guyana's governance.

The people of Guyana need to be grateful to the person who had the presence of mind to record the exchange between the Minister and the observers. Had it not gone viral, the Coalition would have engaged in tyrannical behavior for the duration of the elections process. The ubiquitous cell phone with its myriad of features and applications was to prove the undoing of this elaborate, Tom Sawyer-like adventure.

Mr. Victor Gittens once told of a man from Bridgetown whose bills were piled so high that it depressed him. He lamented his predicament. While pondering his fate, he heard a still, small voice encouraging him to cheer up. Things could be worse! He smiled, thereafter. Lo and behold, things did get worse. And as if things couldn't get worse with Elections

2020, at around 1:30 pm, the RO for Region Four entered the Verification Room of the Command Centre and started to declare his version of the Results of Region Four's unverified results. At 2:30 pm, positioned on the stairway on the Middle Floor of the Command Centre, again, he declared the unsubstantiated results. This was done in the presence of the international observers, representatives of the parties, GECOM's staff and a dozen former Ministers of the Coalition government. A chorus of *"Noooo!"* resonated throughout the building. There was a fish market type atmosphere but with men dressed in business suits and business casual wear and women elegantly and professionally attired. The mood of the place was one of despair, liken to that of waiting for a hurricane to strike and not having immediate protection against it. Shouts and screams, verbal battles and provocations between APNU+AFC and GECOM on the one hand and the PPP-C and the small parties, on the other, took on a sinister overtone.

So concerned were the Western diplomats that a statement was released on behalf of the ABCE countries to the effect that *"Based on our observation of today's GECOM proceedings at their Region 4 office, and the fact that the full count was not completed, we question the credibility of the Region 4 results published by GECOM today. We urge the Guyana Elections Commission, and all relevant actors, to expeditiously complete the tabulation on the basis of the statement of polls. We call on all Guyanese to remain calm and patient, and for all leaders to exercise responsibility and restraint."*

The ever-vigilant PPP-C obtained a High Court injunction, signed off by High Court Judge Navindra Singh, restraining GECOM and the RO from declaring results until the tabulation for Region 4 was completed in compliance with the law. Ranks of the Guyana Police Force conscientiously prevented the Court Marshall from serving the respondents, the CEO and the RO for Region 4.

The first injunction restrained the RO from making any disclosure of the Region Four results unless and until he complied with the statutory procedure set out in Section 84 of the Representation of the People's Act and that procedure was the verification process which was aborted and never completed. The second injunction compelled the Returning Officer to comply with Section 84 of the Representation of the People's Act and to conduct and complete that verification exercise and then make the declaration as the law required it to be done.

The third injunction restrained the Chief Elections Officer (CEO), Mr. Keith Lowenfield, and GECOM from making any declaration of the results of the March 2, 2020, General and Regional elections unless and until the RO complied with that statutory code or verification enunciated in aforementioned Act.

Through Mr. Clairmont Mingo's anamorphic lenses, tabulations took on a magnifying effect for APNU+AFC whilst at the same time, had a reducing effect on PPP-C's totals. With more than 500 SOPs to be verified, he declared results which stated that the incumbent APNU+AFC coalition received 136,458 votes and the PPP-C received 77,329 votes. By 5:30 pm, GECOM, one of the institutions of democracy in Guyana, had released their unverified results to the media and the public at large. Without delay, the Opposition parties called for a recount of the ballots for the entire region.

During the evening hours, at the Lamaha Headquarters of the APNU-coalition, President David A. Granger addressed supporters expressing gratitude to them for another five years of governance. Standing beside President Granger, at the time of the announcement, were the Chairman of the APNU+AFC Campaign, Mr. Joseph Harmon, and Mr. Raphael Trotman and in front of him was a subdued Ms. Simona Broomes, a controversial former minister of government.

Presidential candidate for the PPP-C, Mr. Irfaan Ali, argued that the Statements of Poll (SOPs) gathered by the PPP-C and other parties showed that the PPP-C won 80,920 votes while the APNU+AFC 116, 941 votes in Region Four. This was not reflected because the verification process for the SOPs was not completed and the results were instead arbitrarily declared by Mr. Mingo. On social media, the PPP-C promptly published their Statements of Polls for votes cast in the general elections to strengthen their position and as a strategy to legally combat the outcome of a rigged elections and for the learned people of Guyana to absorb the facts.

There was a larger crack in the seawall of Guyana's democracy and major repairs would have to be undertaken before the flood of conspiracy theories poured in. From the sea of cameras within the Tabulation Centre, social media was buzzing with activity, some flattering, and others dangerously divisive. It was determined that the Chairman of the PNC's signature was that of the only party represented on the declared results certifying the process.

During all the hullabaloo, the Chairman, Justice Singh, was secured in a room on the top floor of the Command Centre which was padlocked. The Deputy CEO, Ms. Roxanne Myers, was the only person who gave permission to enter or exit the room. Two Police ranks stood guard at the door. Those on hand at the Command Centre were very concerned for the health and overall wellbeing of the Chairman, Justice Singh. Though an ambulance arrived, and Emergency Medical Technicians (EMT) were deployed, they were prevented from entering the room in which she was barricaded by officers of the law. Consequently, the First Responders had to leave the building not having completed their mission.

To the shouts of *"Free the Chairman!"* the office next to the one occupied by the Chairman was entered by a large group of brave persons who had expressed an interest in the wellbeing of Justice Singh. This was a room for which they had not received approval to enter. A few of them was arrested and among them was the General Secretary of the TNM, Dr. Josh Kanhai, who as a doctor; had expressed an interest in assisting her. The Chairman was seen stretched out on the floor thereby suggesting a genuine health issue which would have triggered the call for the medical team.

An hour after GECOM declared the Region Four results without the completion of the verification process, ranks of the Tactical Services Unit of the GPF marched into the Command Centre with the express purpose of removing representatives of the political parties from the Tabulation Room. The ranks were disrespectful and unprofessional in their approach to the party agents and observers taking the abrasive and arrogant tone of the deputy CEO, Ms. Roxanne Myers, who had called for the Centre to be rid of the observers and anyone who monitored the process. Commander of the Guyana Police Force Region 4 Division, Commander Ewart Thomas, was stripped of his command for refusing to follow an illegal order to remove international and locally accredited observers and counting agents from GECOM Command Centre. A few good men exist within the Guyana Police Force Region and they must be commended for their noble stand, even honored.

By 8:00 pm, the PPP-C, ANUG, Change Guyana, TNM, LJP and URP leaders held a Press Conference expressing disgust and the need for the Rule of Law to be applied and for GECOM to carry out the work that they were constitutionally appointed to do. Mr. Nigel Hinds lamented the fact that the Coalition was celebrating a *"farcical, fraudulent victory"* while Mr. Rawle Aaron, URP, was of the opinion that the elections were *"seized and hijacked"* and his party had no confidence in GECOM and therefore, in the integrity of the electoral process. Mr. Kian Jabour, an ANUG executive member, called the fraudulent declaration an embarrassment and this was against the backdrop of the arrest of his associate, Dr. Josh Kanhai. Mr. Shuman, LJP, lamented the inaccessibility to the CEO and Chairman of GECOM throughout the day. Collectively, these six parties had called on the international community; more specifically, the ABCE countries to implement sanctions against the authors and implementers of the rigging process.

The small parties served a crucial role in Guyana's Elections 2020. It was their indomitable spirit for the preservation of democracy and their commitment to a process that inevitably highlighted the kinks in the fabric of the electoral process. The lesser parties were the linchpin that united the processes with the people of Guyana in a manner which stripped away the complexities of the crisis.

The supporters of the two largest political parties celebrated in isolation of each other. The political sycophants, wearing their red and green paraphernalia, were joyfully oblivious to the mischief that was created having too much faith in their respective, manipulative leaders. The critical thinking people of Guyana were frustrated and gawked in disbelief as the political theatre of repression unfolded. The climate of fear and uncertainty quickly shrouded Guyana, dark as the night ahead.

There's an African proverb, *"When two elephants fight, it is the grass that gets trampled."* Essentially, as the two major parties continue to fight over the resources of the country, it will be the people of Guyana who will continue to suffer economically, socially, and psychologically. Anxieties will continue to be the order of the day for the people of Guyana unless they play a greater role in the administration of the country's affairs. The year 2020 was the Year of Democracy for the people of Guyana who agitated for a hundred-and fifty-three-day period to ensure that the voice of the majority was heard and respected. During the year 2020, the grass was not trampled, it was merely ruffled.

Around 9:30 am on March 6, 2020, Marshalls[67] of the Court were prevented from entering the GECOM Command Centre and serving the Orders on officers of GECOM. The Orders would be the legal means of ensuring a continuation of the tabulation and verification of the votes for Region Four. The Kalibur Security Guards at the Ashmin's Building along with ranks of the GPF prevented the international and local observers in addition to the patient, party agents from accessing the GECOM Command Centre. The protectors of democracy waited more than three hours behind police barricades waiting for a glimpse of a responsible official from GECOM. At 10:41 am, the Deputy CEO arrived in a Toyota Prado that was heavily tinted and through a series of clandestine maneuverings designed to prevent the observers and party agents detecting her presence, she entered the Command Centre via an escape portal at the back of Ashmin's building.

At 11:45 am, to the surprise of the observers and party agents, a busload of riot police of the GPF was deployed around the GECOM Centre. There was an overwhelming police presence. The GPF was a fit force of political intimidation exposed for the whole world to witness. The unwelcomed observers and party agents unsettled but filled with false expectations of a change in conditions had, at this time, recognized that the tools of repression from the Authoritarian toolbox were being systematically removed and used with deft precision.

Within this uncertain atmosphere, Mr. Shuman of the LJP with bulldog-like tenacity served the papers on GECOM's officials for a recount of Region Four's votes at 11:57 am just three minutes before the statutory deadline expired. On the other hand, the PPP-C, in a masterful application of the law and political strategy; was able to serve the official Letter of Recount upon several Deputy Returning Officers in the absence of the elusive Region Four Returning Officer, Mr. Clairmont Mingo. Mr. Charles Ramson, Counting Agent for the PPP-C, served the Letter of Recount on GECOM having waited for over three hours in the elements. At the mercy of the police guarding the gate to GECOM's treasured personnel, he deposited PPP-C's letter with the Clerk, Ms. Michelle Miles, seven minutes before the deadline.

Like a move out of a spy novel, suspicious activities, and unusually far-fetched requests by GECOM's staff lured Mr. Zulfikar Mustapha[68], the PPP-C's Chief Elections Scrutineer to the GECOM Headquarters in Kingstown, Georgetown where the containers storing unused Statements of Poll (SOP) and other unused documents were located. The Scrutineer in the company of former Attorney General, Mr. Anil Nandlall, refused to open the container to permit access to the SOPs presuming that it would lead to additional mischief by officials of GECOM. The two representatives of the Opposition observed that the lock belonging to the APNU+AFC was unsecured. The locks belonging to the other parties designed to secure the container remained closed. The container could not be opened unless all political parties opened their locks. Consistent intrigue had become the norm during these elections.

Mr. John Rudder, noted for his teaching moments, related how a man who attended a party needed to defecate but all the bathrooms were occupied. He went upstairs and used one of those ventilation holes in the wall, normally found on older buildings of the time. When he returned to the party, no one was present except for the host who was hiding behind the bar. When he asked the whereabouts of everyone, the host responded, *"Where were you when the crap hit the fan?"* Most Guyanese had rightly decided to remain at home while those who felt that their franchise was taken away from them and that democracy was being taken away, once more, took to the streets with an intensity of purpose. Every rational Guyanese remembers exactly what he or she was doing and where he or she was located on that day.

No moral compass could have directed the flow of events of the day as it unfolded, sporadically. The magnetic field of distrust, open defiance and stealthy actions discombobulated the guidance system. The authors of the political chicanery of the last five days could not have anticipated the extent of the protests by supporters of the PPP-C political party nor their passion for a democracy they so earnestly worked and voted for. In the past elections, it was the APNU+AFC sycophants which lined the streets and agitated for fair elections and even caused havoc within communities occupied by PPP-C supporters.

Hundreds of citizens from five of the ten voting district regions organized protests that were violent. The protests in Regions Two, Three, Four, Five and Six were sparked by what the protestors called the lack of verification of General and Regional results from the polls of March 2, 2020, electoral manipulations, and a threatened democracy. Except for Region Four, the other regions where protests were staged were won by the PPP-C with a significantly increased margin over the 2015 votes.

The orchestrators of the election's manipulation had blood on their hand the moment that nineteen-year-old Mr. Devon Hansraj of Cotton Tree Village was fatally shot by the police ranks who opened fire on protestors. The agitated protestors attacked police ranks relentlessly with bottles and other missiles. In Region Five, four schoolchildren sustained head injuries when the bus in which they were travelling from school to their homes was attacked. The Pavlovian effect was the name on the bus, David 'G', one of a series of buses donated by the Government of Guyana bearing the name of the President.

The protests, lasting no more than four hours, resulted in roadblocks consisting of burning tires, torched vehicles and utility poles laid across the road. Within Region Four, more specifically along the East Coast Demerara, the epicenter of protests which kept police ranks active and even disoriented, was Lusignan. Not even the beloved PPP-C's executive members like Dr. Vindhya Persaud, Mr. Anil Nandlall and Pandit Rabindranath Persaud could quell the social disorder of a magnitude Guyana had not seen since the 1960s. The frustration and the commitment were real.

As if the violent protests were not enough to soften the heart of the most implacable of designers of the hardships thrust upon the people of Guyana, the GECOM's CEO[69], Mr. Lowenfield, emailed Justice Singh on the day following the political skirmishes informing the Commissioners that he had received declarations from the Returning Officers from the ten Districts and that he had prepared the Final Report of the General and Regional elections for submission to the Commission in accordance with Cap 1:03 Section 99. A request was made for the Commission to meet at the earliest convenience. However, the Opposition Commissioners refused to meet as it would have constituted contempt of court given that the matter was before the Courts.

To get a sneak peek at the CEO's tabulated results as declared by the Returning Officers (ROs) for all ten Districts in the Regional Elections, APNU+AFC received 237,140 votes while the PPP-C received 229,450 showing that the Coalition government won the elections by 7,690 votes.

Justice Claudette Singh lamented that fact that the injunction had impacted the finalization of the Commission's work but that GECOM, as a *"constitutional agency, it is still subjected to the laws of Guyana."*

In the case that was brought by Mr. Reeaz Holladar, the driver to former Attorney General Mr. Anil Nandlall, Guyana's Chief Justice Roxane George[70] ruled that the declaration made on March 5, 2020, by the Returning Officer of the total votes cast for Region Four was unlawful and in breach of Section 84(1) of the Representation of the People's Act, Chap 1:03 and was null, void and of no effect. Secondly, GECOM could not declare the overall results until the Returning Officer complied with the law. Thirdly, the Returning Officer for District Four, had breached the law in the adding up of Statements of Poll and should either restart or continue from where he left off. Furthermore, as a matter of expediency, the consequential orders were that the Returning Officer or deputy Returning Officer for District Four must return to the process by 11:00 am on Thursday, March 12, 2020, the following day. The Chief Justice lamented the fact that a similar case was ruled on nineteen years ago and that Guyana is once more at the same juncture. She plead for confidence in the electoral process to be restored and noted that *"This is absolutely essential if we as a nation are to move forward and strive to heal the wounds that divide us. Let fairness pervade all of our actions at all times."*

As if things couldn't get any worse, Mr. Reeaz Holladar[71], two weeks after the ruling committed suicide in the presence of his wife. Who's to say whether the court case, personal domestic challenges or any variety of issues were the cause of this most final action that consigned him to the Spirit World?

Liken to a petulant child, Region Four's Returning Officer (RO), Mr. Mingo insisted on following the Chief Justice's orders minimally by reducing the number of local and foreign observers and political agents to a single representative. Initially, the Region Four's RO had informed the observers and party agents that new accreditations were needed. Clearly, the RO was skirting around the Chief Justice's consequential orders to see how far he could push the envelope without being reprimanded by just and fair men.

Tabulation proceedings started around 11:00 am on March 12, 2020. Mr. Mingo was a law unto himself as a pre-prepared spreadsheet was used, once more, in defiance of the Court order. He had obviously not paid attention to Justice Bernard's summing up in 2001 and which was repeated by Justice Roxane George when she said that *"...the role of the Elections Commission and its staff is to take such action as appears necessary to ensure impartiality, fairness and compliance with the provisions of the Constitution and any other acts of Parliament. In the present volatile situation which pervades our country no effort must be spared to assure everyone that the process was fair and impartia*l." The process was suspended when GECOM's Chairman, Justice Claudette Singh, visited the tabulation center because of complaints made by party representatives. She would read and interpret the court orders before pronouncing on the matters at hand.

Within the nearly two hours of tabulations, there was a great deal of arguments and frustration because of the RO's recalcitrance.

Five CARICOM[72] heads led by CARICOM Chairman, the Honourable Mia Mottley Prime Minister of Barbados, arrived in Guyana a day earlier (March 11, 2020) to broker peace between the two major political parties and commit to *"working with the people of Guyana for a free and fair process and transparent process."* The delegation was made up of the Prime Ministers of Trinidad and Tobago, the Honourable Dr. Keith Rowley, the Honourable Dr. Ralph Gonsalves of St Vincent and the Grenadines, the Honourable Mr. Roosevelt Skerrit of Dominica and the Honourable Dr. Keith Mitchell of Grenada. With the exception of the Heads of Government Conference, there hadn't been an assembly of such high-powered leaders from the Region. Prime Minister Mottley reinforced the point that Mr. Clairmont Mingo "holds in his hands the future and stability of Guyana as we go forward, because every vote must be made to count." Clearly Mr. Mingo understood his power which played out in full the following day.

At that critical juncture, GECOM had still not presented its SOPs for perusal by a tired and mentally fatigued nation and neither had the APNU+AFC Coalition party. All political parties except for the Coalition party expressed disgust and grave concern at the haphazard manner of the tabulation and verification process. The Coalition's silence was deafening and far-reaching and baffling at the same time.

March 13, 2020, was a normal tropical day in the life of the average Caribbean person. However, it was a Red-letter day in the lives of the people of Guyana. It started around 9:30 am at the Region Four tabulation center which was relocated to the back of the Ashmin's building.

Fifteen minutes later, party agents and observers were the victims of APNU+AFC's, Ms. Carol Smith Joseph's verbal assaults[73]. The abuse was motivated by the objections and concerns made by those who were there to monitor the process. There were threats of ejection from the Tabulation room by Mr. Mingo should anyone be disruptive or release any information from the Center.

Observers and party agents revealed that the tallies for APNU+AFC were systematically increasing while that of the PPP-C were being decreased and not consistent with the SOPs owned by political party agents. Their appeals went unheeded. Foreign observers felt that the atmosphere was growing too hostile and that they could not be assured of protection. Neither the ranks of the Guyana Police Force nor the staff of GECOM offered any uplifting advice. As a result, the heads of the ABCE Diplomatic Missions abandoned their posts and exited the building. They were promptly followed by members of the smaller political parties.

After a Court Marshall[74] served the RO with court documents, he left for the High Court but returned three hours later after he had suspended the tabulation process. His attitude remained unchanged. A clerk continued the process of reading from a spreadsheet in his absence.

The tabulation process was restarted at 4:48pm at the GECOM Headquarters, Kingstown, Georgetown within the confines of the headquarters. Party agents were unable to read what was projected unto the undulating, presentation screen which was a white bedsheet. Blurred images of the SOPs were being projected. No one was able to scrutinize the SOPs. Ranks of the Guyana Police Force (GPF) were in attendance to ensure compliance and as enforcers of Mr. Mingo's draconian measures.

It is said that when steel hits steel, sparks will fly. That's precisely what happened when Mr. Jonathan Yearwood an ANUG executive member and Ms. Joseph of the APNU+AFC crossed paths. There was a bit of jostling and shouting leading to the arrest of Mr. Yearwood by ranks of the GPF.

11:00 pm was the magical hour when the RO of Region Four, once more, declared the APNU+AFC Coalition took the Region with 136,057 votes while the PPP-C garnered 77,231 votes, a difference of about 58,000 more votes. Again, the results of the Regional and General Elections for Region Four were unverified. The Recount exercise would prove different after many days and many court battles and many challenges. APNU+AFC supporters rejoiced on hearing the news.

The next day, other than the Coalition party, eight other political parties requested a recount only for the requests to be declined by the RO for reasons that were dubious. The RO gave as one of the reasons, the non-adherence to the statutory deadline for the appointment of counting agents. Not much was glimmered from the CEO nor Justice Claudette Singh during this critical period.

In T. S. Elliot's Burnt Norton[75], there's a line that goes, *"Go, go, go, said the bird: humankind cannot bear very much reality."* The stark reality was too much for the local and international observers. Consequently, on March 13, 2020, the OAS Electoral Observation Mission[76] in Guyana, led by the former Prime Minister of Jamaica, Mr. Bruce Golding, pulled out of Guyana stating that the tabulation process for Region Four did not meet the required standards of transparency and fairness. They had much to say about the duplicitous CEO, Region Four's REO, Mr. Mingo and their scant regard for the laws of the land.

Mr. Golding, in the most constrained manner, pronounced that he had *"never seen a more transparent effort to alter the results of an elections. More than a dozen copies of the Statements of Poll are prepared at each polling stations after the ballots are counted… it takes an extraordinary and courageous mind to present fictitious numbers when such a sturdy paper trail exists."* Of course, the International Observers were not to be omitted from providing incontrovertible proof that something was amiss in the Tabulation Centre. A joint statement was issued by the Commonwealth, the European Union and the Carter Center to the effect that the tabulation process was inconsistent with the consequential orders of the Chief Justice and that the SOPs must be displayed as ordered otherwise the election results would not be considered credible.

The Ambassador[77] of the United States of America, H.E. Sarah-Ann Lynch, the British High Commissioner, H.E. Greg Quinn, the Canadian High Commissioner, H.E. Lilian Chatterjee, and the Ambassador of the European Union, H.E. Fernando Ponz-Canto, left the Region Four tabulation process given the lack of credibility of the tabulation process having observed tactics of intimidation against the political agents which were there to ensure that the process ran smoothly.

There was the added caveat that, as friends of Guyana which helped in its development, all parties involved in the electoral process were urged to do all within their powers to prevent Guyana from being isolated. The theme is consistent with that of the U.S. Secretary of State's shot across the bow when he directed his tweet to publicly declare that the *"US is committed to protect Guyana's democracy"* while the State Department's top Latin America official, Mr. Michael G. Kozak[78], stated, *"Democratic nations can't ignore this blatant disregard for rule of law… respect the will of the Guyanese people to choose their leader."*

With her institution crumbling around her, GECOM's Justice Claudette Singh indicated that preparations are in place to facilitate the recounting of the ballots in all the electoral districts. Her decision supplanted many of the Returning Officer's (ROs) denial of recount requests. Meanwhile, CARICOM's Chairperson, Barbadian Prime Minister, the Honourable Mia Mottley, assembled an independent high-level regional team to supervise the recounting process which was requested by incumbent President David A. Granger and agreed to by Opposition Leader, Dr. Bharrat Jagdeo. The OAS General Secretariat openly welcomed the initiative of CARICOM to send a high-level mission to Guyana to supervise the recount of the Region Four ballots and the other nine electoral Districts. The wheels were set in motion for yet another series of sideshows.

CHAPTER 4: GUYANA ELECTIONS COMMISSION
- THE NATIONAL RECOUNT -

"If you look at their voting habits and their eating habits, you realize people are stupid." RuPaul

The National Recount commenced on May 6, 2020, after a few false starts and was completed in 33 days resulting in the swearing in of the President of the Cooperative Republic of Guyana, the His Excellency Dr. Irfaan Ali on August 2, 2020. Initially, on Saturday March 14, 2020, the Chairman of CARICOM[79], the Honourable Mia Amor Mottley announced that she had discussions with His Excellency President David Granger and the Opposition leader, Dr. Bharat Jagdeo and both had requested an independent, high-level team to supervise the Recount process. The political leaders had signed an Aide Memoire on March 16th supported by a Terms of Reference to guide the independent CARICOM team. GECOM's Chairman had assured Chief Justice Madame Roxanne George Wiltshire that there would be a Recount. It was decided that the Recount would be under the supervision of a CARICOM high-level team until a Court of Appeal ruling of April 5, 2020, declared that it was unconstitutional for CARICOM, or any other authority besides GECOM, to supervise any aspect of Guyana's Elections.

On March 15, 2020 the CARICOM high-level team chaired by former Attorney-General and Minister of Foreign Affairs of Dominica, Ms. Francine Baron, and comprised former Minister of Finance of Grenada, Mr. Anthony Boatswain; Senior Lecturer in the Department of Government of UWI, Ms. Cynthia Barrow-Giles; Chief Electoral Officer of Barbados, Ms. Angela Taylor; and Chief Elections Officer of Trinidad and Tobago, Ms. Fern Narcis-Scope were on the ground in Guyana in record time but by March 17, 2020 the team withdrew and departed the shores of

Guyana consequent upon a Court Order issued on the same day granting an injunction restraining GECOM from recounting any ballots of the General and Regional Elections and nullifying the Aide Memoire and the agreement between GECOM and CARICOM. CARICOM's Chairman, the Honourable Mia Mottley[80] alluded to the fact that there were *"forces that do not want to see the votes recounted for whatever reason. Any Government which is sworn in without a credible and fully transparent vote count process would lack legitimacy."* The injunction was filed by Ms. Ulita Moore, an APNU+AFC candidate.

On April 5, 2020, the Court of Appeal determined that GECOM was responsible for supervising the Recount process. Justice Claudette Singh made it clear that her decision to commence a Recount was against the backdrop of Article 162 (1) (b) of the Constitution, which mandates the Commission to *"take such action as appear to it necessary or expedient to ensure impartiality, fairness and compliance with the provisions of the Constitution."* The CARICOM high-level team which was requested for the second time would validate the recount process.

Consequently, the CEO, Mr. Keith Lowenfield, was asked to prepare a Recount Plan taking into consideration the COVID-19 Guidelines. Initially, he returned a Recount period[81] of 156 days for the completion of the Recount exercise which was unacceptable to the GECOM Secretariat, most of the electorate and the Leader of the Opposition. The Plan also specified that each tabulation workstation would have authorized GECOM staff, representatives from each of the contesting political parties and accredited observers. The original Statement of Recount (SoR) would be used to tabulate the votes. 2,339 ballot boxes were to be counted in the ten electoral districts starting with Districts One to Ten chronologically using 10 workstations. Live streaming of the recount was integral to the transparency of the recount process. It is also noteworthy to point out that the Guyana Budget and Policy Institute (GBPI) projected that National Recount process could have been accomplished within roughly 12 days compared to the 25 days proposed by the Chairman of GECOM and 14 days by the Opposition.

The Recount would take place at the Arthur Chung Convention Centre (ACCC) at Pattensen, East Coast Demerara. As a result, on May 5, 2020, the ballot boxes were moved on trucks from GECOM's Headquarters on High and Cowan Street, Kingston, to the Arthur Chung Conference Centre with escort by the Guyana Police Force. For two days, the ACCC was fumigated by the Ministry of Public Health given that a National COVID-19 Task Force was in place and Guyana had reported close to 50 cases of COVID-19 and 6 deaths. The same Task Force denied the Observers from the Carter Centre from returning to Guyana given that the airports were closed and permission was necessary to enter the country.

The second Caribbean Community (CARICOM)[82] high-level team of scrutineers to oversee the recount arrived in Guyana on Friday, May 1, 2020. They were tested for the coronavirus, COVID-19, in their countries before they arrived in Guyana. The new team was led by Ms. Cynthia Barrow-Giles, Senior Lecturer in the Department of Government at the University of the West Indies (UWI), and included Mr. John Jarvis, Commissioner of the Antigua and Barbuda Electoral Commission and Mr. Sylvester King, Deputy Supervisor of Elections of St. Vincent and the Grenadines. The members of the team had previously been to Guyana to participate in the Recount that was subsequently aborted. Fortunately, good sense prevailed and the National COVID-19 Task Force overturned its previous decision that the CARICOM Scrutinizing Team would have had to be quarantined for 14 days on arrival.

During that period between the last declaration by Region Four's RO, Mr. Mingo and the start of the Recount exercise, learned Guyanese voiced their concerns in a modest, lighthearted manner that *"from the sublime to the ridiculous"* was but one step. However, there was a healthy expectation of good governance despite the past shenanigans by the 2 major political parties. Ron Serling describes this period as the *"middle ground between light and shadow, between science and superstition, and it lies between the pit of man's fears and the summit of his knowledge. This is the dimension of imagination. It is an area which we call the Twilight Zone."* No amount of training and knowledge would prepare the average Guyanese for what would unfold and nor any amount of foresight would reveal the baser and compulsive utterances of government and opposition representatives, and reputably, responsible officials of the Embassies of the United States of America and Canada.

Monday March 16, 2020, saw the movement of the ballot boxes by container trucks from GECOM Headquarters in Kingston to the ACCC, Liliendaal as preparation for the Recount process. Except for the containers which stored Region 6 (East Berbice-Corentyne) and Region 4 (Demerara-Mahaica) East Coast Demerara ballots, all ballots were located at the ACCC. Six of the political parties were concerned about the storage of the ballots at two separate locations and voiced their concerns to GECOM. By March 20, 2020, the shipping containers were returned to GECOM[83] Headquarters in Kingston but GECOM had not informed the international/local observers nor the party representatives and this resulted in a mad dash by the party representatives to regroup and unofficially provide surveillance for the containers trucks en route to Kingston location. Even GECOM's Commissioners were unaware of the decision to move the containers.

On that same date, ranks of the Guyana Police Force removed the observers, party representatives and other interested parties from the ACCC's premises without any explanation. GECOM's Commissioner, Mr.

Robeson Benn, was injured as he was being forcibly removed by ranks of the GPF.

On March 19, 2020, Mr. Roy Beepat, the owner of Giftland Mall refused to acknowledge the request of a rank of the Guyana Police Force's Special Branch. The rank indicated to Mr. Beepat that the Mall's security cameras which were directed towards the ACCC were illegally positioned. The ACCC is located a few hundred meters from the Mall complex. According to Mr. Beepat, *"The cameras installed at my premises have been there since the mall was opened and from the inception, [they] were all pointing in the directions that they continue to focus, up to this point in time. The location and focus of these cameras are based upon advice I received from security experts. In light of the dire circumstances that have ensued the March 2nd, 2020 elections which continues to prevail, my security experts have advised that I install the additional cameras to enhance monitoring and security of the premises[84]."*

From the social media comments, one could not help but feel regret and sorrow for the diehard supporters who spewed forth their opposing views laced with racial venom and complete ignorance. But what examples did they have to follow.

On April 30, 2020, the GECOM's Secretariat embarked on a successful training of 80 officials who participated in the Recount process. Staff was acquainted with their roles in the process, the methodology of the recount and an awareness of the strict COVID-19 guidelines. They were responsible for manning the ten workstations and included a Supervisor for each workstation

The Gazetted Order[85] 60/200 dated May 4, 2020, legitimized the Recount process to the satisfaction of the political parties and is a legal document which was requested by CARICOM before they would commit. The Order stipulates the modus operandi throughout the Recount period and defined roles and responsibilities thereby guaranteeing high levels of transparency.

The Order made full use of digitizing devices to ensure capturing of pictures of the state of the ballot boxes, audio feed of the process and audio-visual facility to live-stream the tabulation process from within the Tabulation Centre.

On May 7, 2020, GECOM met and decided on a daily tabulation process between the hours of 5:00 pm and 6:30 pm in the interest of transparency. The process alleviated the concerns of the representatives of the political parties. Furthermore, the Commission decided that the observations for each ballot box based on the Observation Report from each workstation would be recorded during the tabulation. The Statement of Recount (SOR) was projected on a screen to be viewed by observers and the CARICOM scrutineers present and the information shall be input into an Excel Spreadsheet to be viewed simultaneously by all. Invariably, the

Recount would continue daily, inclusive of weekends and holidays between the hours of 8:00 am and 7:00 pm.

In practice, the ballot box was taken from the container and escorted to the workstation by the political party agents and the police. GECOM's Supervisory staff would accept the box and open it in the presence of the party agents and accredited observers where the locks' serial numbers would be recorded. Each folder was opened, and the contents examined. The Counting Clerks counted the votes audibly for the benefit of those present and the general public who were following via social and other forms of media.

Consistent with the narrative of the period and the mischief afoot, on May 7, 2020, the Chairman of a New and United Guyana (ANUG), Mr. Timothy Jonas, received a telephone call from an official of the Ministry of Public Health[86] claiming that he was reported to be demonstrating respiratory symptoms of the novel coronavirus. He was advised to undergo a test for COVID-19 and was found to be COVID-19 free. He believed that the actions taken by the authorities were designed to minimize his efforts at the recounting exercise.

By May 11, 2020, six of the new political parties, namely; Liberty and Justice Party, The New Movement, A New and United Guyana, Change Guyana, the United Republican Party, The Citizenship Initiative and the PPP-C accused the APNU+AFC agents of slowing the recount process by way of demanding that materials, other than those cited by Order 60 be transmitted via live streaming. The Government agents have insisted that the Observation Report be displayed and read out loudly as a provision for the blind and deaf.

APNU+AFC received permission to have the Observation Report linger on the display screen from 10 seconds to 20 seconds - the other party agents considered this to be excessive indicated that this delayed the process. The Chairman of the Private Sector Commission wrote to the Chairman of GECOM, complaining that the *"tabling of these lengthy unverified allegations is the cause of inordinate and unjustified delays of the recount."*

The local and international Observers, party agents and the CARICOM Scrutinizing Team were issued copies of Statements of Recount (SORs) after each ballot box was recounted since the recount process started on May 6, 2020. After 5 days, GECOM abruptly curtailed the practice for the observer teams to be in possession of copies of the SORs. Within a matter of 5 additional days, the country's Attorney General questioned the legitimacy of the National Recount exercise.

On May 12, 2020, seven days into the recount process, GECOM had counted 261 ballot boxes which represented 11% of the total boxes to be counted. The Commission met with a view to reviewing the proposed recount period of 25 days. Consideration was given to increasing the workstations but not before inviting the National COVID-19 Task Force to visit the ACCC to examine the facilities and to consider increasing to the working hours.

The following day, while delivering the preliminary findings of the mission to the Organization of American States' (OAS) Permanent Council, Mr. Golding, the head of the Observer Mission revealed that for ballot box #4062, the Statement of Poll (SoP) had indicated 182 votes for APNU+AFC and 43 votes for the PPP-C. Mr. Mingo's spreadsheet reported the same ballot box results as 292 votes for APNU+AFC and 33 votes for the PPP-C. Based on the recounts to date, the numbers in the Statement of Recount (SoR) were 182 for APNU+AFC and 43 for PPP, "the exact figures that appeared on the statement of poll." He identified three other boxes with similar trends, an inflated number of votes for the APNU+AFC and reduced numbers for the PPP-C[87].

The Guyana Fire Service[88] was called in to investigate a burning smell at the ACCC. The locations were checked by fire fighters and electricians. However, Fire Chief, Mr. Marlon Gentle, reported that they found no evidence of a fire. Such incidences have resulted in reducing the pace at which the votes are counted.

On Tuesday, May 19, 2020, the total ballot boxes recounted were 642 which represented 27% of the ballots cast at the March 2, 2020, General and Regional Elections. During the day, the National COVID-19 Taskforce granted GECOM permission to set up two (2) additional workstations even though a total of six (6) was requested to expedite the process. As the recount continued, there were allegations of discrepancies as purported by agents of the APNU+AFC which further slowed the process of recounting.

On May 29, 2020, the twenty-fourth day of the National Recount and one day before the expiration of the recount deadline, the Gazetted Order # 60/2020 was amended to reflect the new deadline on or before Saturday June 13, 2020. Furthermore, the Order #69/2020[89] provided for the Commission to declare *"the results of the final credible count of the elections held on the 2nd day of March, 2020"* no later than three days after receiving the Election Report. 82 ballot boxes were counted bringing the accumulated total to 1,555 boxes or 66% completed with 784 more boxes to be counted before the deadline expires, again.

Throughout the National Recount period of 35 days, the APNU+AFC Campaign Manager, Mr. Joseph Harmon[90], had complained to the Chairman of GECOM of the high incidences of voter impersonation, voters without Oaths of Identity, unstamped ballots, and other anomalies. However, according to accredited local observers, more specifically, the Georgetown Chamber of Commerce, *"During the recount exercise, at the beginning of the recount for each ballot box, APNU+AFC agents would call out a large list of serial numbers and object to those voters on the grounds that they impersonated the dead or were out of the jurisdiction. They sometimes called serial numbers not related to the ballot box. GECOM staff would then tell the APNU+AFC agents whether any of those serial numbers were marked as voted on the Official List of Electors (OLE). No one was afforded the opportunity to witness the OLEs and verify whether the information being given by GECOM staff was authentic. The APNU+AFC agents never asked. Requests by other party agents were denied."* APNU+AFC's objections formed the basis of the content for the Observation Report which was heavily relied upon by the CEO in the preparation of his Election Report.

On a positive note, the GECOM's staff were operating diligently and often, professionally according to local and international observers. They were complemented by local and international observers for going the extra mile, some 150 days extra; the same could not be said of the CEO and the Deputy CEO.

On day 33 of the National Recount, Sunday June 7, 2020, the final ballot box (Reference 4877/421214D)[91] was removed from the container and recounted. At that moment, the agents from the 11 political parties contesting the elections, joined hands, and celebrated. It was a moment of relief and togetherness. The tabulation of the Statements of Recount (SORs) continued through to June 9, 2020.

Justice Claudette Singh decided to include the votes from 29 ballot[92] boxes that had been under question. The boxes which were from the East Coast Demerara, District 4; were not accompanied by statutory documents but were tabulated as part of the recount process. APNU+AFC objected based on missing documentation and the knowledge that the East Coast is a strong hold for the PPP-C. Consistent with their actions, APNU+AFC refused to sign the Certificates of District Tabulation for District 4[93] as was the process for 8 other electoral districts alleging that dead and migrated persons voted.

The PPP-C Presidential Candidate, Dr. Irfaan Ali[94] continued to appeal to Guyanese and more specifically, his supporters to be patient as they awaited the declaration of the official results from GECOM. He stated, *"I want to assure all Guyanese that as we move towards the next stage of having the report submitted and the declaration, we must act in a responsible manner, we must act in a manner that our countrymen and women expect us to act in as leaders.*

We have to be gracious to each other and we have to move forward in building this country and taking this country forward.

It has been a difficult situation in this country since the No-Confidence motion. Life was never the same. Business was never the same. It is time Guyana gets that space to breathe and move forward. Guyana deserves that."

On the other hand, His Excellency President David A. Granger expressed his concerns as he addressed the nation, *"Everyone is aware of numerous reports of irregularities including unstamped ballots, deceased and migrant voters and missing poll books. Those irregularities appear to have been committed intentionally, not accidentally, and demonstrate a pattern of manipulation of the electoral process.*"

The Chief Elections Officer, Mr. Keith Lowenfield, submitted his first Recount Report to the Chairperson of GECOM on Saturday June 13, 2020. He was required under the gazette order per Paragraph 12 to record that, "*The matrices for the recount of the ten (10) Electoral Districts shall then be tabulated by the Chief Elections Officer (CEO) and shall be submitted in a report, together with a summary of the observation reports for each District, to the Commission on or before the 13th day of June, 2020.*" Instead, the CEO provided details of observations and complaints registered in all 10 Districts. Some of his observation and complaints mirrored those of the ruling party, APNU+AFC which may have been coincidental.

According to the CEO, "*on the basis of the votes counted and the information furnished from the recount, it cannot be ascertained that the results in this District meet the standard of fair and credible elections.*" He listed anomalies for each voting district such as voter impersonation, missing oaths of identity, irregularities, missing polling books and unstamped ballots. According to his Report[95], there were 168 anomalies affecting 7% of all ballot boxes, 947 instances of voter impersonation affecting 41% of all ballot boxes.

Since District Four is the largest electoral district, he reported that "*approximately 55% of all votes cast for general elections stand to be impacted due to either anomalies and/or voter impersonation or unreconciled ballot boxes. Specifically, 7.2% of the votes cast were impacted by anomalies, 39.2% were impacted by voter impersonation, 3.4% impacted by both anomalies/irregularities and voter impersonation, and 5.7% impacted by unreconciled ballot boxes.*" The CEO acted ultra vires of his authority when he analyzed the Recount results instead of reporting as was required by the Constitution and Commission

Furthermore, the CEO reported that the number of valid votes recounted was 269,619 less than the declared votes of 460,295. He allocated 125,010 votes to the APNU+AFC[96] while the PPP-C received 56,628 votes. 60% of the votes cast on March 2, 2020, was deemed invalid by him which legitimately disenfranchised 60% of the electorate.

Again, on June 16, 2020, Justice Singh wrote the CEO requesting the preparation and submission of the Election Report using the results of the recount by 13:00 hrs. on June 8, 2020.

The previous day, Monday, June 15, 2020, the Secretary-General of the Caribbean Community (CARICOM), Ambassador Irwin LaRocque, received the Report of the CARICOM Scrutinizing Team which observed the recount of the General and Regional Elections. The Report was submitted to the Chair of CARICOM, the Honourable Mia Amor Mottley, Prime Minister of Barbados and to the Chairman of GECOM, Madame Justice Claudette Singh. According to the Scrutinizing Team[97], "*We are...of the unshakeable belief that the people of Guyana expressed their will at the ballot box and as a result, the 3 person CARICOM Observer Group concludes that the recount results are completely acceptable...Overall, while we acknowledged that there were some defects in the recount of the March 02, 2020 votes cast for the General and Regional Elections, the team did not witness anything which would render the recount and by extension, the casting of the ballot on March 02, so grievously deficient procedural or technically (despite some irregularities) or sufficiently deficient to have thwarted the will of the people and subsequently prevent the elections results and its declaration by GECOM from reflecting the will of the voters. The actual count of the vote was indeed transparent."*

Since the completion of the Recount process on June 9, 2020, there were two Court challenges against the declaration of the results. The first was by Guyana's Court of Appeal and the second was by the Caribbean Court of Justice (CCJ)[98] where the matter was escalated on June 23, 2020, relative to whether the Court of Appeal had jurisdiction to interpret Article 177 (2) (b) of the Constitution to mean *"more valid votes are cast."*

The Chief Elections Officer (CEO), on Tuesday, June 23 submitted his second Election Report to the Chairman of GECOM, which shows that the APNU+AFC won the 2020 General and Regional Elections by close to 5,500 votes.

Mr. Lowenfield[99] reported that he had *"taken note of the guidance of the Court of Appeal in Eslyn David v Chief Elections Officer et al in the preparation of my Report under Section 96 of the Representation of the People Act and providing advice as required by Article 177 (2) (b) of the Constitution of the Cooperative Republic of Guyana."* As stated in the Election Report, APNU+AFC received 171,825 valid votes [33 parliamentary seats], the PPP-C, 166,343 valid votes [31 parliamentary seats], ANUG and United 1,776 votes, Change Guyana 1,517 votes, and the Liberty and Justice Party (LJP) 1,517 votes. The Joinder List (ANUG, LJP and TNM) secured a total of 3,348 votes [1 parliamentary seat]. There were 347,509 votes cast at the March 2, 200 elections. 115,844 votes or 33% of the electorate were unceremoniously removed and as many electors disenfranchised, again, without an explanation.

After much deliberation by the Caribbean Court of Justice (CCJ) on July 8, 2020, regarding the submission of the CEO's Election Report of June 23, 2020, to the Chairman of GECOM, it ruled that the judgement handed down by the Court of Appeal on June 22, 2020, which the CEO used to invalidate over 115,000 was invalid and that the Election Report was invalid. Their decision was unanimous.

Following the CCJ's decision, the CEO was requested to submit another Election Report on July 11, 2020, in conformity to the ruling and the instructions of the Chairman of GECOM. The CEO submitted figures which closely resembled those declared on March 13, 2020, which were deemed invalid. The Report gave the APNU+AFC party a win and the PPP-C a loss at the polls.

According to Justice Adrian Saunders[100], president of the CCJ, in his ruling, "*Unless and until an election court decides otherwise, the votes already counted by the recount process as valid votes are incapable of being declared invalid by any person or authority.*" The CCJ further stipulated that "*it is for GECOM to ensure the CEO submits a report in accordance with its direction of June 16 in order to proceed along the path directed by the laws of Guyana.*"

Mr. Lowenfield[101] failed to submit another Report as requested by the Chair on Tuesday July 14, 2020, at 2:00 pm. The GECOM Commissioners representing APNU+AFC walked out of the GECOM meeting which was called after the deadline expired for the CEO to present a report of the results of the national vote recount. The meeting was later aborted. Justice Singh had decided that if the CEO failed to present his report in accordance with her directions, the Deputy Chief Elections Officer, Ms. Roxanne Myers[102], would perform the task. Various political parties and the Organization of American States (OAS) had voiced their opinion publicly calling for the removal of the CEO, Mr. Lowenfield.

On July 20, 2020, the Chief Justice, Justice Roxanne George ruled that the High Court had jurisdiction to hear the Misenga Jones[103] case in which she contended that the results of the national recount must be used to declare the results of the March 2, 2020, General and Regional elections. Justice George ruled that the Caribbean Court of Justice (CCJ) endorsed the national vote recount. Ms. Misenga Jones had filed a case in the High Court seeking to prevent GECOM from declaring the results from the recount votes. The Chief Justice concluded that "*the ten declarations cannot be resurrected at this point in time. In this regard, there can no longer be an impasse between the Chairperson and the CEO as to the effect of Article 177 (2) (b) and Section 96 [of the Representation of the People Act]. For the avoidance of doubt as stated in Section 18, the CEO is subject to the direction and control of the Commission.*" It was made explicitly clear that the CEO must obey the instructions of the Chairman of GECOM.

The lawyers for Ms. Misenga Jones escalated the matter to the Court of Appeal upon the dismissal of the High Court case and by July 30, 2020, the Court of Appeal unanimously threw out the Misenga Jones appeal and ruled that recount votes could be used for the declaration of the election results.

On the afternoon of August 2, 2020, the CEO submitted the Elections Report based on the National recount. This was the fourth submission by the CEO and on submission of the Report, the APNU+AFC Commissioners, Mr. Vincent Alexander, Mr. Charles Corbin and Mr. Desmond Trotman walked out.

The Chairman of GECOM, Justice Claudette Singh officially wrote to the Chancellor (ag) of the Judiciary Justice Yonette Cummings-Edwards on the same day informing her that Dr. Mohamed Irfaan Ali had been declared as the 9th Executive President of Guyana and to facilitate arrangements for him to be sworn in. Her correspondence stated, *"In this regard, I take this opportunity to officially inform you of the declaration by the Commission and to request that in your capacity as Chancellor, arrangements are made to facilitate the swearing-in of the new President.*[104]*"*

On August 2, 2020; 153 days from the date of elections, Dr. Mohamed Irfaan Ali, was declared the 9th Executive President of Guyana by GECOM's Chairperson, Justice Claudette Singh[105]. At 40 years old, he was the first Muslim president of Guyana. He held a Quran as he took the Oath of Office.

Sporting a medical face mask, Dr. Ali was sworn in as President at the Arthur Chung Conference Centre by the Chancellor of the Judiciary, Justice Yonette Decina Cummings-Edwards. Former GDF Chief of Staff, Brigadier Mark Anthony Phillips, was sworn in as Prime Minister and former President Bharrat Jagdeo was sworn in as Vice President. Once more, Mr. Anil Nandlall was sworn in as Attorney General and Ms. Gail Teixeira as Minister of Parliamentary Affairs.

On August 8, 2020, for approximately one and a half hours starting at 10:00 am, the Inauguration Ceremony for Dr. Mohammed Irfaan Ali was held at the National Cultural Centre with the normal pomp and ceremony associated. Aside from members of the diplomatic corps, special invitees included the President of the Republic of Suriname, Chandrikapersad Santokhi and his Minister of Foreign Affairs, International Business, and International Politics, Albert Ramdin. Representing the Prime Minister of Barbados was Special Envoy, the Honourable Edmund Hinkson.

The official gazette order, 112/2020 dated August 20, 2020, declared the results of the General Elections held on March 2, 2020, and the National Top-up List as per Articles 60 (2) and 61 in accordance with the Order 60 of 2020.

The following table outlines the status of the results per:

Parliamentary Seat Allocations:

Political Party	No. of Votes	No. of Seats
A New United Guyana (ANUG)	2,313	*
A Partnership for National Unity+Alliance For Change (APNU+AFC)	217,920	31
Change Guyana (CG)	1,953	
Liberty and Justice Party (LJP)	2,657	*
People's Progressive Party/Civic (PPP-C)	233,336	33
People's Republic Party (PRP)	889	
The Citizen's Initiative (TCI)	680	
The New Movement (TNM)	244	* 1

United Republican Party (URP)	36	
Total Valid Votes Cast	460,352	
Rejected Ballots	4, 213	
*Joinder Parties (ANUG, JLP, TNM) share 1 seat		

Table 1: Seat Allocations in the National Assembly

Results by Geographical Constituencies:

General and Regional Elections 2020
Geographical Constituencies

Party	Reg #1	Reg #2	Reg #3	Reg #4	Reg #5	Reg #6	Reg #7	Reg #8	Reg #9	Reg #10	Total Votes
ANUG	-	85	302	1,426	88	164	77	-	-	171	2,313
APNU+AFC	3,909	7,340	23,808	116,941	14,502	20,399	4,813	2,152	4,887	19,169	217,920
CG	-	151	319	935	100	272	67	-	-	109	1,953
LJP	170	121	-	755	-	-	884	450	277	0	2,657
PPP-C	8,002	18,785	47,851	80,920	18,326	43,440	3,728	2,052	7,070	3,162	233,336
PRP	24	57	136	401	52	172	-	-	-	47	889
TCI	-	18	77	466	22	60	-	-	-	37	680
TNM	-	0	56	135	10	16	-	11	-	16	244
URP	6	64	43	98	19	44	23	-	27	36	360
Total Votes	12,111	26,621	72,592	202,077	33,119	64,567	9,592	4,665	12,261	22,747	460,352

Source: Official Gazette 112/2020 August 20, 2020

Table 2: Results by Geographical Constituencies

This was one of the longest periods between the election day and the declaration of the results as per Table 3.

Guyana Polling History 1992-2020

E-Year	Cast Votes	Turnout %	Elections Date	Results Date	Days to Results	Winner	% Win
1992	308,852	81	5-Oct-92	7-Oct-92	2	PPP-C	53
1997	408,057	88	15-Dec-97	19-Dec-97	4	PPP-C	55
2001	403,734	92	19-Mar-01	27-Mar-01	8	PPP-C	53
2006	338,839	69	28-Aug-06	31-Aug-06	3	PPP-C	54
2011	342,126	69	28-Nov-11	1-Dec-11	3	PPP-C	49
2015	412,012	72	11-May-15	16-May-15	5	APNU-AFC	51
2020	460,352	70	2-Mar-20	2-Aug-20	153	PPP-C	51

Sources: Wikipedia/ElectionGuide.org

Table 3: No of days to results

One common factor in all elections in Guyana is that whoever wins, the losing party is never willing to accept defeat. As was portrayed quite dramatically in the Elections 2020, the consequences of the defeated political party's non acceptance of the results of the elections has severe post-elections impact on the psyche of the people of Guyana and on the development of the country. Everything comes to a grinding halt in Guyana from the day of elections until a day or two afterwards when results are made known, and a new leader proclaimed.

There is rarely an occasion when the leaders of the Opposition and the President take the time to shake hand thereby acknowledging that the competition was good and fair and congratulating the winner in the process, a way of conceding defeat. Egos were hurt! Scars ran deep! Reconciliation does not occur as a practice. There is a standing 2020 joke that Guyana was trending in the USA's elections. Strange enough, President Donald Trump the outgoing president of the USA did not attend President-elect Joe Biden's inauguration[106] on January 20, 2021. This was a first in the 152 years of White House tradition and in the history of American politics. President Trump did not invite the president-elect to the White House, neither was there a tea and tour of the White House by the First Ladies.

It is projected, based on historical data, that for the next five years or less, the leaders of both major parties operate in isolation of each other. They do not operate in tandem to solve the problems of the country which further leads to ethnic divisions and short-sighted, development planning that is done in 5-year periods rather than 20–30 year cycles as is the norm in many developing countries.

On June 1, 2021, the chickens came home to roost. Three motions were tabled at GECOM's statutory meeting. The first motion moved by government nominated Commissioner, Mr. Sase Gunraj, called for the immediate dismissal of the CEO, Mr. Keith Lowenfield[107][107]. The second motion which was moved by PPP-C Commissioner, Ms. Bibi Shadick, called for the removal of the DCEO, Ms. Roxanne Myers[108] while the third motion which was moved by Commissioner, Mr. Manoj Narayan sought the immediate dismissal of REO for District Four, Mr. Clairmont Mingo.[109]

The Motion contained 19 reasons supporting the claims for the dismissal of the CEO, 14 reasons for the removal of the DCEO and 27 for the immediate dismissal of the RO supported by orders passed down from the High Court and the Caribbean Court of Justice. The penultimate reason for dismissal in all three cases were the criminal charges being prosecuted by the Guyana Police Force in respect of their numerous infractions of the law.

On June 22, 2021, 1 year 3 months and 20 days after the March 2, 2020, elections; a decision was made by GECOM, unanimously to send the trio of the CEO, DCEO and RO for District 4 on Annual leave. The Annual

Leave would start on Monday June 28, 2021. *"The CEO will proceed on 42 days Annual Leave, the DCEO will be on 120 days leave and Mr. Clairmont Mingo will be on 35 days leave. The Commission intends to conclude these discussions within the shortest possible time[110]."* The decision was deemed necessary to facilitate the Commission's deliberation on the three motions tabled by the Government nominated Commissioners seeking the immediate dismissal of those persons as well as the course of action to be adopted afterwards to conclude the process. On August 12, 2021, the Chief Elections Officer (CEO), Mr. Keith Lowenfield, the Deputy CEO, Ms. Roxanne Myers and Region Four's Returning Officer, Mr. Clairmont Mingo, had their contracts terminated.

Local government elections are constitutionally due in 2021. The Minister of Local Government and Regional Development, the Honorable Mr. Nigel Dharamlall, confirmed in Parliament that the Local Government Elections (LGE) would be held in 2021. However, he stated that systems were being put in place at GECOM such that its administration would fulfil its commitment to democracy. *"We cannot continue to have any elections in this country because anyone who believes in good governance, transparency and accountability can never have Lowenfield, Myers, Mingo at the head of the Secretariat of GECOM. The majority of people in this country will not condone it and we will not condone it.[111]"* Further endorsing his sentiment was President Dr. Irfaan Ali who concluded that *"What we have to do is to fix what is there first and we have to ensure that we have a system that is working, and a system that people trust, and a professional system, and a system that operates in an unbiased manner so that the people of our country can have confidence."*

CHAPTER 5: ELIGIBLE POLITICAL PARTIES

"Neither political party is clean when it comes to tactics that divide our people." Roy Barnes

Triskaidekaphobia is a word which signifies fear of the number thirteen. On January 10, 2020, Nomination Day, Guyanese witnessed thirteen political parties submit their list of candidates to the Guyana Elections Commission (GECOM) at the Umana Yana, Kingston, Georgetown. GECOM approved eleven political parties to contest the March 2, 2020, General and Regional Elections. The approved political parties were A New and United Guyana, A Partnership for National Unity+Alliance for Change, Change Guyana, Federal United Party, Liberty and Justice Party, Organisation for the Victory of the People, People's Republic Party, People's Progressive Party, The Citizenship Initiative, The New Movement, and United Republican Party. This fear of the number thirteen should have caused a Pavlovian effect on the superstitious people of Guyana and would have prepared them for an electoral jolly-ride of epic proportions.

One of the most impressive first timers, A New and United Guyana[112] (ANUG), was launched on January 18, 2019, at Moray House, Camp Street, Georgetown. The Presidential candidate, Mr. Ralph Hari Narayen Ramkarran, is a former executive member of the PPP-C and former Speaker of the National Assembly. The founding members of A New and United Guyana are from a variety of professional backgrounds and include Mr. Kian Jabour, Dr. Henry Jeffrey, Mr. Timothy Jonas, and Mr. Beni Sankar, very influential citizens of Guyana. It contested seven regions in the General and Regional Elections 2020; Regions Two to Seven and Ten and received 2,313 votes. ANUG's primary mission was to *"win enough seats in the National Assembly to prevent a majority government in Parliament and to compel the two major political parties to formally or informally co-operate with each other."* It was one goal that was realized.

ANUG's Manifesto, Creating the Balance, was launched on February 18, 2020, two weeks before elections day. It announced at its launch that there was *"disappointment with the failure of the present regime to implement its core manifesto promise to make constitutional change. The manifesto promised, among other things, to establish a genuine government of national unity. We concluded that there needs to be an active and persistent political catalyst directed towards ending the gridlock caused by the racial/ethnic alliances that have plagued Guyana for all of the 70 or so years of its modern political history. We assessed that we have no other alternative than to call upon the people of Guyana to support another political party to bring about these needed changes."* A political triad of ANUG, TNM and LJP gained one seat in the National Assembly.

During the elections process from March 2, 2020, and beyond, to the final declaration of August 2, 2020, ANUG's role in a free and fair process was unchallenged. Their members were vocal and relentless in their pursuit of democracy and condemnation of threats to the institutions of democracy. On May 30, 2020, its Chairman, Mr. Timothy Jonas, held a Press Conference[113] at the location where the national Recount of ballots was cast on March 2, 2020, the Arthur Chung Conference Center, with a focus on the role of the members of the GECOM Secretariat. Mr. Jonas opined that the Secretariat staff was compromised and singled out the Chief Elections Officer (CEO), Mr. Keith Lowenfield, the Deputy CEO, Ms. Roxanne Myers, the Returning Officer of Region Four, Mr. Clairmont Mingo and even to the Personal Assistant to the CEO, Mr. Duarte Hetsberger.

ANUG's Chairman had to take to the news media to vent his concerns given that complaints made to the Chairman of GECOM went unheeded. Again, on June 3, 2020, during the recount process, he noted that, *"There has been a myriad of little acts of tyranny going on in there. They are designed to frustrate,"* and that a GECOM Supervisor refused to note an objection from ANUG but gave more latitude to the APNU+AFC agents as part of a delay tactic. What was learned from Mr. Jonas and verified by the Kaieteur News[114] was that on that date, on the recounted ballot boxes for Region Four, the Returning Officer's figures differed in a systematic manner to that of the original unverified declaration. APNU+AFC's votes were increased while PPP-C's votes were reduced. It was confirmed that Mr. Mingo had not been dismissed from GECOM though criminal acts were uncovered during the recount process.

The APNU+AFC Coalition came under focused, verbal condemnation on June 14, 2020, by ANUG[115] for lying and deceiving its supporters when President David A. Granger declared that they had won the elections knowing the tabulation by Mr. Clermont Mingo to be false. Leaders of the Coalition were complicit in spreading the unwholesome narrative. According to the ANUG leadership, *"In that recount, the nation learned that*

Mingo had lied, that Granger had lied, that Williams, Patterson, Hughes and the entire contingent of the APNU leadership had lied. On the count of the ballots, PPP leads the APNU by 15,000 votes. APNU supporters have had to swallow the undeniable: that their leaders have lied to them, have deceived them."

On July 12, 2020, ANUG's Chairman, attorney-at-law Mr. Timothy Jonas, called upon Justice Claudette Singh to dismiss the CEO, Mr. Keith Lowenfield, for insubordination consequent upon his refusal to follow instructions issued to him by her. The CEO did not use the results of the national recount which was concluded on June 8, 2020, but had submitted his own computations which gave the incumbents the win.

The controversial Mr. Robert Badal who owns the Pegasus Hotel was Change Guyana's Presidential Candidate while the Prime Ministerial Candidate was Ms. Mishka Puran. Mr. Nigel Hinds, popular newspaper columnist and professional Accountant was the Chairman of Change Guyana. Mr. Badal, at the launch of the party, remarked that the two major political parties have not done enough to address poverty, joblessness, and the poor supply of electricity that have plagued Guyana for far too long, among other burning issues. According to him, there is a *"tale of broken promises and mismanagement throughout post Independent Guyana."*

Change Guyana launched their Manifesto on February 11, 2020, a month short of the March 2, 2020, General and Regional elections. It received 1,953 votes in the General and Regional elections. The Manifesto covered the normal governance issues such as the promise jobs creation, oil and gas, health care, agriculture, governance, community development, crime etc. The party[116] was dissolved by the majority of its leadership on August 24, 2020.

Lots of crazy things happened on March 15, 2020, least of which was the letter from the Chairman of Change Guyana, Mr. Nigel Hinds, to the editor of the Guyana Times[117] newspaper. His letter was a testimony of the authenticity of the 160 Statements of Poll (SOPs) for Region Four which Change Guyana sourced independently of those provided by the PPP-C but contrasted with those provided by the officials of GECOM and the APNU+AFC Coalition. Mr. Hinds chided the GECOM officials for producing a copy of the SOP that was remarkably different to that of the original where the differences were always in favor of the APNU+AFC Coalition. The party recreated the scenarios at the GECOM headquarters where the GECOM representatives read the SOPs at such speed that the Political Party Agents were unable to reconcile the numbers with their figures. The changes in numbers to the other political parties were small to insignificant but the Coalition's numbers were inflated by as conservative as 50% and as high as 200% more.

Mr. Hinds recorded that they *"wish to place in the public domain and state in granite terms that the fabrication, farce and fraud related to the declaration made for*

Region Four election results; amounts to an abortion, aberration and abomination of Guyana's democratic process and the laws and provisions in the Representation of the People Act." On March 14, 2020, Change Guyana filed a request for the recount of the Region Four votes at GECOM pursuant to Section 84 of the Representation of the People Act. It took courage and the defense of democracy to make the action possible.

Lawyers made up the membership of the Federal United Party (FED-UP). The executive members are lawyers from Berbice, Mr. Ryan Crawford, Mr. Horatio Edmonson and Mr. Chandra Sohan. The FED-UP Party was launched was launched on January 12, 2019, at the Central Corentyne Chamber of Commerce building in Rose Hall Town, Williamsburg, Corentyne with its motto being Unite to Survive.

Mr. Chandra Sohan, a former magistrate, advanced the motive for the formation of the party to contest elections on March 2, 2020. *"When we look where Guyana is compared to where other countries are, we really haven't made no progress in this country…At one point in time, we felt disgusted with what we see and… we got more disgusted… we are now just fed up[118]."*

FED-UP's transformative approach would be to introduce a constituency system into the national electoral system that would bridge the racial divide. Persons qualified to represent the people would be the ones who would enter Parliament to represent their people. The party proposed a federal system where the country would be divided into three counties, a combination of the 10 administrative regions, with each having its own administration with a view to removing considerable power from the hands of the Central Government. Constitutional reform and job creation are top on their agenda for Berbice. The FED-UP party contested Regions 5 and 6 in the Regional Elections.

The year 2020 saw an eclectic mix of political parties representing the six races of Guyana. Mr. Lennox Shuman, Presidential Candidate of the Liberty Justice Party (LJP) served as vice- chairman of the National Toshaos Council and Toshao for his village, the St. Cuthbert's Mission in Region Four. Mr. Shuman, a pilot by profession, relinquished his Canadian citizenship to become eligible for election to the National Assembly as stipulated in Article 155 (a) of the Constitution of Guyana. The LJP was launched on January 12, 2019, at the Georgetown Club, Camp Street, Georgetown. This party was founded on the same premise as that of the new political parties but with an emphasis on the representation of Indigenous peoples across Guyana. LJP contested Regions 1, 2, 4, 7, 8 and 9 and received 2, 657 votes.

On July 24, 2020, the LJP[119] released a statement calling for the immediate dismissal of the Chief Elections Officer, Mr. Keith Lowenfield, because of what they referred to as his disrespect of the voting public and the Commission itself. Furthermore, it was pointed out that APNU+AFC's call for open dialogue with the other political parties was duplicitous coming from an entity that had clearly tried to rig the elections and was acting as a demagogue. The LJP leaders had been incensed by the Coalition government's published schedule of meetings across Guyana during the Covid-19 lockdown and demanded that the Guyana Police Force act against the willful, unlawful behavior.

LJP's Presidential candidate was nominated by Prime Minister Mark Phillips and seconded by Minister of Parliamentary Affairs and Governance, Gail Teixeira, on September 1, 2020, to be the deputy Speaker of the House of Assembly of Guyana. Mr. Shuman[120] was the first representative of the combined small parties securing their presence in the twelfth Parliament. He is the first person of Indigenous heritage to hold the position of deputy Speaker.

The Organization for the Victory of the People (OVP)[121] was founded on February 20th, 2015, by members of the Joint Initiative for Human Advancement and Dignity, an organization that was at the forefront of the struggle against the PPP death-squad regime. The OVP contested the 2015 elections but did not win any seats in Parliament. However, it saw itself as the Third Force which would control the balance of power between the two major political parties. Mr. Gerald Pereira of the Organisation for the Victory of the People (OVP) contested the Regional Elections in Region Four only as the leader.

The OVP's symbol, the Black Panther[122], represents strength, power and courage, qualities that are vital in the fight for national liberation. Mr. Perreira pledge *"to work tirelessly to uplift not only poor and struggling Africans, but all oppressed and marginalized citizens in Region 4, regardless of race."*

The dominance of females in organized politics in Guyana was not to be downplayed. The Citizenship Initiative's (TCI)[123] presidential candidate, Ms. Rondha Ann Lam, had enlisted a predominantly female list of members to its political party. The presidential candidate, a forty-year-old teacher by profession, is mother to four children. The party's symbol is a scale that is balancing two water lilies and it was launched at Herdmanston Lodge, Georgetown on October 17, 2019, which exposed a team of young Guyanese professionals. Among the founding members are Mr. Shazaam Ally, Mr. Yonnick David, Mr. Alfonso De Armas Archbold and Mr. Ruel Johnson. The TCI was motivated by the failed national policies of the two largest political parties. Their main focal points would include the bridging of the racial and economic divide. Constitutional reform is a goal of the party along with inclusive governance, accountability, and transparency. TCI contested in Regional and General Elections in Regions 2, 3, 4, 5, 6 and 10 and received 680 votes.

With the stakes rising higher and higher and the risk of the democratic process being eroded, TCI intruded on the unravelling plans of the

APNU+AFC and GECOM coalition by declaring that Mr. Mingo was guilty of dereliction of duty during the tabulation of Region Four's votes of March 13, 2020. On March 15, 2020, as observers to the elections process, TCI[124], a small, newly exposed bastion of democracy testified of the Region Four REO's contempt of the judgement of the Chief Justice, Justice Roxane George-Wiltshire when he continued to use a spreadsheet as opposed to the certified Statements of Poll in the tabulation and verification of votes.

TCI's Presidential Candidate, with academic precision, detailed how Mr. Clairmont Mingo installed a Clerk whose duty was to call out the numbers from their SOPs, the SOPs which were unseen by observers and political agents having been denied by Mr. Mingo, upon requests of the observers and party agents. The Polling Stations' numbers called out did not agree with those of the TCI which was a source of consternation to its Presidential Candidate, Ms. Rondha-Ann Lam. Ms. Lam witnessed the serving of legal notice to Mr. Mingo to appear before the Chief Justice which requested that he should comply with her orders.

The committed Presidential Candidate stated that Mr. Mingo escalated the situation by halting the tabulation process for more than two hours prior to relocating to GECOM's headquarters at Kingston, Georgetown where the media equipment was of a lesser quality than that of the media center at the Ashmin's building. The copies of the SOPs projected were blurred which made it difficult to recognize pertinent details. Ms. Lam, as were members of the smaller political parties along with the local and international observers, remained throughout the entirety of the elections process, frustrated by the transparent way in which the Region Four Returning Officer made efforts to manipulate the election results.

Ms. Lam's final appeal was to the Chairman of GECOM[125], *"We are asking that chairperson, Justice Claudette Singh, ensure that a recount, as she has committed to, take place as the process yesterday (Friday) was so egregiously flawed that the result cannot be taken to be in itself an accurate representation of the will of the people."*

Doctors were among the professionals who dictated the tone of the Elections 2020. The New Movement (TNM)[126] led by Presidential Candidate Dr. Ashley Kissoon and Prime Ministerial Candidate Dr. Gerald Forde launched their party on November 21, 2019. Dr. Ashley Kissoon is a medical doctor who is thirty years old. The party's creation was motivated by the vision to make Guyana the manufacturing hub of South America and the Caribbean. The party's symbol is the Harpy Eagle which depicts the strength to rise above corruption and other ongoing issues in Guyana. The TNM contested in Regions 3, 4, 5, 6, 8 and 10 and received 244 votes.

As to her personal journey into politics, Dr. Kissoon stated, *"I turn to the left, there is one party fighting with another, I turn to the right there is racial barriers, I turn to the left again, there is favoritism in the system so because I was so tired of it, I decided to come forward and work with my colleagues to achieve the vision that we have."* According to the Prime Ministerial candidate, Dr. Forde, *"The average middle, poor and working-class people struggle together in the markets, in the schools, in the hospitals, in the offices, in our communities to make ends meet. We are in a struggle together to realize economic liberation in this generation."*

Dr. Daniel Josh Kanhai, an executive member of the TNM, filed private criminal charges against the GECOM's CEO, Mr. Keith Lowenfield[127] for which he made an appearance at the Georgetown Magistrate's Court on July 24, 2020. Charges were filed at the same time along with Mr. Desmond Morian. The charges claimed that the CEO conspired with person(s) unknown to commit the common law offence of fraud between March 2, 2020 and June 23, 2020 when he submitted his Elections Report of June 23, 2020 and which included figures which altered the results of the elections. The second charge stated that without lawful excuse or justification, the CEO willfully misconducted himself at Georgetown, by ascertaining results of the March 2, 2020 General and Regional Elections for Guyana knowing the said results to be false, the said willful misconduct amounting to a breach of the public's trust in the Office of the CEO of GECOM between March 2, 2020 and June 23, 2020 while Mr. Lowenfield was performing his duty as the CEO. The third charge alleged that the GECOM's CEO conspired with person(s) unknown to commit common law fraud by representing to GECOM, that tables attached to his Election Report dated March 14, 2020 accurately reflected the true results of the said election, in order to materially alter the results of the said election, with intent to defraud, knowing the said tabulation to be false. The matter is still the subject of an ongoing court case.

Another noble profession to join the political fray was the pastors, representatives of the Christian religion of Guyana. The People's Republic Party (PRP)[128] whose Presidential candidate is Dr. Valerie Leung is a political party consisting of Christian leaders and was established on religious principles. Dr. Leung is a pastor and senior lecturer at the University of Guyana. The party's launch was on December 1, 2019, at the Ocean View Hotel at Liliendaal, East Coast Demerara. The members were motivated by the goal to check corruption and the downward moral and ethical spiral of the people of Guyana. The founding members included Pastor Premraj Parshotam, Pastor Patrick Bourne, Glennis Smith, Pastor Timothy Norton, and General Secretary, Pastor Terrence Joseph. The party's symbol is the lantern, depicting light against corruption and it contested in Regions 1-6 and 10 and received 889 votes.

According to Dr. Leung, *"Guyana is plagued by corruption. No country can get past this mud hole…The political leaders are elected to look after our best interests, but they only look after theirs."*

Back in 1985, the United Republican Party (URP) led by Dr. Vishnu Bandhu was formed to bring democracy back to Guyana. The party contested the Regional and General elections in all the 10 regions but received a paltry 360 votes. As more females have been playing a significant role in the leadership of the newer political parties in 2020, Ms. Marcia Allison Lewis, was chosen as the Prime Ministerial candidate. The symbol of the party is the head of the cow which signifies goodness and symbolizes strength and courage while displaying a nurturing and protective nature.

On June 27, 2020, Dr. Bandhu released a Press Statement to the effect that President David. A Granger should concede defeat so that the country could move forward. According to Dr. Bandhu, Guyana has descended to *"the lowest low in the political spectrum to our Caribbean brothers and to the world, we are seen as a nation incompetent of making our own decisions. I am calling on all responsible for this current crisis, to do the sensible and right thing in this situation and let our country move forward."*

The Justice For All Party (JFAP) which is led by Mr. Chandranarine N. Sharma and his wife, after three months of soul-searching, spoke to the people of Guyana in his simple, down to earth style which has led to his popularity and ultimately his success in politics. Mr. Sharma's love for his country and its people are unquestioned. He has travelled the length and breadth of Guyana to help the most vulnerable citizens of all ethnicities. Twenty-three years ago, the inevitable formation of the JFAP was realized when they first contested elections in 1997. His motives were simple. He wanted to highlight the economic struggles of the poor and to fight to improve their quality of life. The Party contested subsequent elections but joined with the APNU+AFC Coalition from 2011.

It was not strange when, on June 19, 2020, Mr. Sharma and his wife expressed gratitude to the people of Guyana for their support during the over two decades of service to them. He further stated that, *"Guyana is a democratic country where Our people have the freedom to vote, freedom to elect a new government every 5 years and interestingly enough Our people have the freedom to be disappointed in the outcome of an election too. With that being said, an election has taken place under the watchful eyes of local and international observers. A National recount was carried out under the eyes of CARICOM. All votes were counted. There is a clear winner. The recount shows that the PPP-C has won the election. Therefore, Mr. Irfaan Ali should be allowed to be sworn in without delay[129]."*

Mr. Sharma and his wife, the General Secretary of JFAP, Ms. Savitree Singh-Sharma appealed to the manipulators of the electoral process not to delay the declaration of results but to let the nation move forward. He recognized that the citizens were suffering because of the Covid-19 pandemic and that a strong, legal government would have to be in place to deal with challenges.

On September 1, 2020, JFAP[130] withdrew from the APNU+AFC Coalition given the changing political landscape and the need to review their *"roles and relationships."* JFAP's leaders felt marginalized as no JFAP Member of Parliament was selected for the National Assembly. Taking just as bold a stand was the Working Peoples Alliance (WPA) whose leaders on August 19, 2020, withdrew from the Coalition citing repeated violations of the principles governing the politics of the Coalition.

Interestingly enough, the merger of the British Guiana Labour Party[131] which was led by Mr. Linden Forbes Sampson Burnham and the Political Affairs Committee[132] led by Dr. Cheddi Jagan created the Peoples Progressive Party (PPP) on January 1, 1950. The PPP was a working class, multi-ethnic party supported by academics until it was split when Mr. Forbes Burnham left the party to form the Peoples National Congress (PNC).

The Peoples Progressive Party-Civic (PPP-C) has held power since 1992 through to 2015. Its symbol is the cup and it is one of the two largest political parties in Guyana. It is the oldest political party in Guyana. The difference between the two major political parties may be the party colors, red versus green but their similarity is the focus on etho-politics, a dangerous game which both major parties have capitalized upon much to the detriment of the people and long-term development of Guyana. While the majority of APNU+AFC sycophants grimace at a victory for the PPP-C, similar reactions are duplicated by the PPP-C yardfowls for an APNU+AFC win. None of the leaders of these two major parties trust each other but respect the levels to which each can sink to win an election.

The leaders of the PPP-C party, on March 5, 2020, urged their supporters to follow the laws of the land as the members and supporters of the party protested against the unverified votes as proclaimed by the Returning Officer of Region Four, Mr. Clairmont Mingo. Violence broke out in Regions Two, Three, Four, Five and Six amidst protests that the APNU+AFC coalition government made attempts to steal the elections.

The Opposition Leader, Dr. Bharat Jagdeo[133], announced, "I want to assure our supporters that we are strong. We are representing you. Granger will not get away with fraud. He will not get away with fraud. And the will of the people will prevail...But do not break the law. Stay at home. Remain calm but vigilant!" The Opposition Leader assured his supporters that members of the international community, including the diplomats from the United States of America, the United Kingdom, Canada and the European Union missions, supported the party's effort to challenge the declaration which were made under suspicious and less than transparent circumstances. He called directly on President David A. Granger not to transition a new government without a proper declaration of results. He called on members of the judiciary and GECOM not to be complicit in electoral fraud. PPP-C

Presidential candidate, Dr. Irfaan Ali, strongly appealed to the supporters to be calm and strong in their defense of democracy.

On March 17, 2020, the PPP-C released a Press Statement[134] considering the second attempt at declaring unsubstantiated results by the same Returning Officer, Mr. Clairmont Mingo. The party pointed out the duplicity of the APNU+AFC Coalition Government which filed an injunction to block a recount and reminded the citizens of Guyana and the international community that it was President David A. Granger who requested a high-level CARICOM team to supervise a recount of the ballots. The PPP-C was skeptical of the Coalition's motive but agreed to the terms and conditions as a means of progressing a solution-oriented approach to the electoral dilemma.

Two days later, Mr. Jagdeo signaled President Granger's delay in signing the aide-memoire in order to undermine the CARICOM Agreement and to resist the Recount given that an APNU+AFC Coalition candidate, Ms. Ulita Moore, filed an injunction to stop the recount.

In its fight for democracy, the PPP-C published copies of the authentic Region Four's Tally Sheets from the various Polling Stations as signed by the Presiding Officers. Their Tally sheets agreed to the Statements of Poll issued by GECOM. Only the APNU+AFC supporters challenged the veracity of those Statements. The party lauded CARICOM's role as interlocutors to arrive at a quick resolution to the impasse.

The PPP-C was pellucid in declaring that they would not accept an illegal government sworn in on fraudulent elections results. They supported the Secretary of State of the USA, Mr. Michael Pompeo's, proposed sanctions for members of the APNU+AFC Coalition, their families and other conspirators who contributed to manipulation of elections. The Secretary of State would visit Guyana on September 17 and 18, 2020 in what some had considered a show of support for a democratically elected government.

They urge all Guyanese, particularly supporters of the PPP, to remain at home until they received instructions from their leaders. They were urged to be vigilant and non-provocative and lawful.

On April 8, 2020, the PPP-C ridiculed a proposal by GECOM to realize a Recount timeframe of 156[135] days. This was seen by the Opposition Party as another protracted engagement by the Coalition government and its cohorts. The entire country's results are normally totaled for the approximately five hundred thousand voters within a 4-days period. The laws of Guyana allow for a 15-day period for elections results to be declared. The then Opposition Party appealed to the Chairman of GECOM, Justice Claudette Singh, to act in a manner consistent with the laws of Guyana and she did. An alternate proposal was made by the PPP-

C's Commissioners of GECOM which found greater favor with the people of Guyana and the Chairman.

A week after the scathing remarks about the Recount proposal, the PPP-C[136] purposed that the APNU+AFC Coalition government having filed a document with the United States Department of Justice's Foreign Agents Registration Act (FARA) Unit by way of the lobbying firm, JJ & B LLC, peddled erroneous information which did not bear any semblance to what occurred post elections day of March 2, 2020. The document titled, Dossier Guyana Elections 2020, consisted of 147 pages and documented the Coalition government's view of occurrences chronicled during the General and Regional elections 2020. It was received on March 31, 2020, by FARA which required that *"certain agents of foreign principals who are engaged in political activities or other activities specified under the statute to make periodic public disclosure of their relationship with the foreign principal, as well as activities, receipts and disbursements in support of those activities*[137]*."*

The Dossier reported how the PPP-C had rigged elections from 1992 to 2015 and were responsible for the spate of violent protests throughout the country. On the other hand, the PPP-C's submission to FARA through the lobbying firm, Mercury Public Affairs[138], LLC, was a 19-page document submitted on March 6, 2020. While President David A. Granger denied the filing of the Dossier, his political colleagues, Mr. Joseph Harmon and Mr. David Patterson, within days of each other, admitted that the process was accomplished by inputs by them to change the political narrative in Guyana.

The PPP-C contended that they were setting the record straight as they responded to the APNU+AFC's dossier. Both major parties were competing for the approval of the U.S. government and any economic benefits that could have resulted from lobbying the National Security Council, U.S. Departments of Justice, State and the Foreign Relations Committees, both Senate and Congress.

Almost weekly, the PPP-C organized live Press Conferences reminding the nation of the fraud perpetrated upon the electors of Guyana and the gradual erosion of democracy in Guyana. The world was listening attentively. Even the government of Venezuela reminded Guyana of its responsibility to the tenets of democracy. On June 18, 2020, the General Secretary[139] of the PPP-C, Dr. Bharat Jagdeo, referred to the APNU+AFC Coalition supporter, Ms Eslyn David's court action to restrain the CEO from complying with the direction of Chairman Justice Claudette Singh as a Coalition "disguised elections petition." The CEO's Report would have allowed the PPP-C to be declared winners of the elections by approximately fifteen thousand votes. On August 22, 2020, the Attorney General and Minister of Legal Affairs, Mr. Anil Nandlall, confirmed Dr. Jagdeo's assertions that the Coalition government financially backed Ms. Eslyn

David in an effort to thwart the declaration of the elections results and to disenfranchise voters.

Mr. Jagdeo asserted that the CEO, Mr. Lowenfield was using his office for the benefit of the APNU+AFC political party. He stated that, *"This seems to be the plot by APNU, they will not give up… you can't disguise anything and put it before the Court of Appeal and rule on technicality. The Court of Appeal we believe has no jurisdiction and we hope the matter will be thrown out in the interest of moving forward[140]."*

PPP-C's Presidential Candidate, Dr. Irfaan Ali[141], made the defining charge to the people of Guyana when he stated on July 13, 2020, that, *"now is the time to fix the fundamentals on which a modern and free society is built. This is the moment to fill the cracks on the pillars of democracy, cast the beams of unity and build the tower of destiny, not by stones and Steel, but by all of us individually and collectively.*

To do this we have to change our mindset and reprogram the way we think and act. My father always said to me, 'Strike the iron whilst it is hot.'

The fight for democracy, rule of law, economic and social development, political will and societal involvement are hot this moment and we must strike it as a nation and shape it into the country that the future generations will be proud of and never again must we find ourselves in this position as a people and country."

By mid-July 2020, the PPP-C's General Secretary lauded the USA's Secretary of State's declaration of sanctions on all those who sought to undermine the democracy of Guyana. Mr. Jagdeo pinpointed leaders of the Coalition government who supported the shenanigans perpetrated by their political party to disenfranchise the electors. That list of persons included Prime Minister, Mr. Moses Nagamootoo, the Head of the Presidential Secretariat, Mr. Joseph Harmon; former Minister of Natural Resources, Mr. Raphael Trotman; former Minister of Public Security, Mr. Khemraj Ramjattan and for Minister of Public Telecommunications, Ms. Cathy Hughes. These ministers of government were scathing in their defense of the sovereignty of Guyana and expressed disdain for those who were critical of the unfolding elections saga.

Mr. Jadgeo, vocal and semi-militant in his engagements, appealed to President David A. Granger to condemn the fraudulent attempts of the Region Four's Returning Officer and the GECOM's CEO. He considered President Granger to be the *"intellectual author and is in charge of the conspiracy to rig the March 2nd, 2020 Election[142]."* His final warning was that the Coalition Government, if they intended to remain in power despite the legal outcome of the court matters, would be *"met by fierce resistance by the PPP and other forces fighting for democracy[143]."*

One of the PPP-C's heroes, somewhat underestimated, was the former Attorney General, Mr. Anil Nandlall, who bestrode the legal waves with the confidence of Plato. He outwitted and outperformed the lawyers who were hired by the Coalition government and their cohorts in every respect. In

September 2020, after Mr. Nandlall had ascended to the office of the Attorney General, he initiated a Special Audit through the Auditor General's office. The office of the Auditor General's purpose was to investigate approximately fifty million dollars[144] of legal fees which was spent by the Coalition government on hiring lawyers for elections-related matters inclusive of the No Confidence Motion, the unilateral appointment of the former Chairman of GECOM and footing the bill for the private citizens who challenged the National Recount results.

Mr. Nandlall was to Mr. Basil Williams what Batman was to the Joker. He was always a step ahead as he responded to the multiple legal challenges designed to prolong the declaration of the elections results and to stifle the democratic process of electing leaders to govern the social, economic development of Guyana. One of his stirring statements made on July 20, 2020, made lucid his approach to the legal maneuverings when he stated that an appeal to the Chief Justice's ruling had no chance of success and *"would be just another shameless attempt to hold on to Government."*

The former Attorney General's relentless efforts were such that the Caribbean Court of Justice's orders of July 31, 2020, awarded costs in the matter of Mohammed Irfaan Ali and Bharrat Jagdeo vs. Eslyn David and others to Dr. Ali and Dr. Jagdeo. The Court ordered the Attorney General, Ms. Eslyn David and Mr. Joseph Harmon to pay costs for two counsels. The legal costs were estimated to be in the millions of Guyanese dollars. Always the one to get in the last words, Mr. Nandlall stated that the costs were "for a frivolous, vexatious and abusive litigation."

On that same date, the Chief Justice[145], Ms. Roxanne George, ruled that the original ten declarations made by the Returning Officers could not be used to declare the March 2, 2020, elections. Furthermore, she ruled that the High Court had jurisdiction to hear the case before her and that the recount results must be used to declare the PPP-C, the winner of the Elections 2020. Chief Justice George referred to the ruling of the Caribbean Court of Justice and the Court of Appeal which reenforced the validity of the National Recount exercise and the Recount Order 60. The matter was Res Judicata. Hence, the GECOM's CEO was required to submit his report from the National Recount results according to Section 18 of the Election Laws (Amendment) Act of 2000.

Within less than a decade, the APNU+AFC has become Guyana's largest coalition political party made up of seven political parties which include the Alliance for Chance (AFC), Guyana Action Party (GAP), Justice For All Party (JFAP), National Democratic Front (NDF), National Front Alliance (NFA), People National Congress (PNC) and the Working People's Alliance (WPA) which governed Guyana from 2015 to August 2, 2020. The second oldest political party in Guyana, the PNC, is the most powerful entity within the APNU+AFC Coalition and dictates how things are done according to the current political maneuverings even with the Cummingsburg Accord in play.

The APNU+AFC's political party's symbol is the Open Hand palm of APNU combined with the Key from the AFC.

Following the 1957 General Elections, Mr. Forbes Burnham split from the PPP and his party was predominantly Afro-Guyanese while the PPP represented the Indo-Guyanese. Mr. Joseph Pryag Lachmansingh was the Chairman of the PNC when Mr. Burnham became its leader. The PNC between 1968 until 1992 governed Guyana until their political leader and the President of Guyana, Mr. Hugh Desmond Hoyte, permitted free and fair elections under the watchful eyes of the Carter Center. It is presumed that all the elections prior to 1992 were rigged by the PNC party. On October 5, 2020, the PNC marked its 63rd anniversary by dedicating the Ranwell Jordan Congress House in Agricola, East Bank Demerara.

The plot thickened as Minister of Public Security[146], Mr. Khemraj Ramjattan and Minister of Public Telecommunications, Ms. Catherine Hughes, addressed journalists at the APNU+AFC Command Centre on Lamaha Street, Georgetown, three days after elections day reporting that there was interference from a group of Russian hackers whose purpose was to change the GECOM's database.

Apparently, three Russians were found and deported on elections day while a fourth Russian escaped. Cyber equipment, flash drives and other high-tech equipment were seized and deposited with the Guyana Police Force. The American Chamber Association of Guyana (AMCHAM Guyana) was implicated in the matter, but they strongly rejected any association with the Russians and any plot to hijack the elections. Persons associated with the PPP-C political party were photographed at the Marriott Hotel speaking with the criminal elements from Russia. However, no proof had ever been presented. None of the culprits had been detained for further questioning nor incarceration.

Ms. Hughes stated, *"We have very clear security channels, the requisite organisations were contacted, fortunately they examined the situation and the information that they received, they deemed it credible and they found three of the four persons, and given that this was occurring on the early morning of the most important day of our history, the decision was taken that they had no grounds for these persons to be here and they were deported."* The idea behind the swift action of deportation was to prevent chaos as Ms. Hughes argued.

AMCHAM Guyana reported that it *"wishes to assure every Guyanese that all of the persons accredited as observers by the Guyana Elections Commission went through a high level of scrutiny by the organisation before their names were submitted to GECOM, and further wishes to state that no Russian citizens (or any of the individuals referred to in Mrs. Hughes' statement for that matter) were submitted by AMCHAM to the Guyana Elections Commission to be accredited. This can easily be verified with the Guyana Elections Commission."*

Ms. Gail Teixeira, an executive member of the PPP-C, opined that the statements made by the Coalition Ministers were fabrications. She added, *"The count in the polling station is done manually not electronically and the Statements of Poll (SOP) are verified and tabulated manually, so there is no electronic systems for Russians or anybody else to hack into."* She believed that Guyana has descended into a police state and provided an example of Mr. Gustavo Arnavat[147], a former US Executive Director of the Inter-American Development Bank (IDB), who visited Opposition leader, Dr. Bharrat Jagdeo. When Mr. Arnavat returned to his hotel room, he was questioned and searched by ranks of the Guyana Police Force. This was merely one example of the multiple incidences.

President David A. Granger addressed the nation on March 9, 2020, assuring the people of Guyana that he acted in accordance with the Constitution and Laws of Guyana. He. reminded all of Guyana that GECOM was an independent constitutional entity over which he did not exercise control. He promised non-interference in the work of GECOM. President Granger systematically explained how the Opposition PPP-C had created *"an atmosphere of intimidation and fear at the office of the Returning Officer of District Number 4"* which led to the interruption of GECOM's work. Furthermore, he implied that the Opposition had approached the Supreme Court to prevent GECOM from making a declaration of the final elections results. The matter was placed before the Chief Justice for March 10, 2020.

On March 6, 2020, the APNU+AFC coalition appealed to the citizens of Guyana to be calm and for them not to disrupt the normal way of life as they awaited the final declaration of results of Monday's general election from the Guyana Elections Commission. This appeal was made because of the series of violent protests which resulted from the two major political parties simultaneously declaring themselves winners of the elections.

The AFC, partners within the Coalition, stated that despite some concerns about the electoral process in specific regions, it believes that the *"elections were generally well conducted within the provisions of the Representation of the People Act. "* They even commended GECOM on the proper administration of the elections. Even more remarkable and paradoxical was the AFC's assertion that it *"believes that the outcome of that process should reflect the political will of the electorate. Equally, it is the AFC's position that there is a clear legal process to be followed if there are disagreements with GECOM's decisions and we urge all concerned – political parties and observers – to embrace and, where appropriate, utilise those processes. All concerns and objections must be clearly documented and addressed within the framework of the law."*

In the strongest terms, the APNU+AFC Coalition condemned the mass infiltration of GECOM's offices by members of the PPP-C and subsequent intimidation of the officials of GECOM. The Coalition accused the PPP-C of hooliganism which created an atmosphere of fear among the staff of GECOM and the unlawful behavior among protestors which emanated from their actions.

As the elections stalemate dragged out, the APNU+AFC Campaign Manager, Mr. Joseph Harmon, on April 16, 2020, explained that the lobbying firm of John, James & Bart Limited Liability Company (JJ&B, LLC) was paid from funds collected from concerned supporters and not out of the government's coffers. The lobbying firm was paid a retainer of US $40,000 or the Guyanese equivalent of $ 8M to stem the false accusations being lodged against the Coalition government by the PPP-C and its agents. Both the major political parties have invested in the tried and tested lobbying firms of the USA to spin their own version of the truth of Elections 2020.

The APNU+AFC party believed that *"if the PPP gets control of Guyana, China and Russia will control the Northern region of South America, from Venezuela to Suriname[148]."* Mr. Harmon stated that the Dossier submitted to the U.S. Department of Justice sought to improve relations between Guyana and the United States of America.

One day later, the Ministry of the Presidency expressed grave concerns of the media's treatment of the details found on the U.S. Department of Justice's web site and the news content of several newspapers published in Guyana on the actual entity which submitted the Dossier. The Government of Guyana clarified that it had not hired JJ&B, LLC and had no contractual obligations to the lobbying firm. The Ministry denied that any government funds were used to recruit the firm and that President David A. Granger was not involved in the hiring of the lobbying firm.

On April 21, 2020, AFC's Leader Mr. Khemraj Ramjattan[149] confirmed that the APNU+AFC Coalition hired JJ&B LLC four days after President David A. Granger, leader of the APNU+AFC political party, disavowed any knowledge of the recruitment of the lobbying firm. All these submissions to the U.S. Department of Justice were done against the backdrop of the threat by the United States Government to implement sanctions against Guyana if a government was sworn in based on fraudulent results.

During the first week of June 2020, the APNU+AFC leaders were adamant that the Recount process had uncovered evidence of *"massive electoral fraud affecting over 84,000 votes."* The Coalition leaders called on GECOM to reject all ballots in all the ten voting districts that could not be validated. Having warned GECOM, the Coalition leaders proceeded to let them know that they could not *"use illegal and fraudulent votes to produce a valid and acceptable result. Fraud cannot produce credibility."* The discoveries were the subject of bitter discourses between June 4, 2020, and June 7, 2020. They contended that within the PPP-C strongholds, specifically on the East

Coast Demerara[150]; sealed ballot boxes were opened, and the relevant documentation was missing.

On June 7, 2020, the Coalition party expressed disappointment that GECOM had decided to tabulate all votes despite their objections. The party declared that they did *"not accept a tabulated vote as a credible vote since in the bundle of tabulated votes rests several votes which are fraudulent."* On that same day, the APNU+AFC refused to sign the Certificates of District Tabulation for District six for the same reasons given to GECOM throughout the Recount period. The reasons would form the basis of a legal defense against the declaration of results within a matter of a fortnight by a private citizen and member of the APNU+AFC party, Ms. Eslyn David. The Coalition[151] registered instances of large numbers of voter impersonation, ghost voting, unstamped and missing ballots, missing poll books and oaths of identity, ballots, and more ballots that electors found in ballot boxes. The other political parties did not concur with the Coalition on these matters.

When Kaieteur News[152] published the names of some of the reputed ghost voters, as many as were listed in the newspaper as having either been dead or migrated turned up at the Newspaper's headquarters or contacted the agency to disprove the assertions made by the Coalition party. With regard to the twenty-nine ballot boxes which the Coalition deemed to have no statutory documents, Mr. Paul Jaisingh, a Deputy Returning Officer (DRO) emailed the Chairman, Justice Singh, to inform her that he and a few other Presiding Officers had received instructions from the Clerk to the Region Four Returning Officer, Ms. Carolyn Duncan, to place the unused ballots in bags and not the ballot boxes.

Eleven days later, His Excellency President David A. Granger addressed the nation informing them that *"an acceptable outcome is expected based on four sequential stages."* He defined the First Stage as the recount of all the ballots which would take 33 days to be completed from May 6, 2020. The Second Stage would the compilation of the Report of the Recount by the CEO. He anticipated a compilation of all discrepancies and tabulated votes to be included, in short, the Observer Report. The report of the CARICOM Scrutinizing Team was deemed to be complimentary to this stage. The Third Stage would be the crucial review of the CEO's Report by GECOM's Commissioners culminating in the final Fourth Stage when the declaration of results would be done by the Chairman of GECOM, the results of which he would accept. The President appealed to the citizens of Guyana to await the completion of the four stages.

The Presidents assured the nation that he would *"accept the declaration of the results by the elections commission, which will allow for a democratically elected government to be sworn into office. I am committed to uphold the Constitution and the rule of law. I respect the integrity and autonomous nature of the elections commission. I will abide by the declarations of the elections commission as I have abided by the rulings of the court[153]."*

On June 19, Mr. Khemraj Ramjattan, leader of the Alliance for Change and the Coalition's Prime Ministerial Candidate, conceded defeat to the PPP-C party when he met with his staff and stated that *"the loss of an election is tremendous. It is a difficult time for me, it's kinda emotional. But at some point in time you have to make a departure because there's always gonna be a winner and a loser...the declaration numbers are against us.[154]"* Nonetheless, Mr. Ramjattan was confident that the Coalition would provide the quality of opposition that was expected. He appealed to his staff and supporters not to despair.

Within a matter of days, the leaders of the APNU+AFC Coalition led a vicious campaign against CARICOM, specific leaders of the Regional governments, and the representatives of the ABCE countries who dared to declare that the elections were free and fair. Former Minister of Foreign Affairs, Mr. Carl Greenidge[155], was the voice of calm and reason from within the APNU+AFC camp. The consummate professional and diplomat, Mr. Greenidge was critical of the utterings of his colleagues in government who launched a verbal attack against the international community. He was adamant that Guyana and Guyanese needed the protection of the foreign powers in the defense of its territory. His comments were underpinned by simultaneous cases before the International Court of Justice (ICJ) with regard to the hearing of the Guyana-Venezuela border case and another one before the Caribbean Court of Justice (CCJ) challenging a ruling by the Court of Appeal in the continuing elections saga.

The former Minister of Foreign Affairs posited that *"you do not have the right to censor other people for pronouncing or giving a view on such matters."* He was alluding to the crude and inappropriate remarks made by Mr. Raphael Trotman, leader of the AFC and the Co-Chairman of the APNU+AFC Election Campaign, Mr. Joseph Harmon, who chastised the Prime Minister of Barbados, the Honorable Mia Mottley, the head of the Commonwealth Observer Mission, the former Prime Minister of Barbados, Mr. Owen Arthur and of the OAS Mission head, former Prime Minister of Jamaica, Mr. Bruce Golding and the Prime Minister of Trinidad and Tobago, Dr. Keith Rowley, for what they considered to be intrusion into the political affairs of Guyana and interfering with its sovereignty. The new Chairman of CARICOM, Prime Minister Dr. Ralph Gonsalves, did not escape the wrath of the APNU+AFC's Elections Campaign co-chairs.

Mr. Greenidge reminded the Coalition that if they have acted with integrity, the Court would have taken those actions into consideration. Censorship should not be used to prove proper conduct of the leadership. Many Guyanese from Generation X would be mindful of Guyana's prominent stance on protestations in the Apartheid fight against South Africa.

As the country's chief spokesperson on matters of diplomatic and other relations, he uttered the teachings that needed to be embraced by way of, *"A country's sovereignty needs to be very clearly separated from the action of any political party…the sovereignty of Guyana has to do with the rights of the people of Guyana to the territory within which they operate…if you are signatory to a treaty, for example, the Treaty of Chaguaramas or Human Rights … or Civil Society agreements then you are subject to those principles which you sign up to."*

During the first week of July 2020, APNU+AFC supporters took to the streets in peaceful protests in New Amsterdam, Linden, Buxton, Vigilance, Mandela Avenue and Sheriff Street in Georgetown[156]. However, prompt police action following the COVID-19 Guidelines caused a quick dispersal of the protestors.

When the U.S. Secretary of State, Mr. Mike Pompeo, on July 15, 2020, announced *"visa restrictions on the individuals responsible for or complicit in undermining democracy in Guyana. Immediate family members and such persons may also be subject to restrictions."* President Granger responded by stating that the Government of Guyana regretted the decision made by the U.S. Department of State as the matter was still before the Court. He maintained that the *"Executive Branch has not participated in the undermining of the electoral process[157]."* The visa restrictions may have been the ace in the hole that caused August 2, 2020, to become a reality sooner than later.

On August 2, 2020, after GECOM's Chairman, Justice Claudette Singh declared the People's Progressive Party-Civic (PPPC) the winner of the March 2, General and Regional Elections, President Irfaan Ali was sworn in. Former President David Granger, leader of APNU+AFC encouraged his supporters to be peaceful as the party continued to fight the results legally through an elections petition.

It didn't take long for the APNU+AFC partnership to display the cracks of a crumbling coalition. By October 4, two months after the elections results were officially declared, the AFC through its National Executive Committee accused APNU of breaching the Cummingsburg Accord[158]. The Accord was signed by five political parties committing to *"shared governance, inclusivity, partnership and mutual respect."* It brought the APNU+AFC into existence at the Georgetown Club on February 14, 2015. However, the new Agreement signed on December 24, 2019, allocated 30 percent of the seats secured by the coalition in the National Assembly to the AFC with APNU taking hold of 70 percent. The new Agreement provided for the allocation of seats at the Regional Democratic Councils (RDCs) level, too[159].

The bone of contention between the APNU and the AFC stemmed from APNU not honoring an agreement to allow the AFC to occupy the Vice-Chairmanship in three regions that it won. Within a matter of days following the election results declaration, two smaller but necessary, political parties, the JFAP and WPA, had already formally withdrawn from the Coalition. The WPA withdrew from the Coalition when they were not consulted on the specifics of the selection of National Assembly representatives and that of Region Four's Regional Democratic Council (RDC). On the other hand, JFAP stated that *"Guyana's political landscape is changing significantly, and it demands a re-examination of roles and relationships."*

CHAPTER 6: ELECTIONS OBSERVERS

"Voting is the most precious right of every citizen, and we have a moral obligation to ensure the integrity of our voting process." Hillary Clinton

Guyana's political landscape demanded the presence of both local and international Electoral Observers to ensure integrity of the electoral process, reduced post elections violence and the participation of citizens in the process. For the past three decades, Guyanese have seen the increase of international and local observers, more specifically, the Carter Centre, the OAS and the Commonwealth Observer Missions not forgetting the significant roles played by the CARICOM Secretariat and local business and social groups.

There is a General Elections (Observers) Act 1990[160] which empowers the President of the Cooperative Republic of Guyana to invite observers at the time of general elections for the purpose of observing the democratic processes and the conduct of the elections. The President consults with the Chairman of the Guyana Elections Commission on the matter of inviting foreign observers to observe the democratic processes and the conduct of the elections as stated in the Constitution of Guyana.

The domestic observers are accredited by GECOM by way of invitation via the news media and they must fulfill the criteria which must include citizenship of Guyana, impartiality in the conduct of their duties, professional independence, demonstrated commitment to democracy and human rights and previous knowledge and/or experience of electoral laws and procedures. There were 10 such qualified groups which included the Georgetown Chamber of Commerce, the Private Sector Commission, and the Guyana Bar Association.

On the other hand, the Ministry of Foreign Affairs was responsible for the accreditation of the international observers. The four Observer

Missions were from the Carter Center, the Commonwealth Secretariat, the European Union, and the Organization of American States. Regionally, CARICOM played a magnanimous role in Guyana's election process that was unparalleled in the history of election monitoring within the Caribbean Community. These international missions were led by bespoke men and women who were either former leaders of governments or heads of Electoral Missions, in the past.

Guyana's 2020 elections were not unlike those of the USA 2020 elections in that the integrity of the election results and voter participation were in question. The closeness of the 2016 USA Presidential election had sparked questions about electoral integrity. As a result, electoral integrity was assured by way of the invitation of international observation missions to monitor the electoral process in all but 13 USA States. The 2016 USA Presidential election was observed by an international Election Observation Mission from the Organization for Security and Cooperation in Europe (OSCE) Office for Democratic Institutions and Human Rights.

The Carter Center[161], like the CARICOM Secretariat, has traction in Guyana. It conducts its election observation missions in accordance with the Declaration of Principles for International Election Observation and Code of Conduct for International Election Observers that was adopted at the United Nations in 2005 and has been endorsed by more than 50 election observation groups. It was formed 38 years ago by a former President of the United States of America, Mr. Jimmy Carter, and his wife Ms. Rosalynn Carter in partnership with the Emory University. In as many years, it has conducted 113 elections in 39 countries.

Ten years after its formation, President Hugh Desmond Hoyte invited the Carter Center, to be included in the observation of elections in Guyana for the first time. Since that time, the Center has been involved in every subsequent election. Elections 2020 was the fifth time that it has been involved in Guyana's elections' process.

A team from the Center made exploratory visits to Guyana in 2019. Four electoral experts and six long-term observers were in Guyana as early as January 2020 engaging government officials, the political parties and other entities that were stakeholders. Prior to polling day, the former Prime Minister of Senegal, Ms. Aminata Touré, and Chairperson of the Carter Center Board of Trustees, Mr. Jason Carter, the grandson of former President Carter, served as co-leaders of the observation delegation and observed that ballot papers were already printed and that electoral preparations were well planned by GECOM within its legal framework.

The team of 41 observers from the Centre, during polling day, observed 220 polling stations throughout Guyana inclusive of the basics of counting, tabulation, and the announcement of results. The Center's report was positive as it related to the organization of the voting procedures.

According to their Report, the voting was peaceful and they commended the professionalism of the GECOM staff. A high level of transparency was noted with the presence of political scrutineers at the stations.

They had observed the proliferation of campaign paraphernalia within 200 yards of the polling stations in violations of the Laws of Guyana. Additionally, they reported that information booths were established within 200 yards of the polling stations which were operated by the APNU+AFC and the PPP-C within Administrative Regions 4, 7, 9 and 10.

On March 5, 2020, the Carter Centre[162] expressed its deep concerns about Mr. Clairmont Mingo's first announcement of unverified election Region 4 results, both vocally and in writing. As diplomatically as they could, they called on GECOM to apply all the rules under the Laws of Guyana to ensure credibility of results and accountability of elections officials.

By March 20, 2020, and after much consideration, the Center withdrew its team of electoral experts and international observers from Guyana indicating that they were willing to return to Guyana when the electoral process resumed and upon the feasibility of travel given the Covid-19 restrictions. They expressed grave concerns about the deteriorating security conditions in the country at the time and described how international observers were threatened and harassed for the world to see. They proffered that the legal challenges which followed the events of March 5, 2020, precluded any electoral activity to be observed.

On May 4, 2020, the United States Embassy reported that, by way of a Diplomatic Note, it had requested permission of the National Covid-19 Task Force and the Guyana Civil Aviation Authority by way of the Ministry of Foreign Affairs to fly to Guyana to monitor the Recount exercise. The request for flights scheduled for May 4, 2020, and May 30, 2020, to return to Guyana was denied. It was noted that the flight to Guyana from the USA scheduled for May 4, 2020, was given approval by the Task Force for permanent residents of the USA, USA citizens and others who wanted to return to their homes given the Covid-19 travel restrictions. However, the Carter Observer Team was outright denied any entry.

Several local, civil organizations rallied the Task Force and urged the Coalition government to invite the Carter Center to return to continue their observation of the Elections 2020 to ensure a speedy and transparent closure to the elections. The Private Sector Commission (PSC) referred to the Carter Center's experience in Guyana for the past 20 years. According to the PSC, *"the Carter Center is an accredited observer to the March 2020 election which remains incomplete until the declaration of the results[163]."* Strong appeals from the ABCE embassies even by way of tweets, went unheeded. The Acting Assistant Secretary for the US Department of State's Bureau of Western Hemisphere Affairs, Mr. Michael Kozak, Organisation for American States

(OAS) Secretary for Strengthening Democracy, Mr. Francisco Guerrero, along with United Nations Representative in Guyana, Ms. Mikkio Tanka; European Union Ambassador, Mr. Fernando Ponz Canto and the Canadian High Commissioner to Guyana, Ms. Lilian Chatterjee called on the Coalition government to approve the flight for the Carter Center Observer Mission to return to Guyana via their Twitter accounts. The strongest sentiments were from Mr. Kozak who wanted to *"ensure a transparent electoral recount."* The fight for democracy was strengthened and ongoing during this period.

Again, on May 15, 2020, the Coalition government refused to allow the Carter Center to participate in the observation of the National Recount. In so doing, the International Republican Institute's (IRI) Advisor was also denied entry even though he was present for the initial March 2 elections. Though the Center was denied, the CARICOM High-Level Team was given permission to enter Guyana to scrutinize the Recount. The foreign employees of the Oil and Gas sector were granted permission to fly to Guyana to continue their work assignments. As the Minister of Foreign Affairs, Dr. Karen Cummings, pointed out to the USA's Ambassador, Ms. Sarah-Ann Lynch; and a handful of US Senators, CARICOM was *"the most legitimate interlocutors in the Guyana situation.[164]."*

On August 3, 2020, the Center congratulated the new President of Guyana, His Excellency Dr. Irfaan Ali, recognized the statesmanship of the outgoing president, Brigadier David Granger for recognizing GECOM's declared results and commended the Chairman of GECOM, Justice Claudette Singh, for finalizing the results of the March 2020 elections. The leaders of Guyana were counselled to begin the inclusive, electoral and constitutional reform process, a recommendation consistent with the advice of the CARICOM High-Level Team. Their message was one of "strike while the iron is hot" as they stand to assist Guyana in the reform effort and to advance democratic principles.

The OAS Electoral Observation Mission[165] which arrived in Guyana on February 20, 2020, was led by the former Prime Minister of Jamaica, the Honorable Bruce Golding and was composed of 17 international observers from 13 countries, including specialists in electoral registries, electoral organization, electoral technology, electoral justice, campaign finance and the political participation of women. The Mission had observed five previous elections in addition to that of March 2, 2020. On February 21, 2020, the Mission observed the voting of the Disciplined Services and the General and Regional elections of March 2, 2020.

On March 13, 2020, the OAS Election Observer Mission was pleased to have declared that the March 2, 2020, poll was, in almost all respects, well executed. The subsequent tabulation of the Statements of Poll in nine of the ten administrative regions was carried out in compliance with the laws of Guyana and concluded that there were no disputations that had arisen in relation to the declaration of results.

"*However, the process employed by the Returning Officer for Region 4 is not transparent and, based on the numbers that have emanated since the process was first disrupted, is unlikely to produce a result that is credible and is able to command public confidence*" and therefore did not meet the standard requirements for fairness and transparency.

The Mission's withdrawal from Guyana, liken to that of the other international Missions, was predicated upon the non-adherence of the Region 4 Election's Officer to obey the legal orders of the High Court, more specifically, the non-display of the Statements of Poll for the Ballots from Region 4. Their concern was for the democracy of the country.

On May 13, 2020, at 10:00 EDT (14:00 GMT), the Permanent Council of the Organization of American States (OAS) held a virtual meeting during which the Chief of Mission presented the Mission's preliminary Report[166] on the Elections in Guyana. While presenting his Report, he paused and ad-libbed his experiences as an observer and described how he had "*never seen a more transparent effort to alter the results of an election.*" As he presented additional polling data to the Permanent Council, he added, "*You know it takes an extraordinarily courageous mind to present fictitious numbers when such a sturdy paper trail exists.[167]*"

These statements, more than any others, encapsulated the ethos of the March 2020 elections. The statements were the final nails in GECOM's and APNU+AFC's coffin of mistrust, lack of transparency and undemocratic values. Within minutes of uttering these words, the Campaign Manager of the APNU+AFC, as he was wont to do, immediately became defensive and sought to besmirch the name of the Chief of Mission, the Honourable Bruce Golding. Mr. Harmon accused Mr. Golding of being a friend of the Leader of the Opposition, Dr. Bharat Jagdeo. He went even further by declaring that Mr. Golding's "*partisanship and unquestionable links to the PPP compromise him and no longer can he be considered an independent observer. He has clearly demonstrated a bias for his close associates and appears to have now become an unabashed co-conspirator of the PPP as they seek to defy the will of the Guyanese people.[168]*"
Bear in mind that the Office of the President and the Ministry of Foreign Affairs had advised the OAS Secretariat that there was "*No Objection[169]*" to appointing the Honourable Bruce Golding as the Chief of Mission of the Electoral Observation Mission to Guyana.

Mr. Golding's final words in the Report were, "*A litmus test of any democracy is the peaceful and orderly transfer of power if that is so ordained by the expressed will of the people. Sadly, Guyana has failed that test. The people of Guyana are not to be blamed. They expressed their will in a commendably peaceful and orderly manner on March 2 but the pernicious actions of a few have wreaked considerable damage to Guyana's image and reputation. Even if this debacle is soon and satisfactorily resolved, it will perhaps take a generation and significant institutional reforms for that damage to be fully repaired. The people of Guyana did not deserve this.*[170]"

The OAS Mission was fully involved in the Recount process. Within the month of June 2020, the OAS had published four preliminary statements on the on-going Recount process. There were concerns about the lack of a credible result in particular because of the global health crisis where decisive actions were crucial in stemming the tide of the corona virus. Another point which was deemed ridiculous by most Guyanese and penned by the OAS Mission was the proposal by the Chief Elections Officer that would have required five months to recount less than 500,000 ballots. Such a proposal was unheard of in any democracy and unacceptable under any set of circumstances. The Mission reported that the review of the ballot boxes was conducted in a *"professional, transparent and impartial fashion,"* which allowed members of GECOM, political parties and other stakeholders to accurately determine the results for each polling station.

The Chief of Mission provided clarity as to the difference between the declarations of the results of Region 4 by the Returning Officer, Mr. Mingo and the results as tabulated during the Recount process. For example, in Ballot box 4062[171], *"the Statement of Poll had indicated 182 votes for APNU and 43 for PPP-C the returning officer reported those results as 292 votes for APNU and 33 votes for PPP."* The Statement of Recount agreed with the Statement of Polls from the March 2, 2020, elections. He quoted a handful of examples with the general trend being an excess of votes for the APNU+AFC while votes were systematically reduced by the RO for the PPP-C.

Due to their concerns over the high level of inaccurate information emanating from GECOM, the Electoral Observation Mission repeatedly requested copies of the Statements of Poll which were prepared at each polling station on the night of March 2, and the Statements of Recount prepared during the Recount process. The purpose of the request was to carry out their own variance analysis of the original and recounted results. The Mission pointed out that the electoral procedures agreement signed between the OAS and GECOM on February 26, 2020, guaranteed access to these materials. GECOM refused to provide the Electoral Observation Mission with the requested documents.

On July 21, 2020, at the request of the Secretary General, Mr. Luis Almagro, a virtual, special meeting of the Permanent Council of the OAS was held from 18:30 GMT to consider the state of the electoral process in Guyana. In attendance were the Minister of Foreign Affairs, Dr. Karen Cummings and the Attorney General, Mr. Basil Williams.

Mr. Williams asserted that the Caribbean Court of Justice *"never made a ruling that the results of the recount must be used by GECOM to determine the results of the elections, that was never a decision of the CCJ.*[172]" A fortnight earlier, the CCJ had ruled that the Recount Order was valid and was to be adhered to. He blamed the PPP-C for the long litigation battles which prevented a quick declaration of the election results.

On the other hand, Dr. Karen Cummings[173] in her presentation, stated that the Executive Branch of the government of Guyana has consistently respected the laws of the land, the Courts and the authority of GECOM. She appealed to the international observers and the ABCE countries not to intervene in Guyana's electoral affairs to dictate a specific outcome, which she deemed premature.

Mr. Anil Nandlall,[174] the former Attorney General who is a representative of the PPP-C, accused both Dr. Cummings and Mr. Williams of misrepresentation of the truth to the Permanent Council, and of uttering lies and fabrications.

Sir Ronald Sanders, Antigua and Barbuda's Permanent Representative to the OAS was passionate of the political impasse in Guyana as was glimmered in his many articles in the Caribbean news media. He believed that democracy was being denied in Guyana. His statement to the people of the Region at the Extraordinary Meeting of the Council, was that, *"The national recount that was certified by each of the supervisors of each of the regions in Guyana, showed that the Peoples Progressive Party/Civic had won the election. But despite, the best efforts of CARICOM, utilizing all its institutions, including the final Appellate Court, the Caribbean Court of Justice (CCJ), one party has persistently delayed acceptance of the result and frustrated a democratic and peaceful end to this matter.[175]"*

On July 30, 2020, the Secretary General of the Organisation of American States (OAS), Mr. Luis Almagro, with some 1.4M Twitter followers, tweeted that *"The right of appeal is a privilege that should not be abused, especially in deferring the will of the people. Guyana has spoken. GECOM must declare results based on the recount,[176]"* and this was an exasperating response after the many legal appeals and counter appeals to the results of the National Recount process. He opined that the judiciary should not be the refuge of those intent on delaying the inevitable results of the General and Regional Elections.

A couple of days later, on August 2, 2020, Secretary-General Mr. Luis Almagro congratulated the new President of Guyana, His Excellency Dr. Mohamed Irfaan Ali, on his ascension to the highest post in the country and the people of Guyana for their patience and the Chairman of GECOM for being resolute in her firm stand against the myriad attempts to undermine the will of the people of Guyana.

One of the most influential bodies to observe elections throughout the Commonwealth was from the Commonwealth Secretariat. Its approach to the monitoring of elections is rooted in the Guidelines for the Establishment of Commonwealth Groups to Observe Elections in Member

Countries, which was adopted at the Commonwealth Heads of Government Meeting in Harare in 1991.[177]

The Commonwealth Secretariat was one of the original signatories to the Declaration of Principles for International Election Observation, agreed at the United Nations in 2005, which is followed by election observers all around the world.

The Commonwealth Observer Groups to Guyana was composed of eminent persons from a range of fields, including electoral commissioners and parliamentarians, and legal, gender and human rights and media experts. The 11-member Mission was led by Rt. Hon Owen Arthur, a former Prime Minister of Barbados; Ms Lebrechtta Nana Oye Bayne, Social Economist and Gender Expert, Antigua and Barbuda; Sir Gerald A. Watt KCN QC, Speaker of the House of Representatives, Antigua and Barbuda; Ms Lisa Shoman, former Foreign Minister, Tribunal Judge and Senior Counsel and Ms Josephine Tamai, Chief Elections Officer of Belize; Mr John Hendra, former United Nations Assistant Secretary-General, Canada; Hon Gitobu Imathiu Imanyara, Former MP, Kenya; Ms Mitra Vasisht, Ambassador of India (Retired), India; Ms Sarah Fradgley, Media Expert, New Zealand; Dr Paikiasothy Saravanamuttu, Executive Director, Centre for Policy Alternatives, Sri Lanka; and Mr Stephen John Hiscock, Retired Diplomat, United Kingdom. It was constituted by the Commonwealth Secretary General, the Rt. Hon. Patricia Scotland QC, following an invitation from the Minister of Foreign Affairs, Dr. Karen Cummings.

The Group arrived in Guyana on February 23, 2020, though some members of staff of the Commonwealth Secretariat were in Guyana a week prior to observe the voting of the Disciplined Services. It was the seventh consecutive election observed by the Group in Guyana.

The Groups' mandate was to observe and consider the factors affecting the credibility of the electoral process in Guyana. The criteria for judging the fairness and credibility were according to the standards for democratic elections to which the government of Guyana had committed, including national legislation and relevant regional, Commonwealth and international commitments.

One of the first statements made by the Group leader was, *"We are aware of the significance of these elections to the people of Guyana and we call on all stakeholders to demonstrate commitment to a peaceful, transparent, credible and inclusive election."*

Between March 5, 2020, and August 3, 2020, the Commonwealth Secretariat issued 11 Press Statements ranging from an assessment of the Region 4 tabulation to a congratulatory message from the Secretary General. Two of the statements were joined with that of other international observer bodies in Guyana, six were penned by the Secretary-General and the remaining three were from the Commonwealth Observer Group.

Noteworthy was the Group's focus on the GECOM[178] Secretariat staff's noncompliance with the mandates of the Courts of Guyana or even that of the CCJ. An appeal was made to the Guyana Elections Commission, inclusive of the Chairperson, the Commissioners, the Chief Elections Officer, and Returning Officer for Region 4 to ensure democracy was preserved in Guyana. The Secretary General warned of the serious violation of the Commonwealth Charter to which Guyana ascribed which recognized the *"inalienable right of individuals to participate in democratic processes, in particular through free and fair elections in shaping the society in which they live.[179]"*

By March 16, 2020; the Secretary General, Baroness Patricia Scotland, welcomed the CARICOM initiative which would facilitate the recounting of ballots given that the tabulation in Region 4 was not conducted in accordance with the unambiguous judgement of the Acting Chief Justice and was therefore not credible, transparent nor inclusive. Therefore, on March 15, 2020, the Group withdrew from Guyana.

Three days later, on 18 March 2020, the Commonwealth Observer Group listed a plethora of challenges which it deemed to be of grave concern during the tabulation process inclusive of the repeated *"cessation of the tabulation process for a variety of irregular reasons,[180]"* the unlawful declaration by Mr. Mingo despite the tabulation process having ceased and Mr. Mingo's non-compliance with the orders and judgements of the Acting Chief Justice of March 11 and March 13.

The Group's Statement was particularly harsh on GECOM's leadership, given its authority, who did not try to correct the blatant deficiencies which were presented for the whole world to witness. Consequently, the Commonwealth Ministerial Action Group (CMAG) set up by the Commonwealth to deal with persistent and serious violators of its shared principles on March 30, 2020 during its 56th meeting called on GECOM *"to immediately fulfil its constitutional mandate and ensure the sovereign right of the people of Guyana to duly elect their Government is respected through a transparent and credible counting and tabulation process."* The meeting was chaired by Ambassador Raychelle Omamo SC, EGH, Cabinet Secretary for Foreign Affairs of Kenya. Ministers and Representatives of Australia, Barbados, Belize, Ghana, Malaysia, Namibia and the United Kingdom also participated in the video conference. It was posited that Guyana would face expulsion from the Commonwealth if it failed to comply with the Charter within a reasonable time.

The Secretary General in congratulating Dr. Irfaan Ali as the new President of Guyana praised the Chairman of GECOM for her courage, the Group and expressed sympathy for the Chairman of the Group, Rt Hon Owen Arthur, former Prime Minister of Barbados, who passed away before the final results were made known, officially.

The European Union (EU)[181]deployed the EU Election Observation Mission to Guyana between January 25 and March 20, 2020, and it was led by Mr. Urmas Paet, a Member of the European Parliament from Estonia. The mission comprised 55 observers from 25 EU member states and Norway. There was a core of 9 team analysts who were based in Georgetown, 14 long term-observers, 20 short-term observers deployed across Guyana in addition to locally recruited short-term observers from EU Delegation and EU member states' diplomatic missions accredited to Guyana. The mission's mandate was to assess the electoral process against international obligations and commitments for democratic elections as well as the laws of Guyana. The Mission was invited by President David A. Granger.

The EU EOM was first in Guyana to observe the 2001 General and Regional Elections. They departed for the EU because of the Covid-19 pandemic fearing for the safety of their team members. The EOM called on all stakeholders to complete the electoral process in a credible and transparent way in accordance with the laws of Guyana. They were the third Mission to depart Guyana at a time when the Region 4 results were in dispute. Furthermore, litigation after litigation prevented an early or timely declaration of a winner.

The EU EOM shared many of the same challenges as those reported by the other international monitors. However, on March 12, 2020 the EOM's Deputy Chief Observer, Mr. Alexander Matus, wrote Region 4's Returning Officer, Mr. Clairmont Mingo and requested that the Statements of Poll (SOPs) be examined from which he prepared his spreadsheet tabulating the votes pursuant to Section 4 (1) and (3) of the General Elections (Observers) Act, as well as Section 6, 7, 8 and 9 of the Administrative Arrangement between the Delegation of the European Union in Guyana and GECOM[182][182]. The request was made after the Chief Justice had ordered Mr. Mingo, who had breached the law, to return to the tabulation process to either start afresh or resume the verification process. Mr. Mingo had continued to use his disputed spreadsheet causing great consternation to all election observers, local and international.

The EOM was most vocal and forthright with regard to GECOM and officials of GECOM. On June 5, 2020, the EU Ambassador to Guyana, Mr. Fernando Ponz Cantó, presented the EOM's Final Report to the Chairperson of GECOM, Justice Claudette Singh at the Arthur Chung Conference Center and it contained some damning content as it related to GECOM. According to the Report, *"Officials of the Guyana Elections Commission (GECOM) acted in blatant violation of the law and High Court orders… By failing to take decisive action as the electoral process derailed into chaos and illegality, GECOM abdicated its constitutional duty to take all actions necessary to ensure compliance with the law by any of its officials, despite unequivocal powers to remove and exercise disciplinary control over them[183].[183]."*

In the Report was contained 26 recommendations for the improvement to the electoral process of which 8 were of high priority. The recommendations covered the electoral legislation, legislative, administrative, the election system and constituency delimitation, election administration and voter registration.

In summary, the high priority recommendations contained a review and consolidation of the fragmented election legislation to strengthen legal clarity and certainty; launching of a national consultation process to overhaul the composition and functioning of GECOM; the development of effective legislation to regulate political finance; and the introduction of a legal and regulatory system that transforms the state-owned media into a genuine public service broadcaster.[184]

In March 2021, the European Union Election Observation Mission (EU EOM) to the 2020 general and regional elections returned to Guyana to present the Report's recommendations to stakeholders to assist in kick-starting election reforms. Mr. Urmas Paet, the Chief Observer of the EU EOM, met with the President Ali, the Speaker of the National Assembly, Mr. Nadir, the Chairperson of the Guyana Elections Commission, Justice Singh, the Leader of the Opposition, Mr. Harmon, the Attorney General, Mr. Nandlall, the Chief Justice, Justice George-Wiltshire and the Minister of Foreign Affairs, Mr. Todd.

Mr. Paet warned at the press conference held to brief the public, *"Now is the time for decisions and actions. For election reform to be effective, its implementation needs to begin well before the next elections are called. Inclusive and transparent reform processes help build confidence in elections and their results.[185]"*

Recommendations By Observers
Appendix 1

Summary of Recommendations	(1)	(2)	(3)	(4)	(5)
1.　Revisit the electoral governance system.	X	X	X	X	X
2.　Political audit of the operations and behavior of GECOM's Commission and Secretariat.	X		X		
3.　Establish a Code of Conduct governing the Political Party Agents/Political Parties.	X				
4.　Launch an investigation into missing 2020 election documents and inquiry into the March2, 2020 elections.	X		X		
5.　Improve voter education among citizens.	X		X	X	
6.　Prohibit the use of state resources for political campaigning to create a more level playing field.		X	X	X	
7.　Provide on-going training for poll workers and other critical support staff.	X				X
8.　Re-registration of all voters in Guyana via House-to-House Registration.	X			X	X

Key: **(1)** - CARICOM Secretariat; **(2)** – Carter Center; **(3)** - Commonwealth Secretariat; **(4)** - European Union; **(5)** - OAS

Summary of Recommendations	(1)	(2)	(3)	(4)	(5)
9. Establishment of an advisory body to serves as a point of communication between political parties and GECOM	X			X	X
10. Review the use of private residences as polling stations					X
11. Identify Polling Stations where the layout takes into account the needs of the elderly & voters with disabilities.			X		
12. Development of an Electoral Operational Manual.	X		X	X	X
13. Development a fully integratable Electoral Management Information system.			X		X
14. Official tabulated elections results should be available online, through GECOM's official web site,			X	X	X
15. Restructuring of GECOM to ensure political independence & confidence by stakeholders.	X	X	X	X	
16. Establishment of a Helpdesk Management system to effectively manage and control the delivery of electoral material.			X		X

Key: **(1)** - CARICOM Secretariat; **(2)** – Carter Center; **(3)** - Commonwealth Secretariat; **(4)** - European Union; **(5)** - OAS

Summary of Recommendations	(1)	(2)	(3)	(4)	(5)
17. Establishment of an election dispute resolution system to address electoral concerns in a timely manner throughout the electoral process.			X	X	
18. Review and harmonize the legal protection of electoral and human rights, especially by incorporating and enacting ratified international law treaties, such as CRPD, ICRMW, UNCAC and ICAC into the national legal framework			X	X	
19. Create a robust domestic mechanism to consider electoral and constitutional reforms.			X	X	
20. Review and consolidate the fragmented election legislation to strengthen legal clarity and certainty.		X	X	X	X
21. Introduce a legal and regulatory system that transforms the state-owned media into a genuine public service broadcaster				X	

Key: **(1)** - CARICOM Secretariat; **(2)** – Carter Center; **(3)** - Commonwealth Secretariat; **(4)** - European Union; **(5)** - OAS

The local observers included the Bar Association of Guyana, the Guyana Public Service Union, the Private Sector Commission, American Chamber of Commerce – Guyana and the Georgetown Chamber of Commerce amongst others whose reputation were such as to warrant accreditation. Together, these local entities championed the cause of democracy at a time when electoral systems appeared to be creaking under the weight of fraud and malicious intent.

The Bar Association of Guyana (BAG), founded in 1980, is a voluntary, unregistered body comprising of Attorneys-at-Law duly admitted to practice law in Guyana. It is the official legal body representing lawyers in Guyana and is governed by a twelve-member Bar Council, elected annually. BAG is made up of a President, two Vice-Presidents, a Secretary, an Assistant Secretary and a Treasurer which comprises the Executive and six Council Members. It was accredited by the Guyana Elections Commission (GECOM) as a Local Observer of the 2020 General and Regional Elections.

On March 4, 2020, BAG reported that GECOM staff had discharged *"their duties on election day with professionalism and competence to ensure free and fair elections throughout Guyana[186]"* and reminded the electorate of the time-consuming nature of the process of declaring accurate results of the elections. BAG had no idea, at the time, that more than 150 days were required. Historically, it took 3-5 days.

However, by March 7, 2020, BAG's Observer team noted the halt to the tabulation process of March 4, 2020, which had not recommenced. Furthermore, it reported that a declaration of results for District/Region 4 was made on March 5, 2020, and therefore, joined with the international Observer Missions and the diplomats of the ABCE countries projecting that there could be no lawful declarations of the results of the General and Regional Elections until all legal requirements have been complied with by GECOM to ensure transparency and credibility of those results.

The Bar Council called on the Chairperson of GECOM, Retired Justice Claudette Singh, to ensure that all necessary steps are taken so that the results would withstand local and international scrutiny and represented the highest international standards as would make all Guyanese proud in the process, before making any declaration required by law. The Council expressed grave concerns about the repercussions of the swearing in of a President of Guyana based on the unlawfully declared results.

On April 16, 2020, BAG beseeched GECOM to act expeditiously to enable an accurate and transparent declaration of results from the March 2 elections noting that a constitutional deadline for the convening of a new Parliament was fast approaching on April 30, 2020, as outlined in Article 69 of the Constitution of Guyana. It chastised GECOM's administration for its less than professional approach to the declaration of results. As a legal body is wont to do, BAG was fired up about the barrage of attacks on the judicial system from all sides of the political divide. They denounced and censored all conducts and actions regarding the political matters before the High Court and the Caribbean Court of Justice designed to interfere with and prejudice the administration of justice.

The Private Sector Commission (PSC) was relentless in its role as an election observer and defender of democracy. Along with 27 NGOs ranging from a wide cross section of civil society, business groups to faith-based organizations, on March 31, it wrote the Executive Secretary of the Inter-American Commission on Human Rights requesting support in the fight to maintain democracy and justice within Guyana. The PSC further appealed *"for the swift assistance of the Inter-American Commission on Human Rights to act to avert a situation that could lead to a humanitarian crisis.[187]"*

It was the PSC that called for a national recount to be broadcasted live on radio and television and streamed live for international observers who were unable to be physically present at the GECOM recount proceedings because of the Covid-19 pandemic. On April 6, 2020, it appealed to the Commonwealth Secretariat, the Organization of American State, the European Union, the Carter Center and the Caribbean Community to return to Guyana for the commencement of the recount by GECOM given that the Guyana Court of Appeal had ruled that GECOM had the power to proceed with a recount of the ballots cast in the March 2nd General and Regional Elections.

The next local heavy roller among the observers was the Georgetown Chamber of Commerce (GCCI) whose President, Mr. Nicholas Deygoo-Boyer, in November 2019 recommended a Code of Ethics to be put in place for the political parties contesting the March 2020 elections. He felt that it was crucial to a peaceful process given the ethnic security challenges in Guyana.

The GGCI's most significant role was played during the Recount Exercise when they collaborated with other accredited Local Observers to cover 100% of the workstations. On June 14, 2020, the GCCI released their Summary Statement of Recount Report[188] which reflected the Observer Team's focus on the legal and policy aspects of the electoral process. Clearly from Mr. Deygoo-Boyer's comments, the Team was looking at the security arrangements, the role of the ranks of the Guyana Police Force, political interference, and administrative short-comings. Of importance to the GCCI's Team was the media perspective as they examined *"the frequency and manner in which pertinent information was provided to the media by GECOM."*

GCCI's Team provided greater details than any other entity which monitored the National Recount and were guests of many TV stations analyzing the tabulation and verification process in a clear and concise manner. Quite reassuring was the Chamber's pronouncement on the claims made by the Coalition government that dead and migrated people voted. GCCI pronounced that no political parties and no observers were given a chance to check whether ballots were issued for these alleged voters since requests to visually confirm serial numbers of ballots in question were denied

Generally, the GGCI's Team was satisfied that the results were free, fair and credible and commended GECOM for their efforts in spite of the lengthy process.

CHAPTER 7: CARICOM

"I hate all politics. I don't like either political party. One should not belong to them - one should be an individual, standing in the middle. Anyone that belongs to a party stops thinking." Ray Bradbury

CARICOM, the Region's 15-member integration body, was the crucial linchpin for securing the principles of electoral integrity in Guyana. It was placed in this unenviable position, when all else appeared to have been lost during Elections 2020. CARICOM was one of the Observer missions which sought to strengthen the transparency of election procedures during the Guyana Elections 2020. Implicit in their role was the promotion of international standards and principles and finally, to recommend reforms which would be implemented at the earliest possible time despite the reluctance on the part of the 2 major parties to have reform recommendations realized.

This has been one of CARICOM's most taxing roles for close to 5 decades. It was being judged by the Government in power, the Opposition, and the people of the Region, more specifically and most harshly, by the people of Guyana. Reference must be made to the initial chapter of the book, Revised Treaty Of Chaguaramas Establishing The Caribbean Community Including The Caricom Single Market And Economy, which makes it pellucid that CARICOM as per Article V of the Revised Treaty Chaguaramas (the CARICOM Treaty), the Charter states that *"The States shall ensure the existence of a fair and open democratic system through the holding of free elections at reasonable intervals, by secret ballot, underpinned by an electoral system in which all can have confidence, and which will ensure the free expression of the will of the people in the choice of their representatives."*

Though the climate in Guyana among the restless Guyanese appeared not to favour CARICOM's participation in their elections, it was not unusual for the CARICOM Elections Observation Mission (CEOM) to fulfill its obligations to Member States as prescribed in the Charter of Civil Society which the Conference of Heads of Government adopted on February 19, 1997. A CEOM was invited to Suriname for the elections of May 25, 2020, and Antigua and Barbuda on March 21, 2018, which was headed by Guyana's CEO of GECOM, Mr. Keith Lowenfield. During the 2020 pandemic, when it was risky to send Observers anywhere throughout the Region, the CEOM monitored the St. Vincent and the Grenadines of November 5, 2020, and that of Belize's elections of November 11, 2020.

By February 28, 2020, all members of the CARICOM[189] Election Observation Mission were in Guyana, to monitor the country's Regional and General Elections and remained until March 4. In November 2019, the Minister of Foreign Affairs of Guyana, the Honorable Dr. Karen Cummings officially informed the CARICOM Secretariat of the proclamation that General and Regional Elections would be held March 2 and as such invited them to ensure the transparency of all electoral processes thereby ensuring a high level of confidence in the elections' results given the history of elections in Guyana.

A Saint Lucian, Ms. Cynthia Cleopatra Combie Martyr, lead the 17-member CEOM. Members of the Mission included electoral management experts such as Mr. John M. Jarvis and Ms. Carolyn Thomas-Parker of Antigua and Barbuda; Mr. Philip Anthony Turner of The Bahamas; Ms. Lesa Collins and Mr. Leonard Walters of Barbados; Ms. Yves-Marie Edouard of Haiti; Mr. Glendon Ricardo Bennett of Jamaica; His Excellency Mr. Lionel Sydney Osborne of St. Kitts and Nevis; Mr. Gaspar Jn. Baptiste of Saint Lucia; Mr. Sylvester Anthony King of St. Vincent and the Grenadines; Ms. Renuka Raghoe of Suriname; and Ms. Fern Narcis-Scope and Dr. Noel Kalicharan of Trinidad and Tobago. The CEOM was fully supported by the Directorate of Foreign and Community Relations of the CARICOM Secretariat.

The Mission[190] outlined it roles, in addition to observing the electoral process, to collect quantitative and qualitative information and observations of the voting process and the results, observe and assess the outcome of the elections and its initial impact on the social and political environment and the preparation of a Final Report on the Elections which would include recommendations as the Mission deems fit. They met with officials of GECOM, 9 leaders of political parties contesting the elections, the Commissioner of Police of the Guyana Police Force, the Ethnic Relations Commission, presidents and members of the 3 leading trade unions along with members of the private sector groups and faith-based organizations. The intent was to get a feel of the political environment in which they would operate. They attended political rallies and visited polling stations.[191]

On March 4, 2020, the CEOM was satisfied that the conduct of the Poll for Regional and General Elections on March 2 in Guyana was *"free, fair and transparent,"* saluted GECOM for their administrative abilities and expressed gratitude to the people of Guyana for the peaceful conduct of their Poll.

Ms. Cynthia Combie Martyr presented CEOM's Preliminary Statement at a Media Briefing at the Headquarters of the CARICOM Secretariat on March 4, 2020, to a room full of heads of governments and members of other regional and international observation missions. Those other Missions included the Organization of American States (OAS), the Commonwealth, the Carter Centre, and the European Union, as well as Ambassadors Accredited to CARICOM who were resident in Guyana and various members of the diplomatic community in Guyana.

Aside from mentioning some minor challenges and delays of an acceptable nature, the report concluded that the issues were not significant enough to *"affect the overall outcome of the poll."* Among those areas is the need for more detailed scrutiny of the fingers and hands of voters for any visible signs of previous voting. However, the report pointed out that the *"process of voter identification was appropriate to avert the possibility of double voting or voter fraud of that kind."*

Another area of concern was the fact that Poll Workers were allowed to leave their respective stations to go and vote at another location. The report noted that there *"were times when poll workers were noticeably absent which could effectively and in some instances, slow down the Polling Process…In this regard, it is one of the recommendations of the CARICOM Observers that provision must be made to include Poll Workers in the ADVANCE POLL."*

Ms. Martyr said the Mission was also concerned about the rejection of a few ballots due to improper folding. *"CARICOM Election Observer Mission was committed to ensuring the preservation of the democratic process and to make certain that every valid vote cast must be counted, in order to be regarded as a vote for the party of the elector's choice."*

The Mission applauded GECOM for a job reasonably well done as it related to the conduct of the poll and poll activities on Polling Day, including the count and issue and presentation of Statements of Poll on Election Day.

On March 6, 2020, due to the suspicious and non-transparent actions of certain members of GECOM, the CEOM stated that the transparent tabulation process which started on March 4, 2020, using the Statements of Poll and was in accord with the legislative provisions of Section 84 of the Representation of the People Act Cap 1.03 Revised Edition of the Laws of Guyana, was interrupted and remained incomplete. The CEOM begged for the resumption of the tabulation of results for Region 4 under the independent control of the Returning Officer, as these scores are necessary and critical, in order to determine the outcome of the National Poll.

Thereafter, the CEOM supported the Joint Statement of March 6, 2020, as issued by the International Observer Missions from the Commonwealth, the Organization of American States, the European Union and the Carter Center. It appealed to GECOM to continue by tabulating the results for Region 4, in accordance with the laws of Guyana. Furthermore, the Mission appealed to the Political Parties and the People of the Cooperative Republic of Guyana to co-operate with the process, by honoring the subscribed codes of conduct.

Corresponding to the statements made to the News Media by Chief of Mission of CEOM, the Chairman of the Caribbean Community, the Honourable Mia Mottley Q.C, MP on March 7, 2020 issued a statement[192] calling on *"the electoral officials in Guyana and the representative political parties to work together to achieve a peaceful and lawful completion of the electoral process in Guyana by ensuring the tabulation of the results in all Regions using the Statement of Polls in a transparent manner in the presence of the representatives of the political parties and the electoral observers.*

Indeed, CARICOM issued a statement on Thursday night and one was also issued yesterday from the Chief of the independent CARICOM Electoral Observation team. Both statements called on GECOM to complete the electoral process.

We are very clear, every vote must be made to count; and transparently so. We have noted that all sides have been making serious allegations against each other.

It is critical that good sense prevail. The Preservation of law and order is paramount and All parties must work hard to ensure that there is peace on the roads and in the communities across Guyana. There has already been one death reported overnight. That is one death too many.

In simple language, we ask the parties to recognise that the primary consideration must not only be who will be President but, moreso, who will be alive come next week or next month, for there cannot be a tolerance for any further loss of life.

I have spoken to both the President and the Leader of the Opposition and indicated that CARICOM stands ready to be able to be there to facilitate further dialogue and any actions that are necessary.

We have done this on many occasions in the past, including in Guyana, when elections have been highly contentious and when social order and the rule of law has been threatened across the region.

We are family and this is what happens when there are disputes in families. We will work together to create the space for dialogue and resolution once there is an acceptance on the part of all parties that there is a higher interest beyond simply the result in this election."

Given the rising political and social tensions following the cessation of the tabulation process for Region 4, covering the period from March 11 to March 12, 2020 in a Press Conference[193] hosted by the Chairman of CARICOM, Prime Minister Mia Mottley of Barbados along with a delegation of CARICOM heads of government including Prime Minister

Roosevelt Skerrit of Dominica; Dr. Keith Mitchell of Grenada; Dr. Ralph Gonsalves of St. Vincent and the Grenadines and Dr. Keith Rowley of Trinidad and Tobago, there was an impassioned plea for a transparent tabulation process, the role of democracy in the Region and they expressed their love for the citizens of Guyana.

The Honourable Mia Mottley stated:

"Thank you very much. Ladies and gentlemen of the media. Caribbean people. As you can see five Prime Ministers of the Community visited Guyana yesterday and we had a series of meetings with different parties. We met with the President and we met with the executive of APNU/AFC. We met with the Leader of the Opposition Bharrat Jagdeo as well as the Presidential candidate Irfan Ali and other members of the executive of PPP. We also met with the representatives of the small parties. We met with the election observers, and then again we met with the President and Mr. Jagdeo very late last night, early into the morning, together, in order to be able to chart a process forward.

We the leaders of the Caribbean Community are committed to working with the people of Guyana for a free and fair process and transparent process. And we made it clear, because there is simply too much at stake for the people of Guyana. Georgetown is the home, the seat of the Caribbean Community. Guyana is a founding member of the Caribbean community and against that background, we are clear that as a community of sovereign Nations we cannot get involved in the in internal processes, but we are family, and family does not stand by and watch others in the family suffer without making themselves available to be able to aid the process.

We have tried to do that. But we are also conscious that we will be as successful as the parties themselves want to be successful and that while we can create the space for them to speak they have to have the will for this to work.

There is no doubt in our minds that there is at stake far more than who will be the president of Guyana. What is at stake is also the lives and the stability of the people of Guyana. We find ourselves today, as we speak, in a world that is exceedingly uncertain that is being challenged in a way that we never contemplated that the third decade of the 21st century would be challenged in this way. It is therefore even more important for us within the Caribbean Community to ensure that there is stability from the North in the Bahamas to the south in Guyana and Suriname, from the West in Belize, to the East in Barbados. And it is against that background that we have appealed to both sides. Both sides committed to the fact that they want to be able to abide by the laws of Guyana and the constitution of Guyana. They have also committed that they believe that there ought to be a free and fair transparent process.

Pursuant to that, they met with the representatives of their own Commissioners with GECOM and we can only hope that both sides therefore will be able to put in place a mechanism that will allow for a fair and transparent process because as I said last Saturday every vote must be counted.

The Chief Justice of Guyana ruled yesterday, and her ruling was absolutely clear. That she expects the returning officer to either start a new or complete the process with respect to the SOPs. And we hope and pray that there will be an adherence to, not just the law of the Judgment, but to the spirit of the Judgment, because she was very clear in the last few paragraphs of her judgment as to what she expected in terms of the spirit and the principal position and the transparent process that is critical if this country is to go forward.

We hope therefore that good sense would prevail on all sides. We have asked both sides to be able to speak to their supporters.

Part of the difficulty in a complex situation like this is that everyone, if they feel that they are a victim then the opportunities for disappointment regrettably are very much there.

Against this background, this morning we have also said clearly that any attempt to be able to stall the process or any attempt to be able to obfuscate the process is one that runs against the spirit of the Chief Justice's judgment. And it is against this background that we pray that even though a statute puts power in the hands of a Returning Officer that that Returning Officer will understand that he holds in his hands the future and stability of Guyana as we go forward, because every vote must be made to count.

We can't say it any clearer. And also it must appear to be so in the presence not just of the Observers but more importantly of all of the parties who contested the election because everyone has a right to be able to determine whether the process is fair to them. And also whether they have the right to ask for a recount.

I'm satisfied that the President and the Leader of the Opposition are aware of our position. I'm satisfied that they too have agreed to act in the best interests of this country. But they must now ensure that all under them too will act in that way. Failing that, we believe that we will have to continue to keep engaged. This is not a single event. This is a process, and we are cognizant that this process didn't get here overnight and it is not necessarily going to be miraculously achieved and changed overnight. But at this point, the most important thing, even as we fight this COVID-19 virus, is for the people of Guyana to remain calm, to remain patient, and to allow us to help both sides and their supporters understand that it is only through a transparent and open process that we can go forward.

I want to say this finally. This country is on the cusp of turning the corner economically, but it must also be on the cusp of making every Guyanese a winner and not a loser. Our fear is that if the process is not transparent that we put at risk too much, and I therefore hope that the people of Guyana will work together to ensure that there is calm; there is peace. One life lost, as I said last week is one life too many. Let us not have any other person's affected at this point. Thank you very much."

On March 17, 2020, CARICOM withdrew the independent High-Level Team it fielded on March 14, 2020, to scrutinize the re-counting of the ballots in Region 4. The Team was mobilized immediately following discussion held at the request of His Excellency David Granger, President of Guyana, on Saturday 14 March 2020. It was important that the Team was viewed as a means of bolstering the transparency of the electoral process and the legitimacy of the recount results.

The members of this first CARICOM Team which were in Guyana waiting patiently for the start of the Recount exercise were Ms. Francine Baron, former Attorney-General and Foreign Minister of Dominica and team leader; Mr Anthony Boatswain, former Minister of Finance of Grenada and Ms Cynthia Barrow-Giles, Senior Lecturer in the Department of Government at the University of the West Indies; Ms Angela Taylor, Chief Elections Officers of Barbados; and Ms Fern Narcis-Scope, the Chief Elections Officers of Trinidad and Tobago.

Clandestine legal maneuverings by members of the APNU+AFC determined that, by way of an injunction, the implementation of the Aide Memoir would not have become a reality within the timeframe allocated by GECOM and CARICOM. A High Court order issued on March 17, 2020, was granted by Judge Franklyn Holder at the request of Ms Ulita Grace Moore, private citizen, and candidate for the APNU+AFC whose lawyer Mr. Mayo Robertson represented the Coalition government in the No Confidence Motion brought against the government. The Court of Appeal subsequently overturned the injunction on April 5, 2020. Every possible solution advanced by rational professionals met with a time delay tactic which was part of an even larger, more complex strategy designed by unnamed sources working behind the scenes.

The Team clearly came to do its job but as one of the GECOM Commissioners, Mr. Vincent Alexander, said of the Team, *"They have not given up on us; they have withdrawn at this point in time; they have indicated that they are still available if the need arises for an intervention to do so."* Such were the utterings of the duplicitous Commissioners of the Coalition government.

On April 6, 2020; the Prime Minister of Trinidad and Tobago, Dr. Keith Rowley was kafuffled by the Guyana Court of Appeal's ruling which found that a CARICOM supervision of a recount of all votes cast on March 2 was illegal and that it was GECOM's responsibility to supervise the elections to ensure fairness and impartiality.

The Honorable Dr. Keith Rowley[194] commented that he found *"that ruling quite disturbing because the ruling was that the actions of CARICOM would deem to be illegal, that finding of a court must be of concern to every member of CARICOM because it would be predicated on an understanding that CARICOM had done something that a court has found to be illegal and I want you to separate that from the actions of individuals within the context of the political environment of Guyana and the political leaders."* He referenced the aide-memoire where the Terms of Reference were clear that the High-Level Team *"would supervise the recount under the auspices of GECOM and would not engage themselves on the actual counting of ballots, their presence is to ensure that the recount is done in a free, fair, transparent and credible manner, meaning scrutiny."*

102 days after the March 2 General Elections and 38 days from the start of the National Recount when legal maneuverings recommenced against

the National Recount Results, the Prime Minister of St. Vincent and the Grenadines, Dr. Ralph Gonsalves (the incoming Chairman of CARICOM at the time) stamped his authority by elucidating that the regional bloc *"will not stand by idly and watch the recount which was properly done for the results to be set aside."* The recount exercise results were clear as to the winner of the General Elections. The Peoples Progressive Party Civic (PPP-C) won the elections with a total of 233,336 votes, 15,416 more votes than the APNU+AFC Coalition. The Honorable Dr. Gonsalves was a thorn in the flesh of the Coalition supporters when he stated that *"When[195] you take part in an election, there is always a chance that you will lose, and if you lose, like Sir Arthur [Lewis] said: 'Take your licks like a man',"* and that CARICOM would not tolerate anyone stealing an election in the Region.

Dr. Gonsalves' statements incurred the wrath of the APNU+AFC Campaign Manager, Mr. Joseph Harmon who was of the opinion that *"CARICOM leaders would refrain from any actions or utterances that could undermine the legitimacy of the process and its credible conclusion."*

On June 12, 2020, Mr. Owen Arthur, the former Prime Minister of Barbados did not take too kindly to Mr. Harmon's verbal attacks on a legitimate head of government and warned Mr. Harmon that he was speaking out of turn. Mr. Arthur, in a non-diplomatic manner; upbraided APNU+AFC's Campaign Manager when he said of him that he should be more respectful and was *"a mere utensil and he is out of order to be speaking to Caribbean leaders in the way in which he is. And if he is speaking with the support of the President of Guyana, who would himself want to sit in Council with other leaders, it would be good for the President of Guyana to tell Mr. Harmon that that is not his responsibility."*

The former Prime Minister of Barbados reminded like-minded citizens of Guyana of the mindset of Mr. Harmon that *"Caribbean[196] countries, including Guyana, have signed a Charter for Civil Society which enjoins upon them the responsibility to have free and fair elections. It would, therefore, be entirely contrary to the provisions of the Charter for Civil Society for CARICOM countries to stand by if an election is being stolen."* Mr. Arthur's concern for the fellowship of goodwill with the other leaders of the Caribbean was a source of great motivation to those who believed in the electoral procedures and the system of democracy.

On June 15, 2020, the Secretary-General of CARICOM, Ambassador Irwin LaRocque, received the Report of the CARICOM High Level Observer Team on the Recount of Guyana's General and Regional Elections. The Team arrived on May 1, 2020, for the recount exercise. The recount exercise finally began on May 6, 2020, after a hard-start and was completed by June 9, 2020. Also receiving a copy of the Report was the Honourable Mia Mottley, Prime Minister Mottley of Barbados and the Chairman of GECOM, Madame Justice (Ret'd.) Claudette Singh

Leading the CARICOM[197][197] High Level Observer Team was Ms. Cynthia Barrow-Giles, Senior Lecturer in the Department of Government at the University of the West Indies (UWI). She was part of the initial CARICOM team which was forced to return due to a court injunction. Her team members included Mr. John Jarvis, Commissioner of the Antigua and Barbuda Electoral Commission and Mr. Sylvester King, Deputy Supervisor of Elections of St. Vincent and the Grenadines.

An aide-memoire was signed on March 16, 2020, between the leader of the PPP-C Opposition party, Dr. Bharrat Jagdeo, the leader of the governing APNU+AFC party, the Honourable David A. Granger and a third signatory, the Secretary-General of CARICOM, Ambassador Irwin LaRoque. The Team was invited to scrutinize the recount by the Chairman of GECOM, Madame Justice (Ret) Claudette Singh and whose Terms of Reference were prepared by GECOM to guide the High-Level Team.

Once more, on June 24, 2020, the Chairman of CARICOM was compelled to express her feeling of sadness regarding the excess of 100 days since the people of Guyana went to the polls with no clear indication of a declared result. She reminded the voters of Guyana and the people of the Caribbean that there was a *"level of gamesmanship that has left much to be desired and has definitely not portrayed our Caribbean region in the best light. This is definitely NOT our finest hour and we MUST NOT shy away from that reality.*

The Caribbean Community (CARICOM) is concerned at reports that the Chief Elections Officer has submitted a Report to the Guyana Elections Commission (GECOM) which is contrary to the directions given by the Commission and which does not reflect the results of the recount process as certified by the very staff of the Guyana Elections Commission and witnessed by representatives of the political parties."

Honourable Mia Mottley commended the CARICOM Observer Team for traveling to Guyana to scrutinize the recount in spite of the pandemic and the risk to themselves and was of the unshakeable belief that the people of Guyana had expressed their will at the ballot box and that the results of the recount certified as valid by the staff of GECOM led to an orderly conclusion on which the declaration of the results of the Election could be made.

Therefore, we must ask – on what grounds and by what form of executive fiat does the Chief Elections Officer determine that he should invalidate 1 vote, far less over 115 000 votes when the votes were already certified as valid by officers of the Guyana Elections Commission in the presence of the political parties.

We must remind all that if there is any evidence of fraudulent or improper conduct then there is a clear and well accepted route to deal with these matters. It is through an Election Petition to an Election Court.[198]

It was after such passionate appeals and direct talk that many Guyanese saw it fit to attack and impugn the character of the Chairman as they questioned the role of CARICOM's impact on the sovereignty of Guyana and the *"intrusion"* of CARICOM into the internal affairs of Guyana. Picketing of the CARICOM Secretariat became a norm thereafter for a few weeks.

On July 3, 2020, CARICOM's Secretary-General Ambassador Irwin LaRocque had not budged as it related to the CARICOM Report which was produced by the high-level CARICOM team that scrutinized the national vote recount for 46 days during the period of the Covid-19 pandemic. During his opening remarks at 20th Special Meeting of CARICOM Heads of Government to hand over the chairmanship from Barbados Prime Minister Mia Mottley to Dr. Ralph Gonsalves of St. Vincent and the Grenadines, he advised that the results of the recount should be used to make a declaration by the Guyana Elections Commission and that the recount results reflected the will of the people who voted on March 2, 2020. Ambassador LaRocque expressed grave concerns in preserving the reputation of the entire 15-nation group of countries. *"We have been grappling with an ongoing electoral crisis in Guyana as we sought to maintain the reputation of the community as a bastion of democracy.*[199]*"*

The CARICOM Report contained observations, commentaries, and recommendations on the 33-day process which it deemed to be an audit rather than a recount. As serious as the Report was to an understanding of the process, the comedy of errors which unfolded not only provided light-hearted humor for the readers but secured an indictment of GECOM's administrative flaws.

The Report lauded Justice Claudette Singh as a strong woman who endured psychological warfare waged against her by the Commissioners within the Secretariat, the political parties, the media and forces external to the GECOM Secretariat who were relentless in their targeted efforts. The citizens of Guyana were indifferent to the *'pressure-cooker'* situation under which she operated yet were inhumanely critical of her.

What emerged clearly from the Report was the passive warmongering of the inept Commissioners on both sides of the political divide in Guyana. First, their political agendas trumped that of the welfare of the nation's electorate. To this end, their *'love vine'* motivation was destroying the very substance which sustained them. Consequently, decisions were never made on time and meaningless discussions continued ad nauseum.

Secondly, ostracizing the Commonwealth advisor to GECOM, Dr. Kwadwo Afari-Gyan, demonstrated an organized effort on the part of the Commissioners not to advance their knowledge base nor their ability to be innovation thinkers who could proactively manage risk. A pool of closed-minded sycophants did not augur well for the effective management of GECOM then nor in the future. The 75-year-old Dr. Kwadwo Afari-Gyan, a former Chairman of the Elections Commission of Ghana, led the electoral commission from 1993 to 2015. He was credited for playing a pivotal role in Ghana's democracy and politics, but his counsel went unheeded in Guyana which resulted in the epileptic approach to the National Recount with regard to many challenges which he had predicted. The political climate in Ghana around election time is not dissimilar to that of Guyana.

Thirdly, another scary predicament recognized by the writers of the Report was that the ethos of the Commissioners *"in ensuring that elections and the electoral environment are conducive to integrity-based elections which will reflect the will of the people.[200]"*

Finally, the most damaging, self-inflicted political wound was captured in the statement from the Report to the effect that the *"Commissioners were therefore complicit in the assault on the legitimacy and independence of that institution.[201]"* The observation stemmed from the Commissioners bizarre references to a string of irregularities to the media whether print, visual or audio which were fiction.

The most important recommendation coming out of the Report was the restructuring of GECOM. There were two models offered. The first would emphasize *"non-partisan and professional body appointed on the basis of merit qualification rather than on the basis of party sympathy or loyalty."* To this end, an Advisory Body, such as the one created in Ghana in 1994, the Inter-Party Advisory Committee (IPAC), would comprise representatives of all political parties which would meet with the Elections Commission body monthly. The recommended approach would reduce the level of friction between contending parties thereby allowing for a permanent conflict resolution platform.

The second model would reflect societal interests and would include representatives of political parties, media and social partners such as the business sector and civil society. The rationale behind this model was that it would reduce the blame game, ensure *"a greater level of consensus,"* lower the high level of partisanship thereby installing confidence and trust in the Commission.

The conclusion of the High-level Team was that they acknowledged *"that there were some defects in the recount of the March 02, 2020 votes cast for the General and Regional elections in Guyana, the Team did not witness anything which would render the recount and by extension the casting of the ballot on March 02, so grievously deficient procedurally or technically, (despite some irregularities), or sufficiently deficient to have thwarted the will of the people and consequently preventing the election results and its declaration by GECOM from reflecting the will of the voters.[202]"*

CHAPTER 8: MEDIA RANTINGS
- PRE & POST ELECTIONS -

"He knows nothing and thinks he knows everything. That points clearly to a political career." George Bernard Shaw

Political party election broadcasts began on radio as far back as 1924 in the United Kingdom when election results were announced intermittently with summaries on the hour. The results of the polling for General Elections could only be heard for 6 hours starting at 9:50 pm as part of a live band performance. Elections campaigning and General Elections overall were not considered appealing to the listening audience, at that time and was viewed as a casual affair.

On the American continent, on the other hand, the first-time election returns were broadcasted live was about a hundred years ago in 1920 on Radio KDKA, Pittsburg, Pennsylvania when Warren G. Harding was elected President of the United States.

However, in February 1950, Grace Wyndham Goldie,[203] a BBC producer signaled the beginning of political elections coverage for the future. Reporters and commentators became the mainstay of the General Elections in the UK which set the tone for the Commonwealth countries thereafter. Television had proven to be a powerful agent of change especially with a viewing audience of over 6 million viewers at the time.

The Elections 2020 was the first time that digital technology was used on such a wide scale which served to enhance the transparency and integrity of elections in Guyana. It is presumed that without the proliferation of digital technology, the Elections 2020 results would have been different. Political parties and their candidates were using newspapers, radio and television media to reach out to members of their constituency, to mobilize their supporters and even to raise funds. On the other hand, political party supporters, used the same media to immerse themselves in campaigns of their parties, and engage politicians and each other about election-related issues and no less, race baiting. Academics, businessmen, students of politics, economics and law, Union leaders and religious leaders were scribes to the nation during the 153 days seize of Guyana's democracy.

The level to which candidates and supporters were wont to sink can only be described as an unfortunate use of the media and an indictment of the underlying racial tensions that have simmered over each election period.

The Broadcasting Act 2011 provides a series of guidelines for the broadcasters inclusive of political broadcasts to encourage broadcasting of the highest professional quality in terms of fairness and impartiality. Specific reference is made to Paragraphs 19 and 20 of the Guidelines. Paragraph 19 is specific to News and Current Affairs Programmes while Paragraph 20[204] relates to Political Broadcasts per:

(a) All paid or free broadcasts in support of political parties or candidates shall be clearly identified before and after the programme;

(b) The public should be provided with information that would enable the electorate to make intelligent choices during elections;

(c) The coverage of political activities shall be objective and impartial;

(d) Political discussion or debates involving partisan speakers or on behalf of political parties should clearly be labelled as such;

(e) Race, ethnicity and/or religious beliefs as a basis for denigration of a person's political affiliation shall not be permitted;

(f) Controversial or offensive references to opponents shall be avoided.

It is clear from the content of the various broadcasting entities and their corresponding behavior that the guidelines were not adhered to in the strictest sense with deviations being glaring and impactful. These guidelines were designed to establish transparency and strengthen the integrity of the electoral processes ensuring that the democratic processes were not eroded. Implementation of the guidelines by the Guyana National Broadcasting Authority (GNBA) is crucial to the success of the Act.

An essential form of documentation which was established in 2001[205] and implemented in the 2015 elections, the Media Code of Conduct,[206] was not completed by the start of the March 2, 2020, General and Regional Elections. This missing piece of documentation was essential for a high standard of media performance and valid content during the elections period especially given the series of events which succeeded the day of elections.

On October 30, 2019, the Chairman of the Board of the Guyana National Broadcasting Authority (GNBA),[207]Mr. Leslie Sobers, met with representatives of the European Union on the matter of content monitoring support for the March 2, 2020, General and Regional elections. Mr. Sobers, an Attorney-At-law, indicated that the GNBA would be working closely with both the Ethnic Relations Commission and GECOM to monitor broadcast content during ice the elections period. A month later, the Guyana Broadcasting Service (GBS) met with GECOM informing them of the Monitoring and Compliance Department's role of monitoring the broadcasters for content that *"may incite racial hatred or crime and public disorder."* The guidelines contain all the elements to inform: rules regarding election coverage; protection for freedom of expression during elections; and implementation/applicability of the guidelines. As March 2, 2020, General and Regional Elections approached, the GNBA noted the increase in broadcasting infractions chief amongst which was the *"unbalanced political commentaries.*[208]*"*

A quick scan of the 64-page Elections Observer Report of the European Union Observer Mission of June 5, 2020, identified two privately owned publications, Stabroek News and Kaieteur News, deemed to be *"rather balanced in their news coverage.*[209]*"* There are four recognized daily newspapers. News Room Guyana was the most professional in its coverage of the elections process.

The GBNA listed ten of the twenty television stations and ten of the thirty radio stations as being Compliant Broadcasters. However, the government owned Guyana Chronicle newspaper along with the National Communication Network Channel 11 TV station, Voice of Guyana radio station and the Department of Public Information, a government agency, carried advertising and programming content that was heavily biased in favour of the APNU+AFC Coalition. The privately owned TV station, Channel 9, continued along the same vein as the government-owned media houses. Coverage of PPP-C activities was largely negative.

On the other hand, the PPP-C affiliated Channel 65 TV station, the Freedom Radio and the Guyana Times newspaper covered a high percentage of PPP-C content and was mostly anti-APNU+AFC in nature. At no time during the 153-days of awaiting election results was the GNBA's mandate realized.

A grant from the American Chamber of Commerce in Guyana (AmCham Guyana)[210]provided for training of journalists who would cover the 2020 elections at the Palm Court on January 26, 2020. The training was a collaborative effort between the Guyana Press Association (GPA), the Guyana Elections Commission (GECOM) and AmCham Guyana. The two-day training provided journalists and reporters with insight into Guyana's electoral laws, understanding manifestos and elections results, elections coverage/media, understanding fake news and social media and disinformation and defamation and political coverage. They learnt of their respective roles during and after elections day.

Justice Claudette Singh in her address to the participants and invitees advised the media persons that they *"must be careful and responsible in your reporting on any Election Day incident. Do not sensationalize your stories. Ensure that you have credible information. Be aware of hearsay reports. Do not act on them unless you have verified your stories[211].*" What the Chairman did not warn them about was that they would not be a welcomed group at GECOM's Command Centre and that security for them would be nonexistent.

The Guyana Press Association (GPA) which was established in 1945 is the sole representative body of media workers in Guyana. It is the second oldest media membership and advocacy body in the English-speaking Caribbean[212]. About 3 days before Election Day, the GPA was concerned about the slothful way GECOM was responding to their queries pertaining to the administration of the elections. The body concluded that GECOM was "complicit in and must be held responsible for imbalanced coverage especially in instances where there are serious accusations and claims being made by the election commissioners, political parties and other stakeholders[213]."

The GPA, on March 15, 2020, registered their condemnation of *"threats and verbal assault on media workers"* by APNU+AFC supporters who had launched an attack outside GECOM's headquarter, Kingston as they carried out their work. It should be noted that though GECOM had established a Media Centre, media workers were prevented from entering the Command Centre and with little to no access to critical electoral information. Media workers were exposed to an agitated and militant crowd without security support from either the staff of GECOM or the ranks of the Guyana Police Force. In a Press Statement, the GPA condemned the *"the threats, verbal assault and attempts of physical attacks of our media workers over the past weeks, including the last two days as they gathered around the GECOM tabulation center and GECOM Secretariat to inform and update the nation about elections. We hold the leaders of the major political parties, Police Commissioner and members of the Guyana Elections Commission responsible for any harm brought to media professionals as they conduct their duties."*

Watching the reporters and journalists around the Command Centre manifested memories of journalists in war-torn and underdeveloped countries. Emotions were real. They were not safe. One reporter cried, yet another ran for safety as the words that were hurled against them were of the most vitriolic nature. They feared for their safety and rightly so. Their enemies were the Corona virus, the APNU+AFC supporters, indifferent police ranks and overzealous GECOM staff. The intimidation tactics were escalating at a rate where a rational human being would flee the location as the Ambassadors of the ABCE countries did during the Region 4 tabulation process.

Guideline 4 of Article 19's Guideline for Election Broadcasting[214] stipulates that *"The authorities should make special efforts to investigate all acts of violence, intimidation or harassment directed against media personnel or the property or premises of a media outlet, and to bring those responsible to justice, particularly where the act was motivated by an intent to interfere with media freedom.*" As the complaints of the GPA fell upon deaf ears, they had a responsibility too to defend democracy and freedom of the press by way of creating a Photographic Wall of Shame and posting the photographs of all the guilty culprits in the various local and Regional newspapers. A Video Mosaic of Political Criminals would have been a source of delight and shame to John Public when viewed on private television stations, on YouTube and other social media channels. The Guyana Police Force would have no choice but to act as the FBI did in the storming of Capitol Hill in the USA. The journalists and reporters were the front liners in the defense of democracy.

For more than 153 days, the news media was at its most active in Guyana. Academics, journalists, home grown reporters, racists, politicians, and political analysts provided more content than anyone had ever witnessed in Guyana. Newspapers were streaming live session on election analysis and projections, daily.

Bright and early on Sundays and for over three decades, Guyanese look forward to reading Stabroek New's Ian On Sunday written by author, poet and veteran journalist, Mr. Ian McDonald. Six days after election day, Mr. McDonald did not write a column. Such an event happens once in a blue moon as it relates to the publication of his column. He regretted not being able to supply a column for his loyal followers and to the devoted readers of Stabroek News. He was, as he reported, "*sick at heart. The events of the last few days have disgraced Guyana. What has happened so far if continued will be an indelible stain in the history of the nation. The affront to democracy is contemptible. In future "My vote counts" will mean nothing – only "Accept what is imposed." It will weaken Guyana's international standing at a vital time. A terrible lesson is being taught to the young people of Guyana.*"

Another journalist who hits hard at the heart of social and political matters in Guyana is Mr. Frederick Kissoon. He is brutally frank. He is a columnist for the Kaieteur News's popular daily column, Freddie Kissoon Column. During the 153 days of elections uncertainty, Mr. Kissoon appeared to have agitated government supporters and his reputed friends alike, even his former colleagues of the Working People's Alliance (WPA). His article of April 4, 2020, provided the gist of his feeling. He wrote, "*Here in Guyana, we have seen the Freudian drives of those who profess to be adherents of democratic principles, but in their souls they care not about rights, justice, rule of law, democracy, Guyana's future; just ethnic domination occupies their mind.*

The 2020 election nightmare has brought out the worst instincts in some humans in Guyana. This is not basic instincts, but uncivilized descent where basic instincts become bestial rampage.

We have seen these bestial directions from all types of people – trade unionists, university lecturers, lawyers, those who call themselves Rodneyites, politicians, etc. They see nothing wrong with what Clairmont Mingo did. They want Guyana to have a new government based on the Mingo declaration."

The Editor-in-Chief of the privately-owned Kaieteur News, Mr. Adam Harris, on March 8, 2020, called the electoral activities of the week following the election day as *"Madness; sheer madness."* He lamented the fact that whenever there is an election, the people of Guyana are anxious. What is more interesting is the comment on the unusual behavioral pattern of the international and local observers when he proffered, *"of interest was the role of the observers. They actually became active participants in the elections, going beyond the scope of observing. But one may argue that this is all well and good, since their actions actually cleared the way for claims of transparency. And the observers are expected to pronounce on the conduct and transparency of the elections."* He concluded that the Carter formula had outlived its usefulness but also made recommendations which paralleled those made by Observer Missions on so many past elections which have never borne fruit.

Kaieteur News political advertising coverage was 40% for the PPP-C and 48% for the APNU+AFC and appeared balanced. News coverage for the APNU+AFC and government was 76%.[215][215].

In contrast to the opinions of the editorial and commentators of the various local and Regional newspapers, the Editor of the Guyana Chronicle bemoaned the PPP-C's manipulation of the people of Guyana. In an editorial captioned, **Yes to a full recount! No to PPP's bullyism**!, of April 12, 2020, it dwelled on the issues of the National Recount and it's undermining by the PPP-C. There were also accusations of the PPP-C cheating the people of Guyana for 23 years and wanting to remove GECOM officials and replacing them with their friends.

In essence, the Editor stated that *"as soon as the court cleared the way for the recount, the PPP began to sing a different tune; it started to back-pedal on everything it agreed to. Suddenly, they only want to count the ballots in Region Four, and have asked for the boxes of the other regions to be excluded. This is nothing short of trickery. Why do they fear a full recount? One can only conclude that because the process in those regions have been so manipulated by the PPP, they fear that this would be exposed by a full and comprehensive recount.[216]"*

It concluded that even though the PPP-C represents a substantial portion of the electorate, GECOM should not allow itself to be bullied by them. During the election period, the news coverage for the combined APNU+AFC and government was at 72% while political advertising was at an all-time high of 91%.

The Guyana Times is part of a triumvirate publishing empire which is owned by Queens Atlantic Investment Inc since 2008. The Radio Guyana Inc and TVG Channel 28 television station constitute the other two components of the empire. In its Editorial of March 15, 2020, titled Granger's Overreach, the Editor expressed disbelief that President David

Granger and his PNC cohorts would have attempted to rig the elections to remain in power given the robust nature of the safeguards in the political process. He took the readers on a memory tour of rigging from the Burnham era. He noted President Granger's indifference to the warnings of the diplomatic community, both internationally and Regionally.

The Editor wrote, *"However, they forgot that the PNC had also resorted to what is referred to as 'brute force and ignorance' in the local idiom to intervene, which left no doubt in the minds of the international community — including Caricom — that they had rigged the elections. This started in 1973, when the Army was mobilised 'to protect the ballot boxes,'* when in fact the hard-won right of the Opposition parties to accompany the boxes to the Counting Office in their Region, was being exercised. Two PPP activists were shot and killed by the army when they attempted to accompany the ballot boxes to the place of counting.[217]" He accused President Granger of misreading the strategic geopolitical approach of the USA in Guyana's neighbor, Venezuela.

As much as 54% of the political advertising was for the PPP-C whereas news coverage was 54% for the PPP-C and 43% for the APNU+AFC Coalition.[218]

Mr. Ravi Dev, one of the weekly columnists for the Guyana Times on March 20, 2020, postulated the Ethnic Security Dilemma, a structuring of the political behavior of the two major ethnic groups. His column is called Roar of Ravi Dev and Mr. Dev has written consistently about the racial, cultural and political nuances which need to be addressed in great earnest for the country to develop. He believed that it was the African Security Dilemma and the Indian Security Dilemma that created the heightened anxieties around elections time rather than a hatred for each other. He suggested that the shift in the demographics of the Indian and African populations, a decrease for the two major ethnic groups and a corresponding increase in the Amerindians and mixed groups redefined the political strategies of this era.

According to him, *"The political African-Guyanese Security Dilemma, therefore, had been resolved: with all ethnic groups now being minorities, African-Guyanese or Indian-Guyanese could now win elections only if they could appeal to voters from "across the divide" or from the Mixed and Amerindian blocks. The Indian Ethnic Security Dilemma, however, still remained, since the Bureaucracy, Police and Army were all still dominated by the PNC's constituency.[219]"* He accused President Granger of alienating the Indo-Guyanese voters being unaware of the paradigm shift.

Stabroek News,[220] founded by a man who believed in freedom of the press, demonstrated the power of the media, when on March 26, 2020, it undertook to publish 116 Statements of Poll (SoPs) that it had collected on the night of the elections and afterwards. It provided evidence of the SoPs which were withheld from the citizens of Guyana by GECOM and the APNU+AFC Coalition. The magnanimous effort on the part of this privately owned newspaper caused much debate and opened the eyes of the electorate to the level of shenanigans involved in the District Four tabulations and the scope of GECOM's involvement in perpetuating a fraud upon the people of Guyana. This was press freedom at its best and wisest. One that the late Mr. David DeCaires would have been proud of.

On April 10, 2020, an editorial in the Trinidad Express titled Guyana Election Merry-Go-Round captured the absurdity of the happenings in Guyana. The Editor wrote that *"Mr Keith Lowenfield has suggested a purported timetable for recounting all of the votes cast in the elections to be completed in 156 days. Such a timetable amounts to 26 days short of a half-year. By any standard, this is nothing short of ludicrous, and points to conclusions long since shared by eminent persons concerned with this situation that dark forces are working to frustrate the will of the Guyanese people."* The views and sentiments of the Regional Newspapers closely matched that of the Trinidad Daily Expres.[221] The critical and unbelieving eyes of the Region were upon Guyana.

The Jamaica Gleaner Newspaper's Editorial of September 30, 2020, titled, **Guyana Must Tread With Care,**[222] was a post-election analysis of Guyana's long drawn-out elections process. The Editor was very concerned about the actions taken by the government and comments made by President Irfaan Ali about cementing the nation in unity at his Inauguration Ceremony. Specifically, the Gleaner introductory statement to the editorial was, *"Using the law to settle political scores is a tactic often employed by authoritarian governments and their leaders, which we hope is not what is happening in Guyana. It has no place in liberal democracy."* The Editor was not in agreement with the CEO's actions and behavioral patterns. However, he warned the government of Guyana of the need to place checks and balances in place before addressing the elephant in the room less it leads to ethnic division. He feared that things may get worse before they got better if the government pursued criminal charges against the CEO as opposed to GECOM from which the case actions ought to have emanated.

In conclusion, he stated that *"The grave danger, in our view, is the potential for the further ethnic polarization of politics in Guyana, and with it ethnic relations. Sometimes, even in the midst of right, or the presumption thereof, it makes sense to tread lightly."* Within three weeks of the Gleaner's Editorial, Dr Vishnu Bisram,[223] a Guyanese and the director of NACTA Polling Institute, responded to the Editor clarifying the CEO's motives and explaining the 153-day siege on Guyana's democracy.

125 days after election day, the Barbados Advocate, one of Barbados' oldest newspapers published an editorial captioned, An Electoral Tragedy.[224] After commenting on the length of the delay in presenting results to the electorate and on the myriad of court cases, the Editor referred to the 153 days election saga as a Caribbean electoral tragedy. Barbadians, back in the 80s; remember reading, at length; of the political leadership struggles and

race baiting in Guyana. Many Guyanese have taken up residence in Barbados because of the past elections' dramas.

The Editor astutely latched on to the nature of the court cases and the context within which they were decided by stating that *"it would be naïve of us not to remark on the ethnic considerations bearing on this matter. It was most noticeable and regrettable in the domestic court decisions where the judges with the recognizably East Indian surnames always appear to differ from the opinions of their learned brothers and sisters of a different racial extraction. This semblance does not breed respect for the judicial process."*

Writers to the four local newspapers dug up political dirt on both sides of the political divide and heaped it so high, it was almost impossible to discern the truth of the results of the elections and the true character of each major political party. The average reader watched as the reputedly learned academics and professionals descended to a level of mudslinging in each daily that caused great rifts in the social fabric of Guyana's society. 2020 was a challenging year and 2021 will have to be the year to regroup and rebuild broken trust and rethink the country's future and the unity of its human resources. Guyanese leaders can learn much from President Joe Biden's Inauguration[225] speech. *"This is democracy's day. A day of history and hope. Of renewal and resolve. Through a crucible for the ages America has been tested anew and America has risen to the challenge.*

Today, we celebrate the triumph not of a candidate, but of a cause, the cause of democracy. The will of the people has been heard and the will of the people has been heeded. We have learned again that democracy is precious. Democracy is fragile. And at this hour, my friends, democracy has prevailed. So now, on this hallowed ground where just days ago violence sought to shake this Capitol's very foundation, we come together as one nation, under God, indivisible, to carry out the peaceful transfer of power as we have for more than two centuries.

We look ahead in our uniquely American way – restless, bold, optimistic – and set our sights on the nation we know we can be and we must be."

Social media is not a misnomer, but it can be anything but social, at times. Within Guyana, Facebook is the social media platform of choice followed by WhatsApp and thereafter by Instagram and Twitter. Facebook lit up in Guyana from January 2020 to the announcement of the results of the General and Regional Elections 2020 on August 2, 2020, and even continued into September 2020.

According to the Edelman Trust Barometer 2020,[226] 57% of media users believe that the content is *"contaminated with untrustworthy information"* and an alarming 76% are worried that fake news will be weaponized. Well, these statistics hold up within the environment that is politically charged. Social media was the major channel of engagement for the political parties and their supporters during the Elections 2020. The WhatsApp Groups were used by those predominately over 30 years old while Facebook was used predominately by the younger, more academic generation.

By April 2019, Facebook had become the largest online social network of which the people of the earth had ever been a part. 30% of the world's population of seven and a half billion are actively using Facebook, monthly. The platform is the largest, most influential media platform[227] in the world. Sneaking up behind is Instagram which has about 50% of Facebook's users while Twitter has about 12% of Facebook's activities. Closer to home, Facebook has about 360,000[228] users and a 45.8% penetration rate which is considerable for a Developing country given an internet penetration of 50.2%, that is, as many persons of voting age. 14.8% of Guyana's population use Instagram,[229] the majority being females with the largest groups of users between the ages of 18 years to 24 years old. This was not the platform of choice between March 2, 2020, and August 2, 2020. On the other hand, much mischief was had through WhatsApp[230] by supporters of the two major parties. WhatsApp, a disruptive technology, has over 2.0 billion users in over 180 countries and is the most popular messaging system in the world. In African and the Caribbean, WhatsApp has been the medium of choice for purveyors of political opinions, factual or fantastical.

It would be prudent to consider the impact of the disruptive nature of social media in two countries; India and Brazil, and to project its impact on Guyana's sensitive ethno-political climate. Facebook's WhatsApp messenger service and Ministry of Electronics and Information Technology of India have agreed to work together to restrict disinformation on its platform. It further added that society must play its role too. The Indian[231] market is WhatsApp's biggest with over 200 million users. The platform's encrypted nature prevents the tracking of the source of messages being shared and the means by which information is shared. In July 2018, disinformation by WhatsApp users caused mass beatings and the lynching of more than five persons in the state of Maharashtra on suspicion of child abduction. WhatsApp had abdicated its responsibility to assist civil society in monitoring such misuse of its system. As a result, it is up to governments, society and telecommunication companies, working in partnership, to tame the disruptive technology beast. It could be surmised that the technology is not the challenge but the criminally, misinformed users of the technology.

In Brazil next door, President Jair Messias Bolsonaro[232] the 38th President of Brazil's campaign of two years ago was a WhatsApp election. Businessmen who supported Mr. Bolsonaro's during the campaign financed the bombardment of hundreds of millions of WhatsApp users in Brazil, of which there are approximately 120 million active users, with fake news about his opponent. The approach was deemed criminal and electoral fraud. The pervasive nature of fake news via WhatsApp was considered an undermining of the democratic process.

Being right in the USA's backyard, the fake news impact on the USA's 2016 elections was swift and mindboggling. President Donald Trump benefitted significantly from the fake news factories of Veles, Macedonia. According to Buzzfeed News,[233] during the last three months of the USA Elections 2016 campaign, the top fake election news stories on Facebook generated more engagement than the top stories from major news outlets such as the New York Times, Washington Post, and the NBC News.

During Guyana's political silly season, social media was used to expose wrongdoings, to monitor elections as was never done before and express opinions that ranged from embracing racism to ones that fought for the preservation of democracy. During the month of February 2020, the Editor-in-Chief of Stabroek News, Mr. Anand Persaud,[234], responded to a fake news story on Facebook which was deemed to have emanated from its media house. It had the look and feel of Stabroek News and would have been accepted as the truth had there not been an adequate level of scrutiny. It is said that imitation is the sincerest form of flattery. If this is anything to go by, Newsroom's fake page which was online for three days, contained many of its authentic stories but also carried anti-President Granger disinformation and unauthenticated content on the APNU+AFC. Editor-in-Chief of Newsroom, Ms. Fareeza Haniff, explained that fake news is a grave concern especially around this time but that it has become a bolder effort by those intent on mischief. She explained, *"There is nothing that we can do per se. At the end of the day we have to guard against what goes out there and how the information reaches the people but it's for the people themselves to also do simple fact-checking on how to spot fake news. Newsroom did its part by putting out a statement saying that the page is fake and we are in no way associated with it and that's the most that we can do."*

Guyana's Cyber Crime Act 2016 was created to deal with the native consequences of this disruptive technology by ensuring that purveyors of racism and disinformation feel the long arms of the law. Section 17 (3) allows for the punishment of culprits who commit *"an offence if the person without lawful excuse or justification establishes a website, with the intent to deceive or mislead a visitor to the website as to the authenticity of the website, for the purpose of gaining unauthorized access to information to commit a further offence."* Furthermore, the offence is punishable for a term of three to five years and a fine of three to five million dollars.

Sections 18 of the Act, (f) determined that publications of a nature "that excites or attempts to excite ethnic divisions among the people of Guyana or hostility or ill-will against any person or class of persons on the ground of race" shall be liable, on conviction, to imprisonment for five years. Based on the numbers of posts which excited ethnic division, it was clear that not even the Ethnic Relations Committee was familiar with most aspects of the 2016 Act and did not respond appropriately.

Every political party, along with most of their staunch supporters, owned a Facebook page which was populated with posts the content of which were skewed towards their party of choice. A detailed scan of social media pages encouraged the spread of fabricated stories that stoked the ethnic fires and political tensions. Friends blocked long-time friends. Expletives became a normal part of comments which hitherto, have never been the norm. There was a need to purge the social media or even participate in a social media diet to purge the mind of the putrid nature of the communications.

Many who professed to be Christians changed their allegiances, Jesus Christ for David Granger or Irfaan Ali or Timothy Jonas and relaxed their gospel principles for approximately 153 days. Given that the separation of private self from public self is impossible, the Christians were encouraged to put their gospel principles to work within the political and cultural context. Religion and politics cannot be separated. Religion must be seen as a force of good within a world that is ever increasingly corrupt and immoral. Politics and religion are intertwined; religion informs politician's moral and ethical code of conduct. However, this mode of thinking was not reflected in the majority in the thousands of posts during the elections process.

Throughout the Elections 2020 campaign and during the tabulation and verification period, social media information bubbles were created by sections of the Press, but more so, by the two major parties and their sycophants. Facebook and Twitter contributed to the filter bubbles by associating links from similar groups of similar ideas and temperament.

There are a group of people who live along the Zambesi River valley in Zimbabwe who are particularly unusual in that they sport only two big toes that are curled inwards and no middle toes. They are referred to as the Ostrich people. Their unusual condition has prevailed for centuries due to intermarriage within the same genetic pool. However, the few Ostrich people who have married into other groups with the normal five toes, bear off springs whose toes are normal.

On social media, the political echo chambers of the APNU+AFC and the PPP-C groups are such that they bore traits of the Ostrich people. There was no cross fertilization of ideas that allowed for critical thinking and active debates nor were they helpful for the development of the country or the growth and healing of its people. The yardfowls of each group continued to peddle narratives that raised the risks of instability and conflict between the two major ethnic groups.

Political Analysts increased in numbers on Facebook via radio shows and personal talk shows. By June 2020, there were over forty such entities broadcasting from Guyana and the USA. Unregulated as to content and abrasive in nature, some were helpful, the handful of which included the Guyanese Critic, NewsRoom and Kaieteur Radio with Mr. Leonard Gilharie and Mr. Yog Mahadeo. These entities kept a sharp eye on Guyana's democracy and were relentless in their defense. One of the voices of reason who stood out on social media was Ms. Denise Herod[235] who in a quiet, calming voice and with over thirty thousand views assured the electors, that as a proud Guyanese without political or religious affiliations, she was disappointed in their embrace of propaganda that divided them. She called for transparency and accountability from our political leaders who live in their magnificent homes and whose children attended private academic institutions while the ordinary citizens lived hand to mouth and have been taught to hate each other. She called for mass education and a movement away from ethnic division and hate.

The Guyanese Critic bestrode the social media wave like an aggressive, foul-mouthed Colossus to champion the cause of the disenfranchised and the voiceless. He served as a voice of reason for the people of Guyana. He found favour with people of all races and religious persuasions who provided documentation, videos, and testimonies of people who witnessed abuse and prejudices first-hand.

The fake news on Facebook was lopsided and favored the ruling APNU+AFC coalition. One fantastic feature noted how the justices of the Caribbean Court of Justice were all paid off to the tune of US $ 500,000 each, hence the reason for their judgements against the coalition. A developing story related how the PPP-C's Prime Ministerial Candidate; Mr. Mark Phillips' was chased out of Freedom House after requesting that Dr. Irfaan Ali should concede defeat as the plots got more elaborate. The fake news coming out of Guyana were being produced at a high rate but were amateurish and comical and lacked the feel and authenticity of those that were manufactured in Veles which were, at least, believable.

The groupings which created the APNU+AFC's filter bubbles included the Chronicle Facebook Page, Mr. Rickford Burke and Mr. Gavin Matthews amongst others. The selection of the Benschop Radio 107.1 FM Facebook page would have, aligned to the side, related pages such as Rickford Burke, APNUAFC, APNUGUYANA among others which, invariably, carried similar content and context. Facebook created those fields of isolation above which the casual browsers do not seem to be able to escape. These men were relentless in their defense of everything that the leaders of their political party had done to win the elections. They shouted foul as the international observers and the judicial system halted their efforts to paint their party in the colors of honesty, decency and integrity, the theme on which they had managed their campaign. By flooding the social media environment with anger cues, the seeds of violence and racial tensions were planted. The supporters of the PPP-C were no different. It was six of one and two threes of the other as the cricket commentators would say. However, the PPP-C's rumor mill was built on anonymity and diversionary tactics and mostly without an identifiable human face whereas APNU+AFC's many faces included Mr. Sherod Duncan and Mr. Christopher Jones.

It was only a matter of time before the Ethnic Relations Commission (ERC) would caution or even prosecute some of these commentators. The Guyana Critic, Mr. Mikhail Rodrigues, on June 17, 2020, was sternly cautioned for using racially insensitive remarks against Afro-Guyanese, Indo-Guyanese and members of the Christian society. He apologized, having accepted his wrongdoing, and declared that his videos would be used to build harmony among Guyanese. The ERC is mandated by Article 212 D (j) & (p) of the Constitution of Guyana, the Racial Hostility Act and the Representation of the People's Act, "to initiate and or launch monitoring and investigations into the utterances of the aforementioned persons on social media, traditional media and the daily newspapers."

The ERC[236] had adopted two approaches to resolve the complaints lodged with them by concerned citizens. On the one hand, they published the posts of those against whom complaints were made and photographs of these culprits while requesting support from the public. On June 24, 2020, the ERC's Facebook[237] page, the faces and comments of 6 such social media commentators were published. On January 20, 2021, Chief Magistrate Ann McLennan charged Ms. Tiffany Greene, Ms. Lashona Chester, Ms. Stacy Smarte and Ms. Glynis Gibson for causing *"racial or ethnic violence or hatred or exciting hostility or ill-will on the basis of race."* Each was fined GY $ 100,000/US $ 500 before being warned by the Magistrate. On the other hand, the ERC and the Cyber Crime Unit of the Guyana Police Force had partnered to solve problems of a criminal nature which did not fall under the purview of the ERC. 87% of the complaints originated via Facebook comments and posts.

On June 17, 2020, a twenty-six-year-old male guard was arrested by the Guyana Police Force (GPF) for threatening violence while brandishing several high-powered weapons. Facebook as his medium of choice. Not to be outdone, a Linder during the month of July, when emotions escalated over the delays of elections results, was arrested by members of the GPF for threatening to kill the Chairman of GECOM, Justice Claudette Singh.

WhatsApp groups were even more confining as groups of like minds volunteered to be members. Fake news items travelled at digital speeds within their network consisting of videos, bulletins and Newsletters that were clearly fictitious and audio that was subversive in nature. Any response to the inaccuracy and unreliability of the source and quality of content of the details shared met with strong opposition and even blocking. Attempts at reasoning met with long gaps of silence and limited flow of additional fake news.

WhatsApp's fake news consisted of a diet of Network News Update Breaking News highlights such as *"US Cuts secret deal with Jagdeo to hand over Guyana"*, as ludicrous as a fake Trinidad and Tobago's *The Guardian* newspaper with headlines to the effect that *"Former Guyanese President Bharat Jagdeo and several others arrested today…"* and a post on news which suggested that the PPP-C leadership was at loggerheads and that the party was disintegrating from within.

The behavioral historian and conflict resolution specialist, Ms. Christiane-Marie Abu Sarah,[238] is driven by the desire to find out why people commit politically motivated violence. She determined that perpetrators of violent acts, through their daily habits contribute to their vengeful behavior. The perpetrators of elections violence enclose themselves in an information bubble with information which they trust even though the information may be unreliable. Decisions based on bad information must result in a bad outcome and therein lies the challenges of political echo chambers or filter bubbles.

The second issue is the Us vs Them or the Green vs Red mentality or the Guyana Amazon Warriors vs the Barbados Tridents which is very dangerous within the political climate of Guyana, both individually and collectively. Group thinking leads to group conformity more so than individual, intelligent critical thinking where recognition of individual worth goes unseen or unrewarded. When Chris Gayle played for the West Indies, he was hailed as a hero by every red-blooded Caribbean man and woman. However, when he played for the Jamaican Tallawahs vs the Guyana Amazon Warriors, he was seen as the enemy in most corners of Guyana. This behavior is important to an understanding of the individual's worth and to see beyond the herd instinct which was pervasive throughout the Silly Season.

The next challenge was the amygdala hijacking, such as an anger cue. The PPP-C's anger cue would have been green and yellow while that of the APNU+AFC would have been red. Back in 2015, the General Secretary of the PPP-C, Mr. Clement Rohee, during a Press Conference[239] regretted that there were green tablecloths along with green suitcases within the Polling Stations during the voting process. Mr. Rohee was livid. On Nominations Day in April 2015 the acting City Hall Clerk, Ms. Carol Sooba, decorated the City Hall Chamber in red much to the consternation of His Worship, Mayor Hamilton Green. The Mayor was incensed. Both major political parties have yet to overcome this paranoia. Other anger cues may include hair texture and skin tones. As Professor Mushtak Al-Atabi pointed out over five years ago, it will take some brain-rewiring to change things for the better within the Guyanese political context.

In a magnanimous stand, the former Minister of Business and the son-in-law of President David A. Granger, Mr. Dominic Gaskin,[240] took to Facebook on March 13th, March 20 and July 17th, 2020, to make known his disappointment in the behavior of his former colleagues in the APNU+AFC coalition government. Mr. Gaskin, a logical thinking and decent politician voiced what every law-abiding Guyanese wanted to say openly without fear of recriminations. He declared that he was not a fan of President Irfaan Ali since he had campaigned against him and his party with all prejudice. He was unconvinced that the declaration of March 5, 2020, by GECOM officials accurately reflected the Statements of Poll (SOP) from the 879 Polling stations. He besought GECOM to publish their SOPs thereby allaying the fears of law abiding Guyanese and reconciling rhetoric with facts.

He lamented the reality of Guyanese turning against each other because of a few bad leaders with the hope that there are many more Guyanese who are of a good law-abiding disposition than those who are of deviant behavior. Mr. Gaskin did not mince his word for the Returning Officer, Mr. Clairmont Mingo, regarding the two false declarations. His numbers did not add up and received *"immediate and widespread rejection of this declaration, based primarily on procedural grounds and a lack of transparency. Who vex, vex!"*

It is interesting to note that the leaders of the European and North American countries resorted to the use social media, chiefly Twitter, to communicate their concerns about the happenings within Guyana during the elections process. On March 6, 2020, Mr. Nils Martin Gunneng, the Kingdom of Norway's Ambassador to Guyana tweeted that Norway called for the finals elections results to be credible and transparent. Over 2,600 of their followers would see this message about the premature declaration of unverified results in the March 2, 2020, elections.

The powerful United States of America through the Acting Assistant Secretary for the U.S. Department of State's Bureau of Western Hemisphere Affairs, Mr. Michael G. Kozak,[241] tweeted that *"any Government sworn in on the basis of that result would not be legitimate."* Among the 81,000 of his followers, Guyana's media houses and supporters of the eleven political parties learnt of the warnings against the perpetration of electoral fraud to form an illegitimate government. With great regularity and with the posting frequency of Donald Trump, the APNU+AFC leaders were warned of the dire consequences of benefitting from electoral fraud. The tweets continued unabated from March 2020 through to August 2020. On March 26, 2020, Guyanese were apprised of the summoning of Guyana's Ambassador to the U.S.A, H.E. Dr. Riyad Insanally to convey his government's firm position that any government sworn in based on flawed election results would not be legitimate. By way of the Department of State's Twitter account with close to six million followers, the Secretary of State, Mr. Mike Pompeo announced the visa and other sanctions on those who played any role in the electoral manipulation in Guyana. The announcements were shared on Facebook and caused much debate on who would be sanctioned.

India's Ministry of External Affairs through @ANI with close to four million followers had, since March 2020, been following the developments with respect to the elections in Guyana. As the largest democracy in the world, the Ministry encouraged credible, fair and transparent electoral process.

Supporters of the eleven political parties were slinging racial slurs for over six months, advocating violence and speaking ill of fellow Guyanese of all skin tones and religious persuasions. It was done with a persistence never witnessed before. Perhaps, it was always there but social media brought it out in the open for the whole world to feast and choke upon. It was surmised that those were some of the coping mechanisms which were reflected on social media, more specifically Facebook and WhatsApp, for partisan-based cognitive dissonance.

Over sixty-three years ago, Leon Festinger wrote *The Theory of Cognitive Dissonance*. He spelt out mankind's innate desire to avoid the discomfort of shame and confusion brought on by serious breaches of trust and the rule of law within groups to which one belongs which does not reconcile with one's own. Here in Guyana, during the Elections 2020, the Guyanese supporting the behavior of their political party which lacked harmony with their own self schema brough on levels of cognitive dissonance that was pronounced and reflected through comments and videos hosted on social media platforms. The abuse of the legal system by the major political parties to which they subscribed and the behavior of the GECOM's leadership and staff to whom they looked for fairness and integrity left the average Guyanese feeling disconnected from reality. The more rational Guyanese felt that they were living in an alternate universe given all the sentiments expressed on social media to which they had become addicted.

Most of the political sycophants supported and accepted the illegal, immoral behavior of these institutions which was difficult to reconcile with their owns beliefs in addition to what was taking place during the electoral process. Consequently, the coping mechanisms which they embraced included rationalizing on how it was better for an APNU+AFC government to be in power to one supported by the PPP-C machinery since they represented another ethnic group. Secondly, like some of the religious members of churches, mosques and temples, they hid their genuine beliefs of obeying the law and being moral and ethical. Thirdly, the political yardfowls attacked those who did not agree with the posture of their political party even to the extent of attacking the ABCE countries, vehemently demanding that Guyana pull out of CARICOM, maligning the justices of the Caribbean Court of Justice and denying that it was their highest Court of Appeal, chastising Prime Ministers, the Honorable Mia Mottley and Dr. Ralph Gonsalves of Barbados and St. Vincent, respectively and spreading dirt on democracy's champions; Mr. Owen Arthur and Bruce Golding of the Commonwealth Observer Mission and the OAS, respectively. The nation was in denial and it had set off a series of deep-rooted prejudices that will continue to simmer under Guyana's current political system of the winner takes all.

The next elections proposed for 2025 will be determined by the level and sophistication of fake news and digital campaigning on Facebook and WhatsApp. The level of animosity, if not quelled by electoral reform, will divide the nation of Guyana once more, oil or not.

CHAPTER 9: ELECTORAL CONSEQUENCES AND RESOLUTIONS

"Every vote should carry a serial number, so that responsibility for harmful or careless use of the vote can be traced. Concealed voting should be outlawed." P. J. O'Rourke

The fairness or freeness of the elections in Guyana have been debated for as long as elections were held, post-Independence. Anecdotes and newspaper archives tell of dark and troubling times, times of pain and the making of dictators. The elections of 1992, under the watchful, eagle eyes of the Carter Centre, were accepted more so than any other elections which followed. Post-election violence, political shenanigans and the likes have been an integral part of post-1992 elections and are getting progressively worse from a psychological viewpoint. Guyana is a powder keg of political energy just waiting to explode with its attendant racial divisiveness and social tensions. It can be stated with great certainty that when the official election results are declared, no losing political party has been able to accept them and as such proclaim victory too. Post-election violence has caused damage to property, injury to children, loss to innocent people and harm to the image of Guyana. Ethnic tension escalates as a result of the nature of the elections campaign driving fear into certain communities while generating uncertainty in the minds of investors.

The Elections 2020, more than any other election in Guyana, saw greater participation by civil society, Regional and international governments and diplomats worldwide.

The Bar Association of Guyana, founded in 1980, is a voluntary body comprised of Attorneys-at-Law duly admitted to practice law in Guyana. As the recognized body representing Attorneys-at-Law in Guyana, it was accredited by the Guyana Elections Commission (GECOM) as a Local

Observer of the 2020 General and Regional Elections. Consequently, it monitored the elections process and dispatched a team to observe the voting process on Election Day in Districts 4, 5 and 6. On March 4, 2020, the Bar Association of Guyana, issued a Statement on their preliminary observations of the General and Regional Elections up to and including the voting process, which were found to be free, fair and transparent.

By March 8, 2020 the Bar Council of the Association was calling on GECOM's Chairman *"to ensure that all necessary steps are taken so that the results can withstand local and international scrutiny and represent the highest international standards as will make all Guyanese proud in the process, before making any declaration required by law to be made by her*[242]*"* and warned that if a President is sworn in on the basis of the unverified declaration, it would have *"far reaching implications."* It joined with international observer missions in calling for the GECOM to comply with the legal requirements to ensure transparency and credibility of the election process. By April 16, 2020, the Bar Council appealed to GECOM to act expeditiously to enable the accurate and transparent declaration of results noting that the constitutional deadline for the convening of a new Parliament was fast approaching on April 30, 2020. It was shocked at the lackadaisical way GECOM was handling a sensitive, political situation given that *"Article 69 of the Constitution*[243] *of Guyana mandates that, on dissolution, the next session of Parliament must commence no later than four (4) months from the end of the preceding session. The last session of Parliament was dissolved on December 30, 2019 . The next session of Parliament must therefore begin no later than April 30, 2020."* Failure to abide by the Constitution, the supreme law of the land, had far reaching effects as it relates to good governance and the rule of law and impacts Guyana, nationally and international. It determined that the absence of parliamentary oversight of those who purport to exercise executive powers, whether de facto or de jure, was of grave concern as it placed the rule of law under siege. The Bar Council further observed that the *"open disregard for truth and decency by certain members of the GECOM Secretariat leaves a feeling of great distaste in the mouths of ordinary Guyanese who have been subjected to scorn, disdain and ridicule by the rest of the world even as we struggle to come to terms with the COVID-19 disaster."*

On July 17, 2020, and on July 25, 2020, the Bar Council of the Association condemned the media and social media attacks, targeted at Attorneys-at-Law and the judges appearing in legal proceedings before the High Court, the Court of Appeal and the Caribbean Court of Justice. The Council spoke of escalated statements aimed at the judiciary in an appalling effort to alter the course of justice. They unreservedly denounced the personal attacks against the judiciary and the professionals who were exercising their professional duties. One of the members of this local observer team, Mr. Selwyn Pieters,[244] was the lynchpin between details emanating from the elections process and relaying clean, unadulterated, addictive video data from cradle to grave thereby providing the people of Guyana and the international community knowledge of the happenings for over 153 days. The critical role that he played in the relentless, defense of democracy cannot be downplayed.

What the erosion of democracy over the 153 days has taught the world is that Guyanese are more resilient and resourceful than was ever imagined. Due to the many court cases and delays in declaring the results of the General and Regional elections, the containers which stored the ballot boxes were located at the GECOM Headquarters, Kingston, Georgetown. As is the practice, one representative from each political party was permitted to watch the containers from within GECOM's compound and across from the Arthur Chung Convention Center.

A group, Guardians of Democracy[245] made up of all the ethnicities of Guyana had ensured that the containers containing the ballot boxes were watched day and night by way of a particularly well-organized system of scheduling. Lack of confidence in GECOM hastened the creation and reason for such a group. Group members sacrificed sleep and time and the fear of contracting corona virus for the sake of democracy. The Group was fully supported by concerned citizens who provided water, coffee, drinks and meals throughout the day and evenings. Even when the pandemic was in full swing, people remained in their vehicles a safe distance away as they practiced social distancing for the cause. Sanitizers were generously donated for the guardians to be safely protected.

Though GECOM opined that the security of the ballot boxes was within the purview of the CEO, legislation does not exist for anyone outside of the GECOM Commission to guard the boxes. The two largest parties, the APNU+AFC and the PPP-C, had placed padlocks on all the containers housing the ballot boxes. Those who were instrumental in the formation of the Guardians of Democracy included Mr. Majeed Hussain, a Justice of the Peace, who died from Covid-19 in January 2021 and was described as a foot soldier in the fight to subvert democracy. Mr. Bryan MacIntosh who played an integral role in the informal group's dynamics, was arrested for issuing threats to public officials through sheer frustration at how the election process was being handled. It may have been because of their efforts that Guyana's President, His Excellency Dr. Irfaan M. Ali, announced on March 2, 2021, the anniversary of the 2020 Elections, the establishment of a national award called the Order of Democracy.

On March 7, 2020, Red Thread called on GECOM to fulfill their legal and statutory obligations to ensure the transparency and credibility of the electoral process for the tabulation, and verification of the cast votes. Aside from condemning the attempts to undermine the electoral process, they apprised the people of Guyana of the level of lawlessness which prevailed. They bemoaned the *"the acts of intimidation, the threats, and verbal attacks including sexual threats to women and girls, the physical violence, the reports of property invasion by groups, attacks on police officers and schoolchildren and ethnicity-based attacks being reported in several communities. Recent reports of the loss of life of one young person points to escalating violence which must cease immediately.[246]"* Their appeal to the people of Guyana to quit the ethnic slurs, to respect the rule of law and to keep the peace, fell on deaf ears.

One week later, the African Cultural and Development Association (ACDA) took umbrage to what they deemed as interference from the Western nations in Guyana' electoral process and an attempt to recolonize the people of a sovereign Guyana by controlling the election process and preventing GECOM from completing its work. ACDA stated that *"This peculiar recolonization effort is displayed in the relentless attempts of some Ambassadors to keep African Guyanese under the control of foreign sovereigns. This view is evidenced by the known fact that one of the vocal Ambassadors in Guyana is seen regularly and intimately in the company of known Opposition activists and another was found aiding the departure of Charandass, who moved to oust the APNU+AFC Government from power.[247]"* They did not have many positive words for the ABCE countries when they stated that *"African Guyanese, reject the dictates of our former colonial power the UK, and its kit(h) and kin the USA, Canada and the EU who seem to think that they have the right to meddle in our electoral process as they see fit, ignore the rule of law and cast aside when they feel like the judgements of our courts."*

By April 9, 2020, the Guyana Consumers Association (GCA) had written GECOM's Chairman to plead for the use of livestreaming of the National Recount exercise to provide credibility to the process. This request, no doubt, had bearing on the deliberations of the GECOM Commission as it did become a partial reality. The GCA argued the merits of the full broadcast of the National Recount to involve the people of Guyana in the elections process, bringing hope to them and the full realization that Guyana was working on strengthening its democracy but more specifically, it would *"eliminate the usual disagreements and acrimony in which the Election affairs have been enveloped over the last month."* This recommendation met with a high measure of success that led to transparency of the recount process.

Protests by the Business Sector:

Aside from the civil society groups offering a wide range of opinions and warnings against the flawed selection of a President of Guyana, the business sector was particularly vigilant and vocal. On March 31, 2020, the Guyana Manufacturing and Services Association (GMSA) urged the political, electoral and other stakeholders to resolve the current impasse which was delaying the election process. The GMSA spelt out the political uncertainty which had a negative impact on the business sector and therefore, the citizens of Guyana. They appealed for a return to the climate of good governance and security of the livelihood of the people of Guyana given the dual impact of Covid-19 and the political impasse on the economy. The President, M. Clinton Williams, stated that *"Business thrives on political stability, and the current impasse is very disruptive. It threatens to erode gains made through the support of our regional and international partners and widens ethnic divisions…Layoffs have already commenced at some companies and may be expanding. We recognize the specific roles ascribed to political parties, civil society, and Guyana Elections Commission (GECOM), as outlined in our Constitution, in consort with the neutral presence of both local and international observers*[248]*"*

By the time, the National Recount had been competed the GMSA had a new President, Mr. Shyam Nokta. His concerns echoed those of the GCCI, the PSA, civil society, and other Chambers of Commerce from Regions 1 to 10 as he called for the declaration of the results based on the National Recount process, and the transition to a new Government which reflected the will of the Guyanese people. He reasoned that *"The political impasse, the absence of a functional Government, the COVID-19 pandemic and the lack of a coherent and comprehensive response, have made it difficult for businesses to operate. As a result, many have closed, resulting in losses of jobs and income for Guyanese. A continuation of this current situation will have disastrous consequences on the business community and the economy.*[249]*"*

Two days later, from the first GMSA's appeal of April 2, 2020, the Private Sector Commission (PSC), an accredited observer for the Elections 2020, and a large number of private sector bodies wrote to the Prime Minister of Barbados who was the chair of CARICOM, the Honourable Mia Mottley, to request that CARICOM continue to engage with Guyana on the elections process. They expressed frustration that the original High-Level team's departure from Guyana filled the air with doom and despair. However, the subsequent return of another CARICOM team to scrutinize the National Recount provided the citizens with hope and expectations. A few days later, the PSC called on the Commissioner of Police to ensure that *"every possible precaution is taken to guarantee the safety and security of the Arthur Chung Convention Centre, the persons of the stakeholders involved, and the process being conducted against any possible attempt to disrupt the procedures being put in place for the recount.*[250]*"* A similar letter was penned to the Executive Secretary of the Inter-American Commission on Human Rights, Mr. Pablo Abrao. The letter laid out the PSC's commitment to maintain democracy and the rule of law and full support for the principles and values established in the Charter of the Organisation of American States (OAS) and the Inter-American Democratic Charter, especially Articles 1 to 3.

It took an extraordinary turn of events for the religious sector to be immersed in political conditions in Guyana. With the erosion of democracy, a certain possibility, the major religious organizations made their feelings known to the people of Guyana and to the international community.

Protests by Academic & Religious Sector:
On March 7, 2020, the Bishop of Georgetown, Bishop Francis Alleyne, rendered his opinion backed up by facts that were known to all but the politicians who were blinded by their power high. He wrote to the Editor of the Stabroek News stating, *"People are dying, people are being wounded, children are*

being traumatized, property is being destroyed, the nation is gripped in fear. This is much too high a cost for a national election and for a nation at any time. There are no words strong enough to express the gravity of the situation and the urgency for it to end.

To all accounts the way forward for the restoration of peace and hope rests with a small group of persons who have been tasked with managing the whole election process. I add my voice to the many others in making strong appeal to the Guyana Elections Commission to expeditiously complete the verification process towards the transparent, formal and lawful declaration of results. Meanwhile, let us keep our heads above the fray and not let the words of our national pledge fall empty ' ... to be loyal to my country, to be obedient to the laws of Guyana, to love my fellow citizens and to dedicate my energies towards the happiness and prosperity of Guyana.' This is something that we can all do. May God Bless Guyana."

On June 29, 2020, the President of the Central Islamic Organisation of Guyana (CIOG), Al-Hajj Shahabudeen Ahmad, called on GECOM to fulfill its constitutionally mandated duty and declare the winner of the 2020 election as soon as the Caribbean Court of Justice (CCJ) made its ruling. Additionally, the CIOG called on the Guyana Police Force (GPF) to uphold the rule of law in a responsible manner. At the same time, the GPF was asked to address and monitor all the inflammatory actions taken by supporters and leaders of political parties by serving all Guyanese citizens. CIOG lauded the citizens of Guyana for their restraint and patience as they awaited the results of the National Recount and pled with GECOM to respect and honor the will of the people as expressed by most of the electorate at the polls.

On July 23, 2020, the Inter Religious Organization (IRO) of Guyana and the Guyana Council of Churches (GCC) in what was described as an uncommon act, issued a joint statement expressing grave concerns at the deteriorating political climate in the country and the negative international image being portrayed. *"As Guyanese, it is imperative that regardless of our political persuasions, that Guyana's interests be paramount in all regards. Further, as religious leaders, we firmly stand on the side of morality and good governance[251]."* The Statements provoked reasons for the political leaders to take the opportunity to permit constitutional reform and betterments for the people of Guyana. The Organizations reasoned that in the absence of a proper solution to the political impasse, the pattern of behavior would be a *"'cancer in the bones' of our beloved nation gnawing away at our national life and progress as a nation"* preventing unity, inclusivity and tolerance.

Beyond the business sector, the politicians, the international community and the attorneys-at-law, diplomats and diplomatic mission had no end of opinions and support for the rule of law in Guyana. The regional critics were particularly aggressive especially those who called Guyana their home at some point of time in the past. During the month of March 2020, the news media was flooded with concerns for the integrity of the elections and appeals to GECOM and the APNU+AFC Coalition government and to a lesser extent, the PPP-C.

On March 22, 2020, the former Guyana Minister of Foreign Affairs, Mr. Rudy Insanally urged President David Granger to remain faithful to his promise of ensuring a recount of votes cast in the March 2, 2020, General and Regional Elections in order to bring an end to the political crisis. As a diplomat, Mr. Insanally warned President Granger of the probably sanctions reserved for Guyana if the government refused to comply with the norms of a responsible government.

He emphasized how, as *"a retired diplomat and technocrat Minister for Foreign Affairs who has served every government and President since Guyana's independence, I believe I have earned the right to express to you the concerns which I have over the current crises, both global and national, as well as the disastrous impact which they may have eventually on our country and its people. I believe that you know me well enough to accept my message as impartial, sincere, and intended only to prevent a descent into anarchy. Not unnaturally, one of my greatest fears is that, having worked for a lifetime to build close and cooperative relations between Guyana and the international community, the resounding furore which followed the recent election and projected us abroad as a racist and undemocratic polity, will most likely reduce our current prestigious world standing to pariah status and public scorn. Not only our domestic policies but also our international initiatives will be seen as mere charade.*[252]*"*

Mr. Insanally bemoaned the impending sanctions; he reminded the President that the sanctions impacted the poor and economically vulnerable with hardly any effect on the rich and powerful. Unfortunately, after urging President Granger to remain faithful to his promises, the appeal fell on deaf ears and the unleashing of legal challenges which constrained the declaration of the results and the naming of a new president. As a diplomat, concerned about the image of Guyana to the rest of the world, he feared that any improvement in Guyana's relations with CARICOM and the rest of the world would be stymied. Mr. Insanally presented a book to President Granger in which he attempted to identify some of the reasons for Guyana's sad state of affairs as an independent nation. The book was titled, *The Guyanese Culture: Fusion or Diffusion.* Some of the reasons included, the psychological damage inflicted by slavery and colonization, the weak and regressive political culture, the growing racial division exploited by unscrupulous politicians, an unstable economic and social environment and the replacement of political democracy by political demagoguery among other reasons.

When Sir Ronald Sanders, Antigua and Barbuda's Ambassador to the USA and the OAS, joined the fray, when diplomacy had long been exhausted and the gloves were off. Sir. Ronald, on March 30, 2020, addressed the issue of the herd mentality that was all pervasive during the 153 days standoff by writing that the attitude that *"international approval is unnecessary and international disapproval, however demonstrated, is both unimportant and incapable of harming the country. Nothing could be further from reality. Should the Guyana general elections be declared, and a government established, without the blessing of the international organizations that the Government invited to observe those elections, Guyana could face suspension from the Commonwealth and from the Organisation of American States (OAS) – two of the most important organisations to which it belongs, for breaches of the Commonwealth 1991 Harare Declaration on the protection and promotion of the fundamental political values of the Commonwealth, and the Inter-American Democratic Charter that guides the OAS.*

Once the machinery of the Commonwealth and the OAS are invoked – as it certainly will be – suspension of Guyana from the councils of both organizations will assuredly follow. The European Union will also take separate action that will be directed at suspending normal terms of trade, aid and investment relations. The latter will have an immediate effect that will be immediately apparent in Guyana."

What Sir Ronald revealed was that if Guyana were suspended from the Councils of the OAS and the Commonwealth, it would not have a voice in these two Organizations and would therefore not be able to argue its case in defense of its sovereignty and territorial integrity in the face of claims by Venezuela. This would leave Guyana vulnerable to Venezuela's claim. Sir Ronald reminded his readers of what Mr. Mike Pompeo, the U.S. Secretary of State, had already said that *"individuals who seek to benefit from electoral fraud and form illegitimate governments/regimes will be subject to a variety of serious consequences from the United States"*. He added that *"it will start with sanctions against state owned enterprise. And that will mean sanctions against any enterprise in Guyana that happens to own oil. The money that would have come to that state enterprise will get frozen and the Guyana Government would not be able to touch it. Now, I am not making this up you can look at the history of several other countries including neighbouring Venezuela to see what has happened to their assets as sanctions have escalated against them. But ultimately, you are a pariah state.*[253]"

As diverse as a former GECOM Chairman such as Brigadier Joseph Singh to a recipient of one of Guyana's highest national honors, the Cacique Crown of Honour, Ms. Supriya Singh-Bodden stated that she could not wear the award with pride and therefore renounced it given that the recent events surrounding the elections process, she feared were wrong. Even former Peoples National Congress Reform (PNC/R) Parliamentarian Anthony Vieira claimed that the PNC-led APNU/AFC coalition was holding on to power through a coup d'etat, since it had been more than 30 days after the 2020 elections and a winner was yet to be announced.

It took Regional academics and retired professionals about four months before the reality of what was happening in Guyana sunk in. For four whole months, the professionals of the CARICOM Region debated whether the electoral farce in Guyana was real or even whether it was prudent to comment on the situation reminiscent of a US-based reality show. Within the last decade, fewer and fewer Caribbean academics have been commenting on the glaring economic and political shifts within the CARICOM Region. Gone are the times when a solid political thrashing would have been unleashed upon the recalcitrant, Caribbean political leaders from the likes of Professor Neville Duncan of the UWI, Jamaica and Dr. Frank Alleyne of the UWI, Barbados.

Around June 6, 2020, one of the most revered and, at the same time, hated analysts and critics of the elections in Guyana was Mr. John Beale, a former Ambassador of Barbados to the USA and to the OAS. Mr. Beale did not expect CARICOM to remain silent as it had done in the past but must speak out as the late Prime Minister of Barbados, Errol Walton Barrow, did when he referred to some of the leaders of the Easter Caribbean as *"bandits."* As a matter of fact, Mr. Beale revealed that President David A. Granger was being called a *"sanctimonious bastard"* within certain circles within the CARICOM Region. He has been an outspoken critic of the CARICOM Region's financial issues and governance. He reminded the Region that the General Secretariat of the OAS stated that *"regrettably the Guyana Elections Commission (GECOM) has refused to provide the OAS Mission with important documents,"* by which he was referring to the SOPs from Region 4.

Mr. Beale stated that *"Numerous opportunities have been given to the President of Guyana, David Granger, to come clean and while he gives the impression that he supports free and fair elections his actions do not. Based on his actions I am prepared to predict that Granger will not accept the results of the elections (the recount, so far, shows that he will lose), and he will do everything possible, including disregarding the rule of law, to remain in power. His actions could include fomenting civil strife in order to declare a state of emergency and martial law, allowing him to rule by decree with the backing of a cabal around him."* His Press Release was counsel to CARICOM for them not to tolerate the Coalition's violations of democracy, the rule of law and political and civil rights because the latter was like a cancer that would spread to all the limbs of the Regional body depriving it of moral and diplomatic standing.

On July 2, 2020, another Barbadian Political Analyst, Professor Andy Knight, Professor of International Relations, University of Alberta, Canada whose work covers international relations, international law and global governance spoke, at length, about Guyana's election impasse and the challenges that Guyana was likely to face in the future. He predicted that Guyana would face sanctions and even removal of membership from such Regional and international bodies as CARICOM, the Commonwealth and even the OAS. He further alluded to the point that the USA would implement sanctions quickly against an illegitimate government. Consistent with his political analysis of Guyana, when the USA's President Donald Trump lost the elections to Mr. Joe Biden and angry protestors made their way to the Capitol, Mr. Knight pronounced that the *"United States' democracy is fragile and the will of the people should never be taken for granted.[254]"* It rang an eerie likeness to that of Guyana.

On the same televised programme, Trinidad and Tobago's CNC 3 television, Mr. Winston Dookeran, a former Senior Economist at the United Nations Economic Commission for Latin America and the Caribbean

(ECLAC), former Governor of the Central Bank of Trinidad and Tobago, and former Minister of Foreign Affairs of Trinidad and Tobago clarified that Guyana's elections were the most outstanding and credible election run by GECOM as witnessed by local and international observers. Hence, the APNU+AFC Coalition government was urged to concede defeat to facilitate a smooth transition for the rightful president to be sworn in and to uphold and preserve democratic governance. He suggested that *"There is no reason to doubt the consensus opinion and veracity of the CARICOM Observer Team, the OAS, the Commonwealth Observation Mission, the Carter Center, the embassies and Ambassadors of European Union, and the United States, the High Commissioners from Canada and the United Kingdom, representatives from Norway, the Elders Group, and the ABCE foreign powers. Several independent bodies in Guyana, including the Guyana Human Rights Association, the Georgetown Chamber of Commerce, the Private Sector Commission, and even partners within the APNU + AFC coalition itself have determined that the 2020 election was free and fair, and that the recount was credible. All of these observers can't be wrong.[255]."*

On July 10, 2020, Guyana's golden son of the soil, Sir Shridath Ramphal, a former Attorney-General and Minister of Foreign Affairs of Guyana; Secretary-General of the Commonwealth; Chairman of the West Indian Commission; and Head of the CARICOM Regional Negotiating Machinery appealed to GECOM, *"fortified by the Court's judgement and the people's demonstrated will"* to sustain democracy in Guyana, it's constitutional duty. Mr. Ramphal was the distinguished international lawyer and member of Guyana's legal team who presented at the public hearing on the question of the jurisdiction of the International Court of Justice in the case concerning the Arbitral Award of 1899 (**Guyana vs Venezuela**) which was held on June 30, 2020, at the Peace Palace in The Hague amidst the political uncertainties and divisiveness.

He appealed to the oneness of Guyanese and called for the destruction of the myth of otherness by cultivating the, by conscious effort, the oneness that is Guyana's historical birthright. When he spoke at the Inauguration of President David A. Granger in 2015, he said, *"At Independence, we aspired to Guyana's worthy destiny through being one nation and one people. We were one people then and have been ever since — save in our politics through which we deceive ourselves into believing that our motto of 'one people' is false. It is not false, and we must not let the vicissitudes of politics and the discord inherent in the democratic process diminish our oneness."*

As a former Secretary General of the Commonwealth for fifteen years, he projected that Caribbean democracy demanded no less and that Guyana, CARICOM and the Western hemisphere even our world would not allow less. He called for all citizens to work hard at realizing the country's motto of One People, One Nation, One Destiny.

Finally, on July 11, 2020, Professor Sir Hillary Beckles, the current Vice-Chancellor of the University of the West Indies joined with the current and past Chairs of CARICOM, the Honourable Ralph Gonsalves and the Honourable Mia Mottley respectively, and with the former Prime Minister of Barbados, the Honourable Owen Arthur, *"in calling for the official embrace of the evidentiary truth of the election. Every hour that the celebration of a new day is allowed to sour, the greater will be the tarnish on the varnish of the history of a great nation.[256]"*

His dispassionate plea for commonsense and unity to prevail in Guyana was a personal rather than political or professional perspective which went beyond the borders of a seemingly divisive circumstance as he outlined the history of his ancestors which intertwined with that of the Barbadians. His Barbadian father who lived in Guyana supported the nation's dream for democratic development and the equality of ethnicities. As a historian, Sir Hillary captured not only the historical ethnic rifts but the beauty of the diversity of the land. He stated that *"above it all, there is also the compelling story, in the history from sea walls to sugar estates, of commitment to the paramount principle that the will of the people should not be toppled, but respected."* He reflected what all other Regional academics has already boldly stated in that the people and the highest court of the land had spoken. CARICOM had reviewed and painstakingly monitored the electoral process and that Guyana's future was assured with compliance of the State to the will of the people.

In keeping with his visionary forecasts, he added, *"Fear of the future is not an acceptable explanation for franchise frustration in the present. Ethical conduct, and not ethnic constructs, is expected to rule when democracy is in need of advocacy. The children of indigenous survivors, the chattel enslaved, the deceived indentured, and others in between, must now converge at the rendezvous of victory. The minority party should stay the course and continue to contribute to the sustainability and maturity of the integrated, multi-racial nation."*

Sir Hillary affirmed that Guyana had much to teach the CARICOM Region and the rest of the world despite the current political challenges. He reflected that this year marked the 40th anniversary of the violent taking of Walter Rodney's life, one of the generations of outstanding Guyanese scholars who was nurtured by his father, an educator. Dr. Rodney's life, he contended, was forfeited *"because of the socially and politically integrated values he held most dear."*

International Protests:

Almost every country from sea to shining sea weighed in on Guyana's political situation. The statements emanating from their respective and equivalent Ministries of Foreign Affairs was to the effect that *"it is imperative that the election authorities in Guyana count every vote in accordance with the established law, procedure and best practices so as to lend credibility to the results."*

From March 22, 2020, through to July 2020, the Governments of St. Vincent and the Grenadines, Dominica, Barbados, Jamaica and Trinidad and Tobago made their concerns as pellucid as the waters of the Caribbean Sea. CARICOM played an integral role in the completion of the process from cradle to grave. It wasn't until the situation on the lengthy period before the declaration of the winner of the elections became unbearable that even the neighboring, Latin American countries started to issue statements on the electoral process.

The Brazilian[257] government, four months after the elections, considered that the delaying of the conclusion of the electoral process posed a serious threat to stability in Guyana and further called on Guyana, an Associated State of MERCOSUR, to remain among the South American nations committed to the highest democratic principles. In March 2019, the governments of Argentina, Brazil, Colombia, Chile, Ecuador, Guyana, Paraguay, and Peru signed the Santiago Declaration to become the original members of PROSUR, a forum for the fostering of regional cooperation and development in South America. It replaced the Union of South American States (UNASUR). One year and four months later, six of the South American members of PROSUR emphasized that one of the essential guidelines of the body is respect for democracy. PROSUR held its first summit in 2019 and excluded Venezuela.

According to Section five of the Santiago Declaration, for which Guyana is a signatory, *"That the essential requirements to participate in this space will be the full validity of democracy, of the respective constitutional orders, respect for the principle of separation of the Powers of the State, and the promotion, protection, respect and guarantee of human rights and fundamental freedoms...[258]"* The countries were fearful that Guyana would slip into anarchy like its neighbor, Venezuela, and have its membership withdrawn.

Further afield, the ABCE countries were relentless in their defense of democracy highlighted by the persistence of their ambassadors and the multiple tweets, social media missives and video proclamations from officials in their respective governments. Particularly blunt were the Acting Assistant Secretary for the United States' Department of State's Bureau of Western Hemisphere Affairs, Mr. Michael G. Kozak, the British Foreign Secretary, Mr. Dominic Raab,[259] the Deputy Director and Senior Analyst at Global Affairs Canada, Mr. Michael Grant, and the Ambassador of the European Union, H.E. Fernando Ponz-Canto.

Though the elections of the United States were no less colorful than that of Guyana for intrigue, riots and invasion of their seat of power, Acting Assistant Secretary for the United States, the Department of State's Bureau of Western Hemisphere Affairs, Mr. Michael G. Kozak, tweeted on March 6, 2020, *"The people of #Guyana deserve a credible election and legitimate transfer of power; the democracies of the region expect that Guyana will uphold our shared values."* Members of the United States Congress were no less deeply concerned. Within days of the tweet, the United States Secretary of State, Mr. Michael Pompeo, posted that the United States was committed to the protection of Guyana's democracy. The United State's vested interest in Guyana's elections went as far back as January 23, 2020, when Congressman Albio Sires (D-NJ), Chairman of the Subcommittee on the Western Hemisphere, Civilian Security, and Trade, lead a congressional delegation to Guyana with Representative Gregory Meeks (D-NY) and Congresswoman Yvette Clarke (D-NY). According to Congressman Sires, the officials visited to *"convey our support for free, fair, and fully democratic elections on March 2, 2020. As we expressed to President Granger, opposition leader Bharrat Jagdeo, election commission members, and other stakeholders, the United States government plans to work closely with the people and government of Guyana, regardless of who wins the March election. Guyana has the potential for a very bright future and, as Chairman of the Western Hemisphere Subcommittee, I will work to deepen relations between our two countries and to support the aspirations of the people of Guyana.[260]."* Again, on July 15, 2020, when the unravelling of the democratic processes proved too much, the three Congresspersons voiced their concerns boldly.

By March 26, 2020, the United States Government[261] had summoned Guyana's Ambassador to the United States, Mr. Riyad Insanally, reinforcing their position of an elected government sworn in by way of using flawed elections results. The United States Ambassador to Guyana, Ms. Sarah Ann-Lynch, issued a statement in defense of the USA's continuous appeals to the Coalition government and GECOM for fair elections. She stated that the actions of the United States government officials could not be interpreted as foreign interference *"but good diplomacy by members of the hemisphere's democratic club."* The citizens of Guyana were not in agreement. Ambassador Lynch reminded the people of Guyana that the government of Guyana, in January 2019, proclaimed that *"that the electoral process that took place in Venezuela on May 20, 2018, lacked legitimacy as it neither included the participation of all political actors in Venezuela, nor did it have the presence of independent international observers, nor did it comply with the necessary guarantees or international standards for a free, fair and transparent election. Accordingly, we do not recognize the legitimacy of the new presidential term of Nicolas Maduro, or his regime, which commences on January 10, 2019."*

After hinting at economic sanctions against the perpetrators of the election fraud, the Chairman of the Senate Committee on Foreign Relations, Senator Jim Risch, on July 15, 2020, endorsed the visa restrictions imposed against Guyanese officials who were seeking to undermine democracy.[262] Other countries followed suit. It was presumed that all their bank accounts and foreign assets abroad would be frozen. Their local Guyana bank accounts would not be able to wire money abroad. Their overseas family members would not be able to receive money. Their businesses would be blacklisted and would not be able to engage in trade and or foreign transactions. Worse, they could face criminal charges in the USA including conspiracy for electoral fraud in Guyana.

On September 18, 2020, almost one month after His Excellency Dr. Mohamed Irfaan Ali was elected President of the Co-operative Republic of Guyana, he met with Mr. Michael Pompeo, Secretary of State of the United States of America in Guyana. It was the first visit by a Secretary of State to

Guyana as a testament to prioritizing the USA's *"relations with the countries of Latin America and the Caribbean.*[263]*"* President Ali confirmed that he was *"grateful to the United States Government and, in particular, to Secretary Pompeo, for their unwavering support for democracy and constitutional order in Guyana, during the recent political and electoral crisis in our country. Secretary Pompeo's visit serves to remind us that the US will continue to be a steadfast partner, as we work with all stakeholders to consolidate our democracy, strengthen our institutions and pursue a path of unprecedented economic growth and development. Secretary Pompeo's visit, moreover, solidifies the bilateral relationship between Guyana and the US and sets the stage for expanding and deepening US cooperation with Guyana.*

I am, therefore, pleased to announce the signing, this morning, of a Framework Agreement between the US Government and the Government of Guyana, to Strengthen Energy and Infrastructure Finance and Market Building Cooperation, in the context of the Growth in the Americas Initiative."

The Framework Agreement would permit the USA's private sector to expand their investment portfolio and to partner with the Guyanese private sector. It would provide more investment opportunities for American firms to explore the tourism and hospitality sector, ICT and food production. The Agreement would deepen cooperation in the areas of security, with specific attention to maritime security and joint patrols, to interdict narcotics trafficking. This would also allow Guyana to improve their technical and human capabilities in monitoring Guyana's Exclusive Economic Zone.

The events of March 5, 2020 resonated as far as the Asian and African countries where the Secretary-General of the African, Caribbean and Pacific Group of States (ACP), H.E. Mr. Georges Rebelo Pinto Chikoti, commended the efforts of the Caribbean Community (CARICOM) and its leadership in their support of a solution to the political situation in Guyana whereas the Elders, Nelson Mandela-founded global peace and human rights non-profit organization, appealed to the Coalition government for the return of the observers of the Carter Center who were barred from re-entering Guyana to complete their tasks during the Recount process.

The Elders consists of former leaders of NGOs and governments from throughout the world, the most famous of which are the former United Nations Secretary General, Mr. Ban Ki-moon, former presidents Ms. Ellen Johnson Sirleaf, of Liberia, Mr. Juan Manuel Santos of Colombia and Martti Ahtisaari of Finland. In addition, former U.S President and founder of the Carter Center, Mr. Jimmy Carter, Bishop Desmond Tutu, Archbishop Emeritus and of Cape Town, South Africa former presidents Ernesto Zedillo of Mexico, Ricardo Lagos of Chile and first women presidents of Ireland and Norway respectively, Ms. Mary Robinson and Ms. Gro Harlem Brundtland are members. The Groups main objectives are to work *"both publicly and through private diplomacy, our mission is to engage with global leaders and civil society at all levels to resolve conflict and address its root causes, to challenge injustice, and to promote ethical leadership and good governance[264].[264]."*

In March 2020 and again in July 2020 spokesperson for India's Ministry of External Affairs, Mr. Anurag Srivastava,[265] Guyana was reminded that *"as a democracy itself, and a time-tested friend of Guyana, India would underline that is important that Guyana's electoral process are credible, fair and transparent."* Ambassador of the Kingdom of Norway, Mr. Nils Martin Genneng, posted on twitter that *"Norway shares concerns expressed regarding recent electoral developments in Guyana. The final election results need to be credible and transparent."* The volatile political situation in Guyana following the presidential election has caused Norway, Guyana's major financial partner on climate change, to block NOK 393 million in climate aid. *"No further decisions will be made on … planning or spending[266]"* of this money until a legitimate government is in place. Up to the time of publishing, Guyana has not received NOK 1 billion in climate aid committed by Norway 11 years ago.

The British, in addition to enforcing visa restrictions much in the same mold as the USA, placed on hold, the funding for key infrastructure projects since September 2019 as a result of the No Confidence Motion. The United Kingdom had deemed the Government unconstitutional and paused funds for the construction of the road between Linden and Mabura and the bridge at Kurupukari. The Kingston-Ogle seawall development project was included in the portfolio of projects on hold.

Oil and Gas Sector:

Guyana's fledgling Oil and Gas industry suffered because of the deviations from the norm during the 153 days of arriving at election results. Guyana is an integral part of Exxon's growth plans. However, Mr. Mark Bynoe, Director of Energy, projected that the evaluation of Exxon's Payara field development plan *"is continuing, but has been impacted by factors outside the control of the Department of Energy,[267]"* referring to the volatility of the political situation. Even though the Covid-19 pandemic had caused considerable rumblings in the Oil and Gas sector, with global project sanctioning declining in 2020 of over 75% from 2019 levels, political uncertainty in Guyana delayed government approvals for the ExxonMobil-operated Stabroek block.

According to Karan Satwani, Energy Service Analyst at Rystad Energy, *"At the beginning of this year, the project commitments forecast for 2020 were expected to be comparable to 2019, but the industry downturn thanks to COVID-19 has caused commitments to fall sharply. Going forward, Rystad Energy estimates that sanctioning will not pick up again and recover to 2019 levels anytime soon.[268]"* ExxonMobil's Payara Development, projected to be sanctioned in 2019 was pushed back to 2020 but the 153-days delay in elections results in Guyana resulted in project sanctioning being further stalled, with approval now likely in 2021. Project delays could reduce the government's take by more than $4.5 billion and could trigger a domino effect by delaying future projects one after the other. Rystad

Energy has projected that a 24-month delay for the Payara development could see Guyana losing as much as 75 million[269] barrels of oil.

Other Issues:

The most harrowing, direct impact of the hijacking of the results of the elections has been the physical and psychological fallout. On June 11, 2020, the US Embassy issued a security alert ahead of the declaration of elections results in Guyana requesting U.S. government personnel to take precautions and to prepare for any unexpected disruptions to their normal routine.

On July 14, 2020, a fire destroyed the office of the Guyana Elections Commission (GECOM) at Wismar Linden just before 2:00 am in what the Guyana Police Force believed to be an act of arson. Three men were remanded to prison for unlawfully and maliciously setting fire to the GECOM building. They were residents of Linden.

On October 31, 2020, Mr. Ryan Williams, a 47-year-old Lindener was the first person to be charged under the Cyber Crime Act, Section 2, Chapter 19:1(b), *"using a computer system to coerce, harass, intimidate or humiliate a person,"* specifically, the Chairman of GECOM, Justice Singh. In a letter to Justice Singh as a condition of having her drop the charges, he apologized publicly. He used a Facebook account under the name *'**Raheem Raahman'**** to threaten the Chairman of GECOM and her family by using a computer system to publish or transmit computer data.

According to the online Cambridge Dictionary, a protest is *"a strong complaint expressing disagreement, disapproval, or opposition."* Political protests have increased in frequency and intensity over the last decade, worldwide. The Carnegie Endowment for International Peace's Global Protest Tracker identifies over 230 significant anti-government protests internationally in more than 110 countries[270]. Unsanctioned, peaceful protests by members and supporters of the PPP-C commenced on March 6, 2020, the day following Mr. Mingo's sleight of hand before escalating into a horrific attack on school children and the Guyana Police Force.

The PPP-C protestors, since September 19, 2019, when they protested the Government's proposed Election date of February 2020 at the Pegasus Hotel where President David A. Granger delivered the address at a luncheon hosted by the Guyana Manufacturing & Services Association, were clearly frustrated by the events of the previous day. They feared a return to a dictatorial regime, the denial of their rights to vote for the leader of their choice and the impact of exercising their franchise on the democratic process. They had firsthand knowledge and accounts from the diplomats, local and foreign observers of credible evidence of fraud in the tallying of the results of votes casted on March 2, 2020.

It was mere coincidence that the protests were launched on the 23rd anniversary of the death of Dr. Cheddie Jagan, a founding member of the PPP and late President of the Cooperative Republic of Guyana. From morning until evening of March 6, 2020, protestors voiced their concerns, at first peacefully, then with increasing vigor as conditions remained unchanged at GECOM. Protests were launched in Berbice, on the East Coast Demerara and on the East Bank Demerara.

Within Region 5, Mahaica-Berbice, stretching from Bush Lot Village to Cotton Tree Village, West Coast Berbice, PPP-C supporters lined the street voicing their concerns to whomsoever would listen. A car was set afire, obstacles were placed on the roadway and burnt inconveniencing the passersby and sending fear throughout the communities. Two buses, bearing the name 'David G' induced a Pavlovian effect resulting in the deliberate pelting of the buses by angry protestors who were unmindful of the innocent children and teachers who were travelling to their respective homes. The unlawful actions of the protestors resulted in broken windows, injuries to seven school children and untold trauma. The children were treated at the Fort Wellington Public Hospital[271] and subsequently released. The attacks on the two buses occurred at Bath Settlement and at Bush Lot as the buses passed through a throng of irate protestors. The six-year-old son of one of the parents who witnessed the episode asked, on seeing the incident and witnessing injured children, asked, "*Daddy, is that going to happen to us and all other children?*"

Ranks of the Guyana Police Force, Sergeant 16999 Punit Nuth Ibarem, Constable Shomeika Wickham, Constable Ron Grant, Constable Jafta Fraser and Constable Tussie Wallerson, along with other colleagues sustained fractures to their ankles, feet and injuries to their heads and hands due to the stone pelting actions of, and severe beatings by, the unrelenting crowd. The ranks were outnumbered and ill-equipped to deal with such large gatherings of demonstrators who, as a consequence of imbibing alcohol, became less friendly and broke the laws of the land with impunity. Racial slurs and an excess of expletives were launched at the riot police, relentlessly.

It ought to be remembered that the Cheddi Jagan government fell in 1953 as a consequence of the conspiracy of the British government. The PPP-C supporters have memories as long as that of an elephant. Accordingly, Sir Alfred Savage, Governor of British Guiana in a speech to the new legislature of British Guiana warned Guyanese that those who feel "*that El Dorado has now been discovered I would say you must not expect too early or too easy a solution to your problems. . . . If labour will give of its best and if capital will deal justly with its employees, the partnership of interests will be more apparent and the general industrial health of this country will be assured. . . . finally, British Guiana has been described as 'the land of six peoples' and a most heartening feature of the recent elections was the absence of racialism.[272]*" Though these words were spoken on May 30, 1953, they apply to the twenty-first century as we substitute for gold, the oil and gas and absorb the principles taught two generations ago but are just as applicable.

"The Police Force in British Guiana is up to strength and as far as we know is not disaffected. The lower ranks are predominantly African which may be a factor of importance if, as seems possible, disturbances are caused by East Indians.[273]*"* Close to seventy years ago, this extract from an internal Colonial Office memorandum on the availability of forces to prevent disturbances in British Guiana still applies. Certainly, the Spanish philosopher, George Santayana's refrain *"those who cannot remember their history are condemned to repeat it"* is most apt even at this most troubling time in Guyana.

By evening of March 6, 2020, the situation was not under control by the authorities, and this led to the death of Mr. Sewdat *'Devon'* Hansraj, a teenager, who was shot by a rank of the Guyana Police Force. The rank was defending his colleague against a cutlass attack from Mr. Hansraj. Homes were broken into, and a handful of businesses were robbed. Lawlessness prevailed and fears went unchecked. Ultimately, the protestors were unwilling to live under the *"rule of a Dictator."*

Protests in several village areas on the West Coast Berbice by PPP-C supporters were not as severe as in East Berbice but protestors blocked the roads with agriculture machinery parts, burning tires and wood. At Canal Number Two, West Bank Demerara, blocked ingresses and egresses resulted in visits by ranks of the Guyana Police Force and the Guyana Fire Service. These events led Superintendent Jairam Ramlakhan, Public Relations and Press Officer of the Guyana Police Force to warn citizens of the impact of their callous disregard for the laws of the land in that *"when protest activities degenerate into public disorder, infringing on the rights of other citizens and putting the protection of life and the safeguard of property at risk, the Guyana Police Force will, as a consequence, take appropriate and condign action against all offenders. Be warned!"*

Meanwhile, on the East Coast Demerara, more specifically Lusignan and Mon Repos, a large cup, the symbol of the PPP-C's party, towered high above the predominantly pro-PPP-C protestors who were just as agitated as those in Berbice. They demanded a recount of the votes within the Region 4 District. The fear of being excluded from a share of Guyana's oil and gas wealth sunk home. The level of aggression, not only equaled but surpassed that of the supporters of the APNU+AFC. Unwilling to listen to the leaders within the PPP-C hierarchy, they burnt abandoned, derelict vehicles, felled utility poles, discarded tires and whatever materials that were combustible to send a clear warning that enough was enough. Thick, billowing black smoke filled the air and could be seen for miles. The main thoroughfare was thick with debris preventing vehicular traffic from moving slowly, if at all.

When the predominantly Afro-Guyanese ranks of the Guyana Police Force, the Riot Squad, arrived the situation escalated leading to ranks' use of teargas and rubber pellets into the unruly crowd. After about four hours, starting from approximately 4:00pm, the crowd dwindled. The crowd had gathered around noon in a sea of red clothing as they waved the PPP-C colors. Throughout the more than 8 hours of protesting, no systems were in place to prevent nor contain the corona virus despite the establishment of a National Covid-19 Task Force and the deadly nature of the pandemic.

Aside from Dr. Vindyha Persaud, Ms. Priya Manickchand and Dr. Frank Anthony, the former Attorney General, Mr. Anand Nandlall, appealed at length to the protestors to return to their homes and to bring calmness to the agitated conditions. They listened but did not respond positively. Mr. Nandlall[274] continued to plead with the unruly supporters by stating that, *"we are trying everything possible to get the verification process completed by the returning officer or the deputy and to have the electoral process restored to normalcy…we are speaking to Washington, we are speaking to the United Kingdom, we are speaking to Canada, we are speaking to the entire Commonwealth and Caribbean. We have the support; we have the full support of the international community. We have the full support of the local organizations in this country, the private sector, the labour movement, the religious organizations are all on the side of democracy…this is not only a PPP issue but this is a countrywide issue ."* The leader of the Opposition, Dr. Bharat Jagdeo released a video statement for his supporters to the effect that *"we will guide you as to what will happen further…stay at home. Remain calm but vigilant!!"* A similar sentiment was offered by President David A. Granger to the people of Guyana to conduct themselves in a peaceful and law-abiding manner. Tensions were at its zenith.

Central Georgetown was almost a ghost town as stores barricaded, schools closed, and the country prepared for the worse. The emotional toll cannot be calculated as persons from both sides of the political divide suffered psychologically as well as physically. Every news channel, more especially social media, recorded the action live and the worse of Guyana was presented to the world at large.

The APNU+AFC supporters were no less distressing to the public and the business sector. The vuvuzelas of the Coalition supporters, whether during the daytime or eventide, were chilling messages of intimidation. On June 18, 2020, Coalition supporters defied the Covid-19 Guidelines and protested without approval in the proximity of the GECOM building, Prince Elizabeth Road, New Amsterdam. The protestors' bone of contention was Justice Singh's decision to order the GECOM's CEO to prepare the final Report from the National Recount. Hundreds of protestors dressed in the traditional party colors of green and yellow chanted, *"GECOM! Get it right![275]"* Law enforcement officers were few but guided the procession instead of dispersing the supporters of the Coalition government. Simultaneously, protests were launched at the GECOM headquarters in Georgetown and a day earlier, Linden was the location of APNU+AFC's protests.

It was not surprising that on July 6, 2020, designated CARICOM Day, that supporters of APNU+AFC, mounted many peaceful protests in Regions 4 and 6 against the Caribbean Court of Justice (CCJ), an institution of CARICOM. The protestors believed that the CCJ has no jurisdiction on the

Guyana elections. Protesters were dispersed by ranks of the Guyana Police Force in keeping with the COVID-19 measures. During July 2020 a wave of intermittent protests was organized by the APNU+AFC organizers starting at the CARICOM Secretariat, and reaching as far as Anna Regina, Region 2, where the common themes were, ***Respect our Sovereignty, Foreign Interference, Valid Votes Only, Swear in David Granger*** and ***CCJ Must Respect the Constitution of Guyana***. The locations targeted included State House, the ABCE Embassies and the Georgetown Chamber of Commerce. At the State House, the Presidential convoy was blocked by supporters, more specifically, a handful of females who laid on the road and who had to be removed by the Presidential guards proving to be a security threat to the President. Their marches were predominately non-violent, noisy but intimidating.

There was no doubt that the protests were essential to the struggle for democracy, more so, during the pandemic period when personal and crowd restrictions were at their highest. However, it will be years within the future before any meaningful political change may be affected. T. Khemraj pointed out that the main driver of political instability is the competition for resources by the two major ethnic voting blocs. Consequently, the discovery of oil and gas may contribute to more intense conflict causing greater political instability in the future.[276]

On April 26, 2021, the Chief Justice (Ag) Roxane George dismissed the Coalition's Elections petition resulting in hundreds of protestors marching along Regent Street, Georgetown. In the past, Georgetown businesses have suffered economic losses of a results of the aggression of the Coalition's protestors, more specifically, the commercial center was a major target of the instability created by the violent protests between 1998-2001. Consequently, businesses closed for security purposes and the flow of traffic was disrupted.

For as long as there has been elections in Guyana, post-Independence, the various elections observer groups have written lengthy recommendations on how the Government of Guyana can resolve many of the pre-election tensions and anxieties and the post-elections violence. The EU Observer Mission Report encapsulated eight priority recommendations comparable to those of the other observer bodies ranging from the simplest one of adopting clear written procedures for the transmission and tabulation of election results, to fostering transparency and accountability in online and offline campaigning, and finally, to the review and consolidation of the fragmented election legislation to strengthen legal clarity and certainty and the launching of a national consultation process to overhaul the composition and functioning of GECOM.[277]

Very few of the recommendations have been implemented yet the Observers rehash the same recommendation threads in 5-year electoral cycles.

Electoral reform has always been at the top of the recommendations received with much indifference by the two major parties.

The International Development Law Organization (IDLO) has been active in Kenya, a country which shares similar ethnic mobilization and violence as Guyana, for over a decade. The IDLO's mandate is in *"promoting the rule of law. IDLO works to enable governments and empower people to reform laws and strengthen institutions to promote peace, justice, sustainable development and economic opportunity.*[278]*"* Aside from helping to build the capacity of the justice sector and legal profession in Kenya, it provided technical support to institutions *"mandated to implement or monitor the constitutional implementation process."* Where the IDLO's capacity building would be of greatest need is in the creation of *"strong judicial electoral dispute resolution mechanism"* to increase the electorates confidence in the electoral system and the systems to allow for political participation by the people of Guyana. Ms. Irene Khan, the IDLO Director-General has stated that *"as a contest for political power, elections by their nature invite disputes. Effective electoral dispute resolution is therefore key to preventing electoral violence and ensuring legitimacy of the results.*[279]*"* Of course, for this judicial electoral dispute resolution system to work in Guyana, the combined political will of the two largest political parties must be aligned and engaged. As has been noted through the escalation of court cases from the High Court through to the Court of Appeal and finally, the Caribbean Court of Justice, the politically charged electoral cases cannot be treated as other legal matters. Election petitions are filed expeditiously and the quick time in which election cases must be handled dictates an efficient judiciary system especially under the threat of ethnic tensions.

GECOM may wish to consider the immediate dismissal of members of staff who are guilty of criminal activities, in particular, as it impacts the transparency of the process and the outcome of the results. A quick response lends to the building of confidence in the integrity of the electoral system and an assurance of the quality of staff on board. On August 12, 2021, the Chief Elections Officer (CEO), Mr. Keith Lowenfield, the Deputy CEO, Ms. Roxanne Myers and Region Four's Returning Officer, Mr. Clairmont Mingo, had their contracts terminated. It took 526 days to arrive at that decision on staff that were charged for misconduct in Public Office and being charged for defrauding the electors. The Commission knew that the three staffers were contractual officers who could have been removed by giving them three months' notice or payment in lieu of. On any timescale, it was 525 days too many, leading to doubts and increased concerns that wrongs would not be righted in the grand scheme of things.

The slow decision-making process is symptomatic of deeper governance challenges within the electoral administration. It is a recipe for mass frustration, doubt by the electorate and political parties in the administration of any future elections and the subliminal repetition of the phrase, *"Well, you know, this is Guyana!"*

Guyana's electoral management body, GECOM, may wish to consider a voter registration system which has already been successfully implemented in Sweden where the government automatically registers all eligible voters using data from the national population database. The current voter registration system is tedious to manage and has been unreliable for years. A complete sanitization is necessary prior to the next elections in 2024/2025.

Guyana's voter participation has never approached 90% as in Australia[280] where citizens may be fined a small fee for not voting. Voting is mandatory in Australia and is an approach that the former president of the United States of America, Mr. Barack Obama had entertained. Campaign monies can therefore be spent on content rather than mobilizing voters.

In the months of March and July 2020, a group of supporters of the APNU+AFC assembled at the Seven Ponds in the Botanical Gardens and at the Square of the Revolutions,[281] respectively to perform spiritual works of the Obeah kind. The *"Spiritual wuk"* was designed to change the outcome of the National Recount thereby paving a way for the incumbent president to remain in office. Through the chanting at the Botanical Gardens where the Burnham Mausoleum is located, supporters called on the spirit Aka Kabaka (the Late Sampson Forbes Burnham) to deliver the results in favour of the APNU+AFC Coalition while at the Square of the Revolution, a tri-lingual Spiritualist, accompanied by drumming and chanting and the pouring of much oil on the waters of the fountain, pled for favourable electoral results for the APNU+AFC party.

Three years ago, Guyana's Attorney General, Mr. Basil Williams,[282] announced that he planned to remove mandatory fines and jail terms for people who practiced Voodoo, Obeah or witchcraft. No one was charged with any criminal activities related to the elaborate, public sessions as no police ranks were present. It takes a unique mindset, even one tainted with desperation, to abandon the gospel principles of a people who are predominantly Christian to embrace Obeah as a mechanism to change what the Fates had already decided.

But when all is said and done, and as the citizens of Guyana have lamented the embarrassment, partial isolation and pain of the 153 days, what has been concluded is that Guyana's democracy liken to that of the United States of America, is a fragile, counterfeit democracy. There were hardly any major differences between the elections of 2020 held in the United States of America and the Caribbean country of Guyana located on the South American continent. The leaders had much in common as they were unwilling to relinquish power as decided upon by the electorate. As faded mandarins, inciting violent protests appeared to have been the hallmark of their campaign rhetoric.

The similarities between the elections held in each country were glaring and manifested themselves in frivolous lawsuits, claims and counter claims of victory, violent protests, and the revelation of cracks in the democratic foundation of each country.

The U.S. President, Mr. Donald Trump,[283] months after President-elect Joe Biden was declared the winner of the 2020 presidential race, had not accepted the results of the election. His non-acceptance went beyond 153 days. However, a major difference was in the structure of the USA's electoral administrative system and the people of America's desire to move forward for the sake of the majority and to save face.

Secondly, the frivolous lawsuits encouraged by the APNU+AFC Coalition were part of a flawed strategy to deliberately forestall the announcement of the results of the elections and had no merit in law as the outcome was predictable. The lawsuits were instruments applied to the salvaging of what was left of Guyana's democracy. None of the APNU+AFC and PPP-C lawyers have been penalized for the improper lawsuits, not even a slap on the wrist by the Bar Association of Guyana who had denounced attacks on the justices of the CCJ and the lawyers representing their clients during the legal episodes. On the other hand, in the USA, the Trump campaign filed several lawsuits and petitions seeking to overturn or block election results in many of the battleground States, many of which were denied or just plain thrown out. Some Governors had reacted by asking judges to impose fines on the plaintiffs' lawyers or have disciplinary bodies disbar and reprimand the attorneys. There was no such luck in Guyana other than the Chief Justice demanding that the losing side pay for the court costs.

On a lighter note, one of the highlights of the 153-days saga was the collection of songs of unity and protest written within a short period of time on matters of governance and high-profile electoral fraud. Over a dozen calypsos and chutney songs, acts of resistance against a tainted democratic system, played increasingly on YouTube and Facebook during the suspension of belief for a third of the year. The ball started with Mahendra Ramkellawan's *Go Na Granga*[284] on the matter of the No Confidence Motion against the Coalition government but was sustained during the 2020 elections by the unflappable Terry Gajraj[285] and Wataflow[286] whose well-produced hits were also songs of support and healing and unification of the citizens of Guyana. Some of the Chutney Soca singers appealed to a higher power to intervene to resolve the impasse. Other singers appealed to the hearts of the electorate to be critical thinkers, an exemplar being Romeo Mystic's *Live Life Like We At De Cricket.*[287]

Between 1986 and 1991, the Estonians used choral music against their occupiers, the Soviet Union successfully. Using nonviolent methods, a choir of Estonian singers gathered in the thousands to celebrate their heritage by singing national songs. The music awoke the consciousness of their citizens. It was called the Singing Revolution which led to their Independence against the powerful Soviet Union. They had used music as a political weapon for centuries. Calypso music originated as a mean for slaves to communicate and protest against their masters and oppressors. It was a way for them to gain solidarity. On the other hand, a fusion of calypso and Indian rhythms, the blending of the Afro and Indo Caribbean styles is the conscience and mind of the people of the CARICOM Region born out of struggle and defiance. The Chutney Soca singers, in the face of delays by GECOM and protests from both the major parties, sought to awaken the minds of the citizens of Guyana through sounds like *Mr. Rigga, OMG Guyana, Stop The Delay*, and *Granger Yuh Wrong*.

For democracy in Guyana to survive and to be strengthened continuously, it will need the collective, unrelenting efforts of the local champions of democracy, an unbiased judiciary and a vigilant electorate not driven by fake news and racial taunts. Fast forward four years into the future and the election year appears just as bleak as it did in 2020. One advantage of the electoral manipulations was the unification of unlikely foes, a greater commitment for reform by the electorate and the emergence of additional political parties to split the votes of the major political parties. In hindsight, the APNU+AFC could have saved face by accepting the results and be better prepared to entice the 30,000 voters or more within the next 4 years to win the next election. That works out to be close to 7,500 voters per year, approximately 650 per month or 22 persons per day. A good, professional political strategist could make that work.

In essence, the political pundits and prognosticators from both the major political parties could benefit from a healthy dose of good governance and keen, project management and marketing skills. Any being or group of beings who repeat the same mistakes beyond a generation is unlikely to learn anything new of consequence except under duress. Therein lies the recipe for dictatorship. The stakes may be even higher when the next elections are due. Democracy is collective hard work by all the citizens of Guyana working every hour of every day, 365 days a year to preserve the institutions of democracy. Relying primarily on outsiders or international support is sheer mental laziness on the part of the electors and represents the non-self-reliant attitude of mendicants.

Edmund Burke, an Irish statesman, economist and philosopher who served as a member of parliament (MP) between 1766 and 1794 in the House of Commons of Great Britain, in a letter to a member of the National Assembly, named four institutions which would always help the electors in their pursuit of freedom, namely, religious, political, social and economic institutions. Let us rally around his visionary statements, *"Men are qualified for civil liberty in exact proportion to their disposition to put moral chains upon their own appetites, — in proportion as their love to justice is above their rapacity,—in proportion as their soundness and sobriety of understanding is above their vanity and presumption,—in proportion as they are more disposed to listen to the counsels of the wise and good, in preference to the flattery of knaves.*[288]"

Let the chips fall where they may, a Joker-effect may be the only thing that will effect changes to the five-year cycle of political and social self-abuse. Whatever form that Joker-effect takes, it will have to surpass the Covid-19 pandemic in deaths, the 2005 deluge in devastation and the Venezuelan intermittent takeover bids in fear. The refrain in the minds of all Guyanese must be, ***One People, One Nation, One Destiny!***

ABOUT THE AUTHOR

Wayne Westphal Barrow is originally from Barbados but is now a citizen of Guyana and is a Business Development Consultant who moves vulnerable citizens from poverty to prosperity through the teaching of self-reliance principles. He studied Management Information Systems at West London College, UK and received his Masters in Project Management from OBS Business School, University of Barcelona, Spain.

He has published articles in Barbados' New Bajan Magazine and has written for the leading Guyanese Newspapers dealing with a range of social issues inclusive of police brutality, child & spousal abuse, garbage management, schools information management systems and entrepreneurship. He created and produced a television show of 12 episodes dealing with the role of Information and Communication Technology in Guyana.

He is married and has three children each sporting a different Caribbean nationality; Guyanese, Barbadian and Trinidadian.

Chapter 1: Pre-Elections Activities

[1] World Health Organization, - https://covto "id19.who.int/   [Accessed April 5, 2020]

[2] A Bicentennial Proclamation to the World,
 https://www.churchofjesuschrist.org/study/scriptures/the-restoration-of-the-fulness-of-the-gospel-of-jesus-christ/a-bicentennial-proclamation-to-the-world?lang=eng [Accessed April 5, 2020]

[3] Guyana Elections 2020, - https://www.gecom.org.gy/home/gre2020 [Accessed April 5, 2020]

[4] Exxon Mobil, https://corporate.exxonmobil.com/locations/guyana [Accessed August 4, 2020]

[5] https://guyanachronicle.com/2020/04/24/revenue-from-first-crude-shipment-in-federal-reserve-bank/ [Accessed June 4, 2020]

[6] 'The Economy in the Time ofCOVID19,
https://caribbeanbusinessreport.com/news/world-bank-predicts-growth-for-guyana/ [Accessed May 25, 2020]

[7] NASDAQ, Prableen Bajpai, https://www.nasdaq.com/articles/the-5-fastest-growing-economies-in-the-world-2019-06-27 [Accessed May 25, 2020]

[8] The Charter of Civil Society for the Caribbean Community, Page 51,
https://caricom.org/documents/12060-charter_of_civil_society.pdf [Accessed August 4, 2020]

[9] The Inter-American Democratic Charter of the OAS,
http://www.oas.org/OASpage/eng/Documents/Democractic_Charter.htm [Accessed May 25, 2020]

[10] Denis Chabrol, July 12, 2020, Demerara Waves,
https://demerarawaves.com/2020/07/12/small-sparsely-populated-caribbean-islands-must-keep-out-of-the-guyana-problem-raphael-trotman/ [Accessed August 2, 2020]

[11] http://www.guyanaembassyusa.org/permanent-mission-of-guyana-to-the-organization-of-american-states-oas/ [Accessed August 6, 2020]

[12] Economist Intelligence Unit's Democracy Index,
https://statisticstimes.com/ranking/democracy-index.php [Accessed August 5, 2020]

[13] Guyana Elections Commission [GECOM],
https://www.gecom.org.gy/home/faqs [Accessed August 2, 2020]

[14] Guyana Elections Commission [GECOM],

https://www.gecom.org.gy/home/about_gecom [Accessed August 2, 2020]

[15] Caribbean Court of Justice, https://ccj.org/wp-content/uploads/2019/06/MEDIA-RELEASE-Mustapha-v-AG-Chairman-GECOM3.pdf [Accessed August 2, 2020]

[16] New York Times, https://www.nytimes.com/2018/12/22/world/americas/guyana-government-falls.html [Accessed April 7, 2020]

[17] Caribbean Court of Justice, https://ccj.org/wp-content/uploads/2019/06/Press-Release-CCJ-Affirms-Guyanas-No-Confidence-Motion.pdf [Accessed April 7, 2020]

[18] Kaieteur News, https://www.kaieteurnewsonline.com/2020/09/01/apnuafc-lodges-election-petition-in-the-high-court/ [Accessed September 5, 2020]

Chapter 2: Electoral Manipulation – Invisible Rigging

[19] Nic Cheeseman and Brian Klaas, How to Rig an Election, Page 23, [Accessed July 5, 2020]

[20] Global Corruption Barometer – LATIN AMERICA & THE CARIBBEAN 2019, Page 51 https://www.transparency.org/en/gcb/latin-america/latin-america-and-the-caribbean-x-edition-2019 [Accessed August 2, 2020]

[21] https://knowledgehub.transparency.org/helpdesk/overview-of-corruption-and-anti-corruption-in-guyana-with-reference-to-natu [Accessed June 21, 2020]

[22] Kaieteur News, https://www.kaieteurnewsonline.com/2019/10/27/guyana-remains-a-hub-for-the-trafficking-of-drugs-nana-director/ [Accessed August 10, 2020]

[23] https://www.worldatlas.com/articles/biggest-cities-in-the-united-kingdom-great-britain.html [Accessed August 13, 2020]

[24] Radio Times, https://www.radiotimes.com/news/2017-06-08/8-fascinating-facts-about-the-early-days-of-bbc-election-night-broadcasts/ [Access June 13, 2020]

[25] https://en.wikipedia.org/wiki/United_States#cite_note-largestcountry-13 [Accessed August 11, 2020]

[26] William Scarborough, Masters of the Big House, p. 289 [Accessed August 13, 2020]

[27] https://ponyexpress.org/pony-express-historical-timeline/ [Accessed August 13, 2020]

[28] https://www.uvm.edu/~dguber/POLS125/articles/pomper.htm [Accessed August 13, 2020]

[29] https://www.history.com/this-day-in-history/al-gore-concedes-presidential-election [Accessed August 13, 2020]

[30] Guinness Book of World records, https://www.guinnessworldrecords.com/world-records/longest-time-without-

a-government-as-a-result-of-conflict [Accessed June 27, 2020]
31 https://www.guinnessworldrecords.com/world-records/96893-longest-time-without-a-government-in-peacetime [Accessed June 27, 2020]
32 https://en.wikipedia.org/wiki/Electoral_fraud [Accessed August 13, 2020]
33 Stabroek News, https://www.stabroeknews.com/2020/01/05/news/guyana/ppp-c-asks-cops-to-probe-alleged-attack-on-campaigners-in-sophia/ [Accessed August 13, 2020]
34 Georgetown Chamber of Commerce, https://gcci.gy/press-statement-gcci-condemns-aggressive-posture-taken-by-gpf-and-political-interference-in-electoral-process/[Accessed August 13, 2020]
35 https://guyanatimesgy.com/open-letter-to-guyanas-commissioner-of-police/?fbclid=IwAR00ajWXrql7vleNjGUxP3NfqJMZOgsFO96ocORtrteLQIp71Pul yF3z0Qk [Accessed August 13, 2020]
36 https://newssourcegy.com/news/political-parties-sign-code-of-conduct-for-elections/ [Accessed August 13, 2020]
37 Guyana Chronicle, https://guyanachronicle.com/2020/08/12/437244/ [Accessed August 13, 2020]
38 Dr. Tara Singh https://www.stabroeknews.com/2020/02/02/opinion/letters/statistically-impossible-for-ole-to-have-661028-eligible-voters/ [Accessed March 10, 2020]
39 2012 Population & Housing Census Final Results, May 10, 2016 Page 2, https://statisticsguyana.gov.gy/wp-content/uploads/2019/10/Final_2012_Census_Count-1.pdf [Accesses June 2, 2020]
40 Claims and Objections Exercise https://www.kaieteurnewsonline.com/2019/09/28/gecoms-claims-and-objections-exercise-will-commence-october-1/ [Accessed August 13, 2020]
41 http://www.ipsnews.net/2016/11/high-voter-turnout-at-u-s-elections-a-public-good/ [Accessed August 13, 2020]
42 Inter Press Service News Agency, http://www.ipsnews.net/2001/01/politics-guyana-general-elections-declared-null-and-void-3-years-later/ [Accessed August 16, 2020]
43 News Room, https://newsroom.gy/2019/11/29/campaign-finance-legislation-full-disclosure-of-oil-monies-in-ppp-c-manifesto/ [Accesses August 15, 2020]
44 Guyana Standard, https://www.guyanastandard.com/2020/02/11/citizenship-initiative-releases-campaign-finance-information/ [Accessed August 15, 2020]
45 https://www.kaieteurnewsonline.com/2020/08/11/50m-tax-not-pnc-r-paid-for-buju-banton-concert-tickets/ [Accessed August 15, 2020]
46 https://nsarchive.gwu.edu/briefing-book/human-rights/2020-06-13/the-walter-rodney-murder-mystery-in-guyana-40-years-later [Accessed August 15, 2020]

Chapter 3: Guyana Elections Commission - Elections Process

[47] iNews Guyana, https://www.inewsguyana.com/5-4-billion-set-aside-for-gecom-for-2020-polls/ [Accessed March 7, 2020]

[48] GECOM's Web Site, https://guyanaelectionsresults.com/about/ [Accessed April 1, 2020]

[49] https://www.gecom.org.gy/home/about_gecom [Accessed August 15, 2020]

[50] Carter Center 2015 Final Report, [Accessed April 2, 2020]

[51] iNews Guyana, https://www.inewsguyana.com/10000-guyanese-to-vote-in-49-polling-stations-located-in-tents/ [Accessed March 3, 2020]

[52] Stabroek News, https://www.inewsguyana.com/opposition-leader-says-govt-conspiring-with-gecom-to-rig-elections/ [Accessed March 7, 2020]

[53] iNews Guyana, https://www.inewsguyana.com/opposition-says-will-not-recognise-voters-list-arising-from-present-house-to-house-registration/ [Accessed August 1, 2020]

[54] Demerara Waves, https://demerarawaves.com/2019/09/30/granger-constitutionally-declares-march-2-2020-as-general-elections-date/ [Accessed March 12, 2020]

[55] iNews Guyana, https://www.inewsguyana.com/81-8-turnout-at-joint-services-voting-gecom/ [Accessed August 3, 2020]

[56] Guyana Chronicle, https://guyanachronicle.com/2020/06/01/the-joint-services-vote-must-be-counted/ [August 4, 2020]

[57] iNews Guyana, https://www.inewsguyana.com/ppp-objects-to-govt-financiers-aircraft-being-used-as-gecoms-movable-polling-station/ [Accessed August 20]

[58] Guyana Chronicle, http://guyanachronicle.com/2020/03/01/giftland-chairman-offers-tips-to-eliminate-post-election-worries [Accessed August 3, 2020]

[59] https://newsroom.gy/2020/03/03/elections-2020-oas-says-modern-tabulation-systems-needed-for-early-declaration-of-results/ [Accessed March 05, 2020]

[60] News Room Guyana, https://newsroom.gy/2020/03/03/ppp-calls-on-top-cop-to-protect-all-govt-offices/[Accessed March 12, 2020]

[61] Georgetown Chamber of Commerce, https://www.facebook.com/gtchamber/videos/551191515494690 [Accessed August 20, 2020]

[62] The Standard, https://www.standardmedia.co.ke/the-standard/article/1144001701/if-kivuitu-were-to-speak-what-would-be-the-punch [Accessed August 28, 2020]

[63] https://www.youtube.com/watch?v=tbPOjGzk-YM [Accessed August 28, 2020]

[64] https://www.facebook.com/watch/?v=551191515494690 [Accessed August

28, 2020]

65 News Room Guyana, https://newsroom.gy/2020/08/27/gecoms-staff-in-elections-flash-drive-scandal-arrested/ [Accessed August 20, 2020]

66 Trinidad Express, https://trinidadexpress.com/news/local/chief-election-observer-process-was-not-followed/article_26298b08-5f4f-11ea-9386-eb633146a99a.html [Accessed August 20, 2020]

67 https://www.facebook.com/lenox.shuman/videos/10163009501540291 [Accessed August 20, 2020]

68 https://guyanatimesgy.com/attempt-to-steal-blank-sops-for-further-rigging-thwarted/ [Accessed April 1, 2020]

69 Guyana Chronicle, https://guyanachronicle.com/2020/03/08/final-report-of-elections-prepared [Accessed April 1, 2020]

70 Guyana Bar Association, http://guyanabarassociation.org/decision/reeaz-holladar-v-returning-officer-et-al/ [Accessed April 1, 2020]

71 News Room Guyana, https://newsroom.gy/2020/03/28/nandlall-mourns-loss-of-driver-to-suicide/ [Accessed April 1, 2020]

72 https://today.caricom.org/2020/03/12/caribbean-community-leaders-are-committed-to-working-with-the-people-of-guyana-mottley/ [Accessed April 2, 2020]

73 Stabroek News, https://www.stabroeknews.com/2020/03/13/news/guyana/mingo-completes-discredited-count-for-region-four/ [Accessed April 2, 2020]

74 http://www.landofsixpeoples.com/news2002/ns20062902.htm [Accessed April 2, 2020]

75 http://www.paikassociates.com/pdf/fourquartets.pdf [Accessed October 16, 2020]

76 http://www.landofsixpeoples.com/gynewsjs.htm [Accessed October 16, 2020]

77 News Room Guyana, https://newsroom.gy/2020/03/13/us-britain-canada-eu-warn-guyana-could-be-isolated-if-reg-4-vote-count-is-not-credible/ [Accessed October 16, 2020]

78 New York Times, https://www.nytimes.com/2020/03/14/world/americas/guyana-election-winner-granger.html?searchResultPosition=1 [Accesses April 2, 2020]

Chapter 4: Guyana Elections Commission – The National Recount

79 CARICOM Secretariat, https://caricom.org/statement-by-hon-mia-amor-mottley-q-c-m-p-re-caricom-team-to-supervise-guyana-elections-recount/ [Accessed March 20, 2020]

80 iNews Guyana, https://www.inewsguyana.com/caricom-chair-there-are-forces-that-dont-want-the-recount/ [Accessed March 20, 2020]

81 News Room, https://newsroom.gy/2020/04/09/lowenfield-to-tweak-

recount-plan-to-reduce-time/ [Accessed April 12, 2020]
[82] CARICOM Secretariat, https://today.caricom.org/2020/05/01/caricom-observer-team-for-guyana-elections-recount-arrives/ [Accessed May 20, 2020]
[83] News Room, https://www.facebook.com/newsroomgy/videos/626154634833743 [Accessed March 25, 2020]
[84] Stabroek News, https://www.stabroeknews.com/2020/03/21/news/guyana/alleged-instruction-on-giftland-security-cameras-raises-eyebrows/ [Accessed March 25, 2020]
[85] https://www.gecom.org.gy/assets/docs/Press_Releases/2020/Gazetted_Order_Recount_5May2020.pdf [Accessed May 20, 2020]
[86] News Room, https://newsroom.gy/2020/05/08/jonas-believes-sinister-plot-afoot-to-claim-he-has-covid-19/ [Accessed March 12, 2020]
[87] News Room, https://newsroom.gy/2020/05/08/recount-shows-mingo-figures-were-inflated-in-favor-of-apnuafc/ [Accessed March 20, 2020]
[88] Demerara Waves, https://demerarawaves.com/2020/05/13/no-evidence-of-fire-at-vote-recount-centre-fire-chief/ [Accessed March 20, 2020]
[89] The Official Gazette of Guyana, https://officialgazette.gov.gy/images/gazette2020/may/Extra_29MAY2020AddOrd60of2020.pdf [Accessed June 5, 2020]
[90] Department of Public Information, https://www.youtube.com/watch?v=BJLRJC7rq2A&t=15s [Accessed June 30 2020]
[91] Stabroek News, https://www.stabroeknews.com/2020/06/07/news/guyana/all-ballot-boxes-recounted/ [Accessed June 10, 2020]
[92] Stabroek News, https://www.stabroeknews.com/2020/06/08/news/guyana/gecom-chair-says-yes-to-votes-from-29-challenged-ballot-boxes/ [Accessed June 10, 2020]
[93] Kaieteur News, https://www.kaieteurnewsonline.com/2020/06/10/region-4-recount-certified-coalition-refuses-to-sign-on/ [Accessed June 20, 2020]
[94] News Room, https://newsroom.gy/2020/06/07/recount-shows-ppp-in-the-lead-by-over-13000-votes-indicating-a-ppp-win/ [Accessed June 10, 2020]
[95] Kaieteur News, http://www.landofsixpeoples.com/news2001/h2pict.htm [Accessed June 20, 2020]
[96] Stabroek News, https://www.stabroeknews.com/2020/06/17/news/guyana/gecom-chair-rules-that-recount-result-be-used/ [Accessed June 20, 2020]
[97] News Room, https://newsroom.gy/2020/06/15/caricom-team-says-recount-results-completely-acceptable/ [Accessed June 20, 2020]
[98] Caribbean Court of Justice, https://www.caribbean-council.org/ccj-halts-

questionable-declaration-of-guyana-election-recount/ [Accessed June 30, 2020]

99 Guyana Chronicle Newspaper, https://guyanachronicle.com/2020/06/24/ceo-submits-report-on-valid-votes/ [Accessed June 26, 2020]

100 Caribbean Court of Justice, https://ccj.org/wp-content/uploads/2020/07/Media-Release-Mohammed-Ifraan-Ali-et-al-v-Eslyn-David-et-al6.pdf [Accessed July 15, 2020]

101 https://newsroom.gy/2020/07/14/no-report-from-lowenfield-again/ [Accessed July 15, 2020]

102 https://newsroom.gy/2020/07/14/no-report-from-lowenfield-again/ [Accessed July 15, 2020]

103 Guyana Chronicle, https://guyanachronicle.com/2020/07/21/high-court-rules-recount-data-legit/ [Accessed July 25, 2020]

104 News Room, https://newsroom.gy/2020/08/02/gecom-chair-tells-chancellor-to-make-preparations-for-swearing-in-of-irfaan-ali/ [Accessed August 2, 2020]

105 News Room, https://www.facebook.com/watch/live/?v=632169060743468&ref=watch_permalink [Accessed August 2, 2020]

106 BBC News, https://www.bbc.com/news/world-us-canada-55736856 [Accessed January 21, 2021]

107 News Room, https://newsroom.gy/wp-content/uploads/2021/06/scan0127.pdf [Accessed June 14, 2021]

108 News Room, https://newsroom.gy/wp-content/uploads/2021/06/scan0128.pdf [Accessed June 14, 2021]

109 News Room, https://newsroom.gy/wp-content/uploads/2021/06/scan0129.pdf [Accessed June 14, 2021]

110 https://www.facebook.com/LGE2018/photos/a.310093939776066/947896459329141/ [Accessed June 24, 2021]

111 https://dpi.gov.gy/lge-will-be-held-in-2021/ [Accessed June 24, 2021]

Chapter 5: Eligible Political Parties

112 Kaieteur News, https://www.kaieteurnewsonline.com/2019/01/19/a-new-and-united-guyana-launched/ [Accessed September 11, 2020]

113 Kaieteur News, https://www.kaieteurnewsonline.com/2020/05/31/gecom-secretariat-compromised-anug/ [Accessed September 11, 2020]

114 Kaieteur News, https://www.kaieteurnewsonline.com/2020/06/04/gecom-should-note-mingos-inflated-votes-during-recount-tabulation-anug-chair/ [Accessed September 11, 2020]

115 Kaieteur News, https://www.kaieteurnewsonline.com/2020/06/15/anug-

says-coalition-repeatedly-lies-to-its-supporters/ [Accessed September 11, 2020]

[116] Kaieteur News, https://www.kaieteurnewsonline.com/2020/08/24/change-guyana-dissolved-by-majority-vote/ [September 10, 2020]

[117] Guyana Times, https://guyanatimesgy.com/farce-fraud-in-region-4-results-amount-to-an-abortion-of-guyanas-democratic-process/ [Accessed March 21, 2020]

[118] Stabroek News, https://www.stabroeknews.com/2019/01/12/news/guyana/fed-up-berbice-attorneys-launch-new-political-party/ [Accessed March 20, 2020]

[119] Stabroek News, https://www.stabroeknews.com/2020/07/24/news/guyana/ljp-spurs-offer-of-talks-from-apnuafc/ [Accessed September 11, 2020]

[120] Guyana Chronicle, https://guyanachronicle.com/2020/09/02/manzoor-nadir-elected-speaker-shuman-deputy/ [Accessed September 11, 2020]

[121] https://www.ovpguyana.org/about-us/ [Accessed March 20, 2020]

[122] https://www.ovpguyana.org/elections-2020/ [Accessed March 20, 2020]

[123] https://www.facebook.com/1204467483041050/videos/989153991430577 [Accessed September 11, 2020]

[124] Guyana Chronicle, http://guyanachronicle.com/2020/03/15/tci-presidential-candidate-decries-mingos-counting-methodology [Accessed March 21, 2020]

[125] Guyana Chronicle, http://guyanachronicle.com/2020/03/15/tci-presidential-candidate-decries-mingos-counting-methodology [Accessed March 21, 2020]

[126] News Room, https://newsroom.gy/2019/11/21/new-political-party-led-by-female-presidential-candidate-launched/ [Accessed September 11, 2020]

[127] Kaieteur News, https://www.kaieteurnewsonline.com/2020/07/25/lowenfield-released-on-450000-bail-for-fraud-charges/ [Accessed September 11, 2020]

[128] Stabroek News, https://www.stabroeknews.com/2019/12/01/news/guyana/pastors-launch-political-party/ [Accessed September 11, 2020]

[129] News Room Guyana, https://newsroom.gy/2020/06/19/cn-sharma-says-ppp-is-clear-winner-of-elections-irfaan-ali-should-be-sworn-in-without-delay/ [Accessed July 2, 2020]

[130] Stabroek News, https://www.stabroeknews.com/2020/09/05/news/guyana/justice-for-all-party-quits-apnu/ [Accessed September 20, 2020]

[131] https://en.wikipedia.org/wiki/British_Guiana_Labour_Party [Accessed April 20, 2020]

[132] https://en.wikipedia.org/wiki/Political_Affairs_Committee_(British_Guiana) [Accessed April 20, 2020]

[133] Stabroek News, https://www.stabroeknews.com/2020/03/07/news/guyana/ppp-tells-

supporters-to-respect-laws-stay-at-home/ [Accessed September 11, 2020]
134 News Room Guyana, https://newsroom.gy/2020/03/17/process-to-finalise-elections-results-continues-to-be-undermined-ppp/ [Accessed April 20, 2020]
135 News Room Guyana, https://newsroom.gy/2020/04/08/156-day-period-for-recount-is-ridiculous-ppp/?utm_source=News+Room&utm_campaign=a7de95c3c9-EMAIL_CAMPAIGN_2020_04_09_12_06&utm_medium=email&utm_term=0_6 5252e1518-a7de95c3c9-76544049 [Accessed April 20, 2020]
136 https://newsroom.gy/2020/04/15/govt-forking-out-millions-to-u-s-firm-to-spread-lies-about-elections-ppp/ [Accessed April 20, 2020]
137 https://www.justice.gov/nsd-fara [Accessed October 6, 2020]
138 https://efile.fara.gov/docs/6170-Informational-Materials-20200306-312.pdf [Accessed August 30, 2020]
139 https://newsroom.gy/2020/06/18/apnuafc-using-gangsterism-and-crookery-to-delay-elections-declaration-jagdeo/ [Accessed August 30, 2020]
140 https://newsroom.gy/2020/06/18/apnuafc-using-gangsterism-and-crookery-to-delay-elections-declaration-jagdeo/ [Accessed August 30, 2020]
141 https://newsroom.gy/2020/07/13/never-again-must-we-find-ourselves-in-this-position-as-a-country-ali/ [Accessed August 30, 2020]
142 https://www.inewsguyana.com/sanctions-against-granger-govt-electoral-officials-justified-ppp/ [Accessed August 30, 2020]
143 https://newsroom.gy/2020/07/23/jagdeo-says-granger-acting-in-defiance-of-court-gecom-intl-community/ [Accessed August 30, 2020]
144 Kaieteur News, https://www.kaieteurnewsonline.com/2020/08/23/coalition-used-close-to-50m-in-tax-dollars-to-pay-for-elections-other-court-cases/ [Accessed August 30, 2020]
145 Daily Guyana News, https://www.dailynewsguyana.com/appeal-of-ruling-is-a-shameless-attempt-to-hold-on-to-govt-nandlall/ [Accessed August 30, 2020]
146 Guyana Chronicle, https://guyanachronicle.com/2020/03/06/allegations-of-russian-meddling-surface [Accessed October 6, 2020]
147 Stabroek News, https://www.stabroeknews.com/2020/03/11/news/guyana/teixeira-dismisses-comical-govt-claim-of-russian-plot-to-interfere-in-polls/ [Accessed October 6, 2020]
148 News Room Guyana, https://newsroom.gy/2020/04/16/upset-supporters-paid-for-firm-hired-to-push-back-against-elections-narrative/ [Accessed October 6, 2020]
149 News Room Guyana, http://newsroom.gy/2020/04/21/apnuafc-hired-lobby-firm-not-the-govt-ramjattan/ [Accessed May 5, 2020]
150 News Room Guyana, https://newsroom.gy/2020/06/07/apnuafc-says-gecom-cannot-use-recount-to-produce-credible-result/ [Accessed October 6, 2020]

151 http://afcguyana.com/afcnew/?p=6608 [Accessed October 6, 2020]

152 Kaieteur News, https://www.kaieteurnewsonline.com/2020/07/29/smoke-and-mirrors-how-apnuafc-failed-to-fool-the-international-community/ [Accessed October 6, 2020]

153 Guyana Chronicle, https://guyanachronicle.com/2020/06/08/tabulation-is-not-validation [Accessed June 10, 2020]

154 Kaieteur News, https://www.kaieteurnewsonline.com/2020/06/20/ramjattan-privately-concedes-loss-in-meeting-with-unit-heads/ [Accessed June 22, 2020]

155 https://www.facebook.com/guyanasouthamerica/videos/737434887082143 [Accessed July 1, 2020]

156 News Room Guyana,https://newsroom.gy/2020/07/06/apnuafc-mounts-countrywide-protests-ahead-of-ccj-ruling/ [Accessed July 8, 2020]

157 Demerara Waves, https://demerarawaves.com/2020/07/15/guyana-govt-regrets-us-visa-sanctions-over-election-results/ [Accessed July 17, 2020]

158 News Room Guyana, https://newsroom.gy/2020/10/05/afc-insists-apnu-breached-cummingsburg-accord-asks-patterson-to-reconsider-resignation/ [Accessed October 6, 2020]

159 Stabroek News, https://www.stabroeknews.com/2020/01/07/news/guyana/full-revised-cummingsburg-accord-wont-be-released-harmon/ [Accessed January 5, 2020]

Chapter 6: Elections Observers

160 General Elections Observer Act 1990, https://parliament.gov.gy/documents/acts/8496-act_17_of_1990_general_election_observers.pdf [Accessed June 21, 2020]

161 The Carter Center, https://cartercenter.org/news/pr/2020/guyana-022020.html [Accessed June 21, 2020]

162 The Carter Center, https://cartercenter.org/news/pr/2020/region-4-election-results.html [Accessed June 21, 2020]

163 Kaieteur News, https://www.kaieteurnewsonline.com/2020/05/04/carter-center-observers-blocked-from-flight-arriving-today/ [Accessed May 30, 2020]

164 Kaieteur News, https://www.kaieteurnewsonline.com/2020/05/16/carter-center-blocked-by-govt-for-3rd-time/ [Accessed May 30, 2020]

165 Organization of American States, https://www.oas.org/en/media_center/press_release.asp?sCodigo=S-010/20 [Accessed May 21, 2020]

166 UPDATE ON THE ELECTORAL PROCESS IN GUYANA OAS ElectoralObservation Mission in Guyana, http://scm.oas.org/pdfs/2020/CP42690TSTATEMENTCHIEF.pdf [Accessed May 21, 2020]

167 Stabroek News,

https://www.stabroeknews.com/2020/05/14/news/guyana/golding-exposes-electoral-fraud-at-oas-meeting/ [Accessed May 21, 2020]
168 Department of Public Information, https://dpi.gov.gy/govt-says-goldings-statement-partisan-biased-and-lacks-credibility/ [Accessed May 20, 2020]
169 The Jamaican Observer, https://www.jamaicaobserver.com/the-agenda/attacking-bruce-golding-doesn-t-change-guyana-elections-mess_194223?profile=1096 [Accessed May 20, 2020]
170 UPDATE ON THE ELECTORAL PROCESS IN GUYANA OAS Electoral Observation Mission in Guyana, http://scm.oas.org/pdfs/2020/CP42690TSTATEMENTCHIEF.pdf p.4 [Accessed May 20, 2020]
171 Kaieteur News, https://www.kaieteurnewsonline.com/2020/05/14/mingo-presented-fictitious-numbers-in-transparent-attempt-to-alter-election-results/?fbclid=IwAR3qRY86epXNi4FQYjg8-TuHdkEA2cTojFQBezqQJGk_NmBq8j5JBShail [Accessed May 22, 2020]
172 The Guyana Times, https://guyanatimesgy.com/basil-williams-karen-cummings-lie-to-oas-permanent-council/ [Accessed August 5, 2020]
173 http://scm.oas.org/pdfs/2020/CP42682ENOTEGUYANA.pdf [Accessed August 5, 2020]
174 News Room, https://newsroom.gy/2020/07/21/basil-williams-accused-of-misrepresentations-lies-and-fabrications-at-oas-meeting/ [Accessed August 5, 2020]
175News Room, https://newsroom.gy/2020/07/21/democracy-being-denied-in-guyana-sir-ronald-sanders-tell-oas/ [Accessed August 5, 2020]
176
https://twitter.com/almagro_oea2015/status/1288982344418852867?lang=en [Accessed August 2, 2020]
177
https://thecommonwealth.org/sites/default/files/inline/GPD_Handbook_Election_Observation.PDF [Accessed March 13, 2020]
178 Reports of the Commonwealth Observer Group, Guyana General and Regional Elections, 2 March 2020, https://thecommonwealth.org/media/news/statement-secretary-general-commonwealth-guyana, p.67, [Accessed August 4, 2020]
179 https://thecommonwealth.org/media/news/statement-secretary-general-commonwealth-guyana [Accessed August 5, 2020]
180 https://thecommonwealth.org/media/news/18-march-statement-commonwealth-observer-group-guyana [Accessed August 4, 2020]
181 European Union Elections Observer Mission Guyana Mission, Final Report Guyana General and Regional Elections, 2 March 2020, https://eeas.europa.eu/sites/default/files/eu_eom_guyana_2020_-_final_report_0.pdf, p.8 [Accessed August 4, 2020]
182 News Room, https://newsroom.gy/2020/03/12/eu-wants-to-see-sops-from-

which-mingo-prepared-spreadsheet/?fbclid=IwAR3NnSjhJnDOJ3aybnHdE_2QaDidhMsgLiX9KhIzxVJ2vhOxAHdiQv3N0_c [Accessed August 4, 020]

[183] European Union Elections Observer Mission Guyana Mission, Final Report Guyana General and Regional Elections, 2 March 2020, https://eeas.europa.eu/sites/default/files/eu_eom_guyana_2020_-_final_report_0.pdf p.4 [Accessed August 4, 2020]

[184] https://eeas.europa.eu/election-observation-missions/eom-guyana-2020/80416/european-union-election-observation-mission-presents-final-report-recommendations-future_en [Accessed August 4, 2020]

[185] https://eeas.europa.eu/election-observation-missions/eom-guyana-2020/95330/european-union-election-observation-mission-returns-guyana-present-recommendations-and-help_en [Accessed August May 20, 2021]

[186] http://guyanabarassociation.org/release/statement-by-the-bar-association-ofguyana-on-their-preliminary-observations-of-the-2020-general-and-regionalelections-held-on-march-2-2020/ [Accessed May 2, 2020]

[187] News Room, https://newsroom.gy/2020/04/06/private-sector-writes-inter-american-commission-on-human-rights/ [Accessed May 5, 2020]

[188] https://gcci.gy/press-release-gcci-summary-statement-of-recount-report/ [Accessed July 4, 2020]

Chapter 7: CARICOM

[189] CARICOM Secretariat, https://today.caricom.org/2020/02/25/caricom-secretariat-mounting-election-observation-mission-to-guyana/ [Accessed March 30, 2020]

[190] CARICOM Secretariat, https://today.caricom.org/2020/02/28/arrival-statement-caricom-election-observation-mission-to-guyanas-elections/ [Accessed March 30, 2020]

[191] CARICOM Secretariat, https://today.caricom.org/2020/02/29/caricom-observers-make-pre-election-day-visits-to-polling-places/ [Accessed March 30, 2020]

[192] Stabroek News, https://www.stabroeknews.com/2020/03/07/news/guyana/caricom-chair-calls-for-transparent-tabulation-of-voting-in-all-regions/ [Accessed March 30, 2020]

[193] CARICOM Secretariat, https://today.caricom.org/2020/03/12/caribbean-community-leaders-are-committed-to-working-with-the-people-of-guyana-mottley/ [Accessed March 30, 2020]

[194] News Room, https://newsroom.gy/2020/04/06/rowley-says-courts-ruling-on-caricoms-role-of-recount-disturbing/ [Accessed August 3, 2020]

[195] iNews Guyana, https://www.inewsguyana.com/caricom-will-not-tolerate-the-setting-aside-of-recount-results-incoming-chair/ [Accessed August 3, 2020]

196 News Room, https://newsroom.gy/2020/06/12/ralph-gonsalves-perfectly-in-order-owen-arthur-says-harmon-should-not-be-attacking-caribbean-leaders/?fbclid=IwAR1M14vwpdFRCSbY_dSCP2rMErnVhWZWB3cQXvxjgBACZvTeC0NOnT9pNHQ [Accessed August 3, 2020]

197 iNews Guyana, https://www.inewsguyana.com/caricom-team-thanked-for-professionalism-integrity/?fbclid=IwAR2kyREQpeM0tzIlOqatg4JoI9v4ph1RlJjygn7E2oxGwCUsqAIARtkH85M [Accessed August 3, 2020]

198 CARICOM Secretariat, https://today.caricom.org/2020/06/24/statement-by-the-chair-of-the-caribbean-community-caricom-the-honourable-mia-amor-mottley-prime-minister-of-barbados-on-the-electoral-crisis-following-guyanas-general-and-regional-electi/?fbclid=IwAR3j2sMjmllZglhY6igl6HquTCri6GDIn7urvztluzZ7J3vl39IaqmTbmCI [Accessed August 3, 2020]

199 News Room Guyana, https://newsroom.gy/2020/07/03/caricom-secretary-general-has-every-confidence-in-recount-report-from-scrutineers/ [Accessed August 3, 2020]

200 Report of the CARICOM Observer Team For The Recount Of The Guyana March 02, 2020 Elections, Ms. Cynthia Barrow-Giles, Mr. Sylvester King, Mr. John Jarvis, June 13, 2020 p.58

201 Report of the CARICOM Observer Team For The Recount Of The Guyana March 02, 2020 Elections, Ms. Cynthia Barrow-Giles, Mr. Sylvester King, Mr. John Jarvis, June 13, 2020 p.58

202 Report of the CARICOM Observer Team For The Recount Of The Guyana March 02, 2020 Elections, Ms. Cynthia Barrow-Giles, Mr. Sylvester King, Mr. John Jarvis, June 13, 2020 p.58

Chapter 8: Media Rantings - Pre & Post Elections

203 Radio Times, https://www.radiotimes.com/news/2017-06-08/8-fascinating-facts-about-the-early-days-of-bbc-election-night-broadcasts/ [Accessed March 20, 2020]

204 Guyana National Broadcasting Authority, http://gnba.gov.gy/wp-content/uploads/2017/10/Guidelines-for-Broadcasters-.pdf [Accessed March 20, 2020]

205 Media Code of Conduct, https://www.gecom.org.gy/archived/pdf/MEDIA%20CODE%20OF%20CONDUCT.pdf [Accessed February 2020]

206 Guyana Chronicle, https://guyanachronicle.com/2020/01/23/gecoms-draft-media-code-of-conduct-in-the-works/ [Accessed February 1, 2020]

207 Department of Public Information, https://dpi.gov.gy/european-union-representatives-engage-gnba-on-broadcasting-sector-in-light-of-impending-elections/ [Accessed November 1, 2020]

208 Stabroek News,
https://www.stabroeknews.com/2019/12/13/news/guyana/broadcasting-authority-finds-rise-in-infractions/ [Accessed January 20, 2020]
209 European Union Election Observer Mission Guyana 2020 Final Report,
https://eeas.europa.eu/sites/eeas/files/eu_eom_guyana_2020_-_final_report_0.pdf, Page 24 [Accessed June 30, 2020]
210 Guyana Times, https://guyanatimesgy.com/amcham-pledges-support-to-gecom-for-free-fair-elections/ [Accessed January 26, 2020]
211 Stabroek News,
https://www.stabroeknews.com/2020/01/26/news/guyana/gecom-chair-says-elections-will-be-free-and-fair/ [Accessed January 26, 2020]
212 Guyana Press Association, https://pressassociation.gy/ [Accessed January 26, 2020]
213 Stabroek News,
https://www.stabroeknews.com/2020/02/27/news/guyana/press-association-flays-gecom-over-access-to-info/ [Accessed March 3, 2020]
214 Article 19,
https://en.unesco.org/sites/default/files/guidelines_for_election_broadcasting_en.pdf [Accessed March 21, 2020]
215 European Union Election Observer Mission Guyana 2020 Final Report,
https://eeas.europa.eu/sites/eeas/files/eu_eom_guyana_2020_-_final_report_0.pdf, Page 24 [Accessed June 30, 2020]
216 Guyana Chronicle, https://guyanachronicle.com/2020/04/12/yes-to-a-full-recount-no-to-ppps-bullyism/ [Accessed April 14, 2020]
217 Guyana Times, https://guyanatimesgy.com/grangers-overreach/ [Accessed March 30, 2020]
218 European Union Election Observer Mission Guyana 2020 Final Report,
https://eeas.europa.eu/sites/eeas/files/eu_eom_guyana_2020_-_final_report_0.pdf, Page 24 [Accessed June 30, 2020]
219 Guyana Times, https://guyanatimesgy.com/granger-rejects-democratic-legitimacy/ [Accessed March 30, 2020]
220 Stabroek News,
https://www.stabroeknews.com/2020/03/26/news/guyana/stabroek-news-publishes-116-region-four-statements-of-poll/ [Accessed March 21, 2020]
221 Trinidad Daily Express Newspaper,
https://trinidadexpress.com/opinion/editorials/guyana-election-merry-go-round/article_73c8ab96-7b88-11ea-8645-8fc703d5474d.html?fbclid=IwAR1hpaVMp-nRs6JJMKmU-r0JGLMQ4Y-ylObs9papG8Y3la57lgY6_Z5JB8w [Accessed April 12, 2020]
222 Jamaica Gleaner Newspaper, http://jamaica-gleaner.com/article/commentary/20200930/editorial-guyana-must-tread-care [Accessed October 5, 2020]
223 Jamaica Gleaner Newspaper, http://jamaica-

gleaner.com/article/commentary/20201023/vishnu-bisram-guyana-election-agents-charges-not-govt-supported [Accessed October 30, 2020]

224 The Barbados Advocate, https://www.barbadosadvocate.com/columns/editorial-electoral-tragedy [Accessed July 30, 2020]

225 https://www.whitehouse.gov/briefing-room/speeches-remarks/2021/01/20/inaugural-address-by-president-joseph-r-biden-jr/ [Accessed January 255, 2021]

226 20th Annual Edelman Trust Barometer Global Report, 2020, Page 16. https://www.edelman.com/sites/g/files/aatuss191/files/2020-01/2020%20Edelman%20Trust%20Barometer%20Global%20Report_LIVE.pdf

227 https://www.guinnessworldrecords.com/world-records/largest-online-social-network[Accessed July 16, 2020]

228 https://www.internetworldstats.com/south.htm [Accessed July 16, 2020]

229 https://napoleoncat.com/stats/instagram-users-in-guyana/2019/04[Accessed July 16, 2020]

230 https://www.businessofapps.com/data/whatsapp-statistics/[Accessed July 16, 2020]

231 https://venturebeat.com/2018/07/04/whatsapp-says-collective-action-required-to-combat-the-spread-of-misinformation-in-india/ [Accessed July 16, 2020]

232 The Guardian, https://www.theguardian.com/world/2018/oct/18/brazil-jair-bolsonaro-whatsapp-fake-news-campaign[Accessed July 16, 2020]

233 Buzzfeed News, https://www.buzzfeednews.com/article/craigsilverman/viral-fake-election-news-outperformed-real-news-on-facebook#.bp90yKJ1W[Accessed July 16, 2020]

234 Guyana Chronicle, https://guyanachronicle.com/2020/02/27/stabroek-news-distances-self-from-fake-exit-polls-on-joint-services-vote/[Accessed July 16, 2020]

235 Ms. Denise Herod, https://youtu.be/EkgNKhREIck [Accessed July 16, 2020]

236 Ethnic Relations Commission, https://www.facebook.com/permalink.php?story_fbid=813722966032853&id=318337545571400&__tn__=K-R[Accessed July 16, 2020]

237 Ethnic Relations Commission, https://www.facebook.com/Ethnic-Relations-Commission-318337545571400/photos/pcb.763290264409457/763217791083371 [Accessed June 30, 2020]

238 TedX Talks, https://www.ted.com/talks/christiane_marie_abu_sarah_how_do_daily_habits_lead_to_political_violence?utm_source=newsletter_daily&utm_campaign=daily&utm_medium=email&utm_content=button__2020-09-03#t-383164[Accessed July 16, 2020]

239 HGPTV Channel 16,
https://www.youtube.com/watch?v=kUfYJdRqJvY[Accessed July 16, 2020]
240 News Room, https://newsroom.gy/2020/03/13/dominic-gaskin-says-there-are-more-good-guyanese-than-rotten-ones/ [Accessed July 17, 2020]
241 Twitter, @WHAAsstSecty, [Accessed July 20, 2020]

Chapter 9: Electoral Consequences and Resolutions

242 Stabroek News,
https://www.stabroeknews.com/2020/03/08/news/guyana/guyana-bar-council-alarmed-at-potential-swearing-in/ [Accessed July 20, 2020]
243 Stabroek News,
https://www.stabroeknews.com/2020/04/16/news/guyana/bar-association-calls-on-gecom-for-swift-final-election-result-to-enable-new-parliament-by-constitutional-deadline/ [Accessed July 20, 2020]
244

https://www.facebook.com/DistinguishedRadical/videos/10158329572770799 [Accessed July 20, 2020]
245 https://www.inewsguyana.com/attacking-golding-does-not-change-demand-for-credible-guyana-elections-result/ [Accessed April 2, 2020]
246

https://www.stabroeknews.com/2020/03/08/opinion/letters/condemnation-of-attempts-to-undermine-the-electoral-process/ [Accessed March 12, 2020]
247 http://demerarawaves.com/2020/03/13/acda-calls-on-western-nations-to-stop-recolonisation-intervention-in-guyanas-electoral-process/ [Accesses March 15, 2020]
248 https://www.inewsguyana.com/political-impasse-taking-a-toll-on-economy-creating-hardships-for-all-manufacturing-body/ [Accessed May 5, 2020]
249 https://www.inewsguyana.com/gmsa-calls-for-swift-declaration-of-recount-results-transition-to-new-govt/ [Accessed July 15, 2020]
250

https://www.facebook.com/privatesectorcommissiongy/posts/2663980310557803 [Accessed May 5, 2020]
251 https://theworldnews.net/gy-news/current-electoral-impasse-provides-opportunities-for-constitutional-reforms-iro-gcc [Accessed August 3, 2020]
252 https://www.facebook.com/Rudy-Insanally-1142329102509814/ [Accessed May 5, 2020]
253 https://oilnow.gy/featured/under-sanctions-oil-money-could-be-frozen-sir-ronald-sanders/ [Accessed July 20, 2020]
254 https://www.cnc3.co.tt/professor-andy-knight-us-democracy-fragile/ [Accessed June 3, 2021]
255 https://newsroom.gy/2020/07/03/do-the-right-thing-and-demit-office-caribbean-scholars-urge-g ranger/ [August 2, 2020]

256 https://newsroom.gy/2020/07/11/uwi-vice-chancellor-says-only-recount-results-would-be-acceptable-to-the-caribbean-wider-world/ [Accessed August 3, 2020]

257 https://www.inewsguyana.com/brazil-calls-for-elections-declaration-based-on-recount-results/ [Accessed August 3, 2020]

258 https://www.kaieteurnewsonline.com/2020/07/24/six-south-american-nations-say-declare-caricom-certified-recount-figures/ [Accessed August 3, 2020]

259 https://www.gov.uk/government/news/foreign-secretary-statement-on-guyana-24-march-2020 [Accessed August 4, 2020]

260 https://sires.house.gov/media-center/press-releases/congressman-sires-leads-congressional-delegation-to-guyana [Accessed August 2, 2020]

261 https://twitter.com/whaasstsecty/status/1243300538063650818?lang=en [Accessed April 12, 2020]

262 https://twitter.com/SenateForeign/status/1283461545255743490 [Accessed August 2, 2020]

263 https://www.miamiherald.com/news/nation-world/world/americas/article245760395.html [Accessed October 2, 2020]

264 https://twitter.com/TheElders/status/1267810968253263872 [Accessed June 30, 2020]

265 https://newsroom.gy/2020/07/25/india-urges-early-conclusion-to-elections-impasse-hopes-outcome-is-respected-by-all-parties/ [Accessed August 22, 2020]

266 https://www.development-today.com/archive/dt-2020/dt-2--2020/norway-puts-brakes-on-climate-aid-to-guyana-amid-post-election-chaos [Accessed August 2, 2020]

267 https://www.reuters.com/article/us-global-oil-exxonmobil-guyana-idUSKBN21P2J3 [Accessed June 3, 2020]

268 https://www.miamiherald.com/opinion/op-ed/article244604897.html [Accessed August 2, 20200]

269 https://oilnow.gy/featured/stabroek-block-consortium-looking-to-move-forward-expeditiously-with-payara-once-guyana-elections-impasse-is-resolved/ [Accessed August 2, 2020]

270 https://carnegieendowment.org/publications/interactive/protest-tracker# [Accessed January 2021]

271 https://issuu.com/guyanachroniclee-paper/docs/guyana_chronicle_e-paper_3-7-2020 [Accessed June 3, 2020]

272 http://www.guyana.org/govt/declassified_british_documents_1953.htm [Accessed March 25 2020]

273 Internal Colonial Office Memorandum On Availability Of Forces To Prevent Disturbances In British Guiana, http://www.guyana.org/govt/declassified_british_documents_1953.html [Accessed April 24, 2020]

[274] News Source Guyana, https://www.facebook.com/watch/?v=1645521928919053 [Accessed April 24, 2020]

[275] https://www.facebook.com/watch/?v=596263437939253 [Accessed August June 20, 2020]

[276] Khemraj, T. (2020). Two ethnic security dilemmas and their economic origin. Special Edition Working Paper No. 4, Faculty of Social Sciences, University of West Indies, Cave Hill Campus

[277] European Union Elections Observer Mission Guyana Mission, Final Report Guyana General and Regional Elections, 2 March 2020, https://eeas.europa.eu/sites/default/files/eu_eom_guyana_2020_-_final_report_0.pdf p.7 [Accessed August 4, 2020]

[278] https://www.idlo.int/about-idlo/about-idlo [Accessed August 2, 2020]

[279] http://www.ipsnews.net/2017/05/strong-dispute-resolution-system-key-to-2017-kenya-elections/ [Accessed August 2, 2020]

[280] https://www.mic.com/articles/118598/7-facts-from-the-around-the-world-show-how-absurd-america-s-elections-really-are [Accessed August 2, 2020]

[281] https://www.facebook.com/jermaine.gentle.98/videos/180703546784304 [Accessed July 29, 2020]

[282] https://www.caribbeanlifenews.com/guyana-scrubs-witchcraft-colonial-laws/ [Accesses August 4, 2020]

[283] https://apnews.com/article/election-2020-ap-fact-check-joe-biden-donald-trump-technology-49a24edd6d10888dbad61689c24b05a5 [Accessed January 5, 2021]

[284] https://www.youtube.com/watch?v=-cxBngWmjcY [Accessed March 25, 2020]

[285] https://www.youtube.com/watch?v=VlEaWShDvyc [Accessed March 25, 2020]

[286] https://www.youtube.com/watch?v=1eeX_Qp3yy0 [Accessed March 25, 2020]

[287] https://www.youtube.com/watch?v=trVdZXLUKvA [Accessed March 25, 2020]

[288] https://www.goodreads.com/quotes/293641-men-are-qualified-for-civil-liberty-in-exact-proportion-to [Accessed August 25, 2020]